PRAISE FOR DAVID MICHIE'S EARLIER BOOKS

"Michie demystifies the ancient teachings of Buddha
and writes about them in an easy style."
—*Sunday Mail*

"Michie is as adept at the storytelling as he is at making the
ancient tenets of the faith and meditation methods
understandable and applicable to daily life."
—*Huffington Post*

"For those who have been searching for a sincere, accessible
introduction to Tibetan Buddhism…this is your book…Michie
employs storytelling and humor without being falsely
enthusiastic or superficial."
—*Shambhala Sun*

"…a humorous, wry look at Western problems that shows us how
to use time-honored meditation techniques to find our way to
the heart of Buddha's wisdom, and to distinguish between lasting
happiness and temporary pleasure."
—*Mandala* magazine

"Michie condenses the virtues of Buddhism into a reasonably easy-
to-navigate text that may go some way toward answering the big
question, or at least provide a starting point for introspection."
—*Herald Sun*

T0060277

"These were among the fastest 200+ pages I ever read. If Buddhism is a 'mirror,' then Michie kindly holds it up for the reader. Here's the essence of Buddhism, and better—
why it matters and how to access it."
—*Elephant Journal*

"The pursuit of happiness is a time-consuming rollercoaster ride with plenty of ups and downs—especially when we allow our galloping desires and our entrenched aversions to dominate our emotions each and every day. Tibetan Buddhism offers an alternative to this frenzied ride and David Michie…describes this inner path to a more peaceful and rounded life."
—*Spirituality and Practice*

"You get the sense that this guy practices what he preaches. There's a confidence and peace that inspires."
—*Modern Sage Magazine*

Enlightenment to Go

SHANTIDEVA AND THE
POWER OF COMPASSION
TO TRANSFORM YOUR LIFE

David Michie

WISDOM PUBLICATIONS • BOSTON

Wisdom Publications
199 Elm Street
Somerville MA 02144 USA
www.wisdompubs.org

Copyright © 2012 Mosaic Reputation Management (David Michie)

All rights reserved.

No part of this book may be reproduced in any form or by any means, electronic or mechanical, including photography, recording, or by any information storage and retrieval system or technologies now known or later developed, without permission in writing from the publisher.

Library of Congress Cataloging-in-Publication Data

Michie, David.
 Enlightenment to go : shantideva and the power of compassion to transform your life / David Michie.
    p. cm.
 Includes bibliographical references (p.   ) and index.
 ISBN 0-86171-757-0 (pbk. : alk. paper)
 1.   Santideva, 7th cent. Bodhicaryavatara. 2.   Mahayana Buddhism—Doctrines. 3. Meditation—Buddhism. I. Title.
 BQ3147.M53 2012
 294.3'85—dc23

                          2011030585

ISBN 978-0-86171-757-6
eBook ISBN 978-0-86171-694-4

15 14 13 12 11
5 4 3 2 1

Cover design by Phil Pascuzzo. Interior design by Gopa&Ted2. Set in Fairfield LT Std 11/14.95. First published in 2010 in Australia.

Wisdom Publications' books are printed on acid-free paper and meet the guidelines for permanence and durability of the Production Guidelines for Book Longevity of the Council on Library Resources.

Printed in the United States of America.

MIX
Paper
FSC FSC® C011935
This book was produced with environmental mindfulness. We have elected to print this title on 30% PCW recycled paper. As a result, we have saved the following resources: 20 trees, 8 million BTUs of energy, 2,005 lbs. of greenhouse gases, 9,040 gallons of water, and 573 lbs. of solid waste. For more information, please visit our website, www.wisdompubs.org. This paper is also FSC® certified. For more information, please visit www.fscus.org.

Contents

This book is dedicated with heartfelt gratitude to my Dharma teachers: Geshe Acharya Thubten Loden, Founder of the Tibetan Buddhist Society, and Les Sheehy, Director of the Tibetan Buddhist Society in Perth, Western Australia, whose kindness I can never repay and without whom this book could never have been written.

Introduction

"If I have any understanding of compassion and the practice
of the bodhisattva path, it is entirely on the basis of
this text that I possess it."

THE DALAI LAMA SPEAKING ABOUT SHANTIDEVA'S
GUIDE TO THE BODHISATTVA'S WAY OF LIFE

OFTEN WHEN the Dalai Lama ends a public speech, a member of
the audience will ask: "Can you recommend a book that explains
how to put Buddhist ideas into practice?"

In all his forty years of teaching, the Dalai Lama has been remarkably consistent in the way he answers this question: "Read Shantideva's *Guide to the Bodhisattva's Way of Life*." One of the great classics
of Tibetan Buddhism, its pages contain all the advice and motivation
you need to make Buddha's teachings part of your daily reality.

Shantideva's *Guide* is not only one of the most revered texts in
Tibetan Buddhism, it is arguably one of the most remarkable books
ever written. Composed by an eighth-century Buddhist monk in
India around the same time as one of the earliest English-language
compositions, the epic work of fiction *Beowulf*, Shantideva's *Guide*
is a manual of advanced psychology. Writing to motivate his own
practice, Shantideva authored what could well be called the world's
first self-help book, outlining specific techniques to "reframe" our
experience of reality to achieve greater happiness and inner peace.

More than this, the *Guide* outlines a structured approach to the whole Tibetan Buddhist path, beginning with simple but powerful analytical tools and leading us, step by step, to the most profound realizations about the true nature of reality—and of ourselves. The word "bodhisattva" in the title of Shantideva's book describes a person who wishes to achieve enlightenment to help free all other beings from suffering. The bodhisattva way of life may therefore be regarded as the ultimate expression of compassion.

Shantideva's *Guide* is extraordinary for many reasons. One thing I find amazing is that even though he wrote it in the eighth century, the wisdom it contains still has a direct application for us, here and now, in the twenty-first. More than twelve hundred years separate us from Shantideva, scratching at his parchment, trying to ignore the flicker of his oil lamp; nowadays we sit tapping at our computers, trying to ignore the ping of our email inbox. But in a more important sense, nothing has changed. Human nature is the same. We still strive for the same things. And no one has a more profound under-standing of human nature than Shantideva.

Like all great spiritual teachers, Shantideva understood the power of metaphor to make explanations come alive. Like an embroidered tapestry his instructions are richly illuminated with images that tumble off the pages—vivid, earthy, and often quite unexpected. Shantideva had a poet's understanding of language, and some of his stanzas are expressed with such poignancy and beauty that they rival the most lyrical passages of Shakespeare. I gather there are some verses that still move the Dalai Lama to tears, despite his years of familiarity with them.

THE BEST OF SHANTIDEVA

But the most astonishing thing of all about Shantideva's *Guide* is that it is still so little known in the West. Ask most people who Shan-tideva was and chances are you'll be met with a blank expression, or a hesitant guess—an Indian soccer player? A Bollywood actor? Before

I became a regular Buddhist-class attendee in my early thirties, I had never heard of him, even though I am an arts graduate with a supposedly well-rounded education. Such is the parochial nature of Western culture that if you go into any reasonably well-stocked bookstore you'll be sure to turn up a volume on Aristotle, Descartes, or Freud. But Shantideva? We'll have to order that in for you, sir.

Even specialist Buddhist sections are likely to stock a variety of books by Buddhist lamas and other teachers, all of whom would readily acknowledge the preeminence of Shantideva, but not the great man himself.

This is perhaps understandable. Sitting down to read Shantideva unplugged can be daunting. In the same way that someone unfamiliar with classical music might be intimidated by the prospect of sitting through an entire Beethoven symphony, or a stranger to art might hesitate on the steps of a famous gallery, even though we may feel drawn to some new field of endeavor we face a simple problem: Where on earth do we begin? Even the name of his *Guide*, sometimes published under its multisyllabic Sanskrit title, the *Bodhicharyavatara*, is somewhat confronting. Without someone to give us the background, to explain the significance of this symbol or that reference, and to target the new material to our own experience and understanding, it's easy to put any such new interest in the "too hard" basket.

But with a guide to point out features of importance, and above all, to bring the whole subject alive with his or her own enthusiasm and purpose, then our new interest can quite naturally develop as a source of fresh inspiration.

In writing this book, I hope to be just such a guide. *Enlightenment to Go* is not a scholarly discourse on Shantideva—there are plenty of those already. Nor does it provide a comprehensive analysis of every one of his eight hundred stanzas—rather, only seventy-five of them. I have not slavishly followed the sequence of the verses presented in his teachings because, like a composer of a grand classical piece of music, Shantideva returned to several of the same key themes in different parts of his discourse, often with a different emphasis or turn of phrase. To enhance the practical application of his teachings for readers today, I have presented them thematically, rather than in the order they appear in the *Guide* (though in its own way, the *Guide* is also arranged according to different themes).

Part I of this book discusses the compassionate mind of enlightenment from a Buddhist perspective. In Buddhism the word "mind" is often used to mean "state of mind," and we look at how such states of mind can be developed, what the benefits of developing them can be, and how they may differ from the mind states we currently experience.

Part II moves from theory to practice. Exactly how do we set about cultivating an enlightened way of being? What precisely does this entail? What are the nuts and bolts—the psychological tools, the meditation practices, the methods and techniques—we can apply to effect personal transformation at the most profound level?

Like my book *Buddhism for Busy People*, *Enlightenment to Go* also provides a very personal account of how I've come to terms with Buddhist teachings in my own life. I offer my story not because I think I'm something special but for the very opposite reason. I know that the challenges and the frustrations, the happiness and the inner peace I continue to experience on my personal journey are not particular to me. Sure, I may experience them in a particular way, but they are experiences common to all busy people who seek to put Buddha's teachings into practice.

Enlightenment to Go is not the book for readers preferring a rigorous textbook approach to Shantideva. However, I hope that those of you who join me on this highlight tour will find in my autobiographical passages something you can relate to: reassurance, perhaps, that you are far from alone as you make your way along this tried and tested path.

A STRUCTURED MEDITATION PROGRAM

One way to use this book is simply to read it from start to finish like any other. And because most readers are busy people with precious little time to spare, I have written fairly short, easily digestable chapters that may be read during the course of a train commute, or perhaps in bed at night before turning out the light.

However, *Enlightenment to Go* has also been designed to provide a kind of guided analytical meditation program. Each chapter is on a different theme and ends with suggested points for reflection or action. These meditations and exercises are based on traditional practices, some of which I have adapted a little to suit our contemporary needs. There are eighteen chapters in all, covering the full Tibetan Buddhist path. It is my heartfelt wish that many of you will find this book helpful not only as an introduction to Shantideva, but as a means to become acquainted with the most important Buddhist teachings in a truly life-enhancing way.

What is the difference between practicing analytical meditation and simply reading something? In brief, our depth of understanding. While the intellectual knowledge we gain from reading can be helpful, if the significance of what we read is to have real meaning for us—if there is to be any possibility of it changing our view of ourselves and the world around us—we need to understand it on a deeper basis. Ultimately we need to experience it at a direct or nonconceptual level.

THE IMPACT OF REALIZATION

To illustrate, not so long ago I saw a TV news item about workers on a cacao plantation in West Africa. Although they'd been harvesting cacao beans for many years, each season dispatching large sacks to chocolate factories in Europe, the majority of plantation workers had never actually seen chocolate, let alone tasted it. They had, of course, heard about it. They possessed a good intellectual knowledge of chocolate: they knew that it was sweet, that it contained condensed milk, that it had a firm texture but melted in the mouth. And they knew that Europeans loved eating it. But despite having this intellectual knowledge, they couldn't fully understand the ever-growing demand for the small bitter beans they harvested each year.

That is, until the day a TV crew arrived, bringing a variety of chocolate products. There was something compelling about watching the cacao workers undo the foil wrappers, scrutinize the mysterious brown tablets—and take their first bite. Seeing the expressions on their faces suddenly change as they realized: *this* is why people can't get enough cacao beans! Their understanding was no longer intellectual. It was firsthand and nonconceptual. They had experienced it directly.

When we meditate, we create the possibility of experiencing ideas directly. We take our first bite of reality. While most of us have no shortage of notions about who we are and the world around us, and many of the other subjects Shantideva writes about, like the plantation workers before the TV crew arrived, our understanding is mostly intellectual and therefore necessarily limited.

The word "realization" is sometimes used in Buddhism to describe the point when our understanding of a particular subject ripens to the extent that it changes our behavior. The middle-aged executive may know he needs to work less and exercise more, but perhaps he will only fully *realize* this in the back of an ambulance on his way to hospital having suffered a heart attack. Realizations may also refer to changes in attitude. Like the crusty old homophobe I introduced to a gay friend—of whom, after a thoroughly enjoyable dinner, he couldn't speak highly enough. When I told him my friend was gay, there was a marked shift in his hitherto incorrigible prejudices: a realization had been made!

Through meditation we can go beyond a surface or intellectual understanding of a subject toward achieving truly life-enhancing realizations. And the curriculum provided by Shantideva offers the most profound benefits of all. We all know that every day of our life could be our last and that we shouldn't take a single moment of it for granted—but do we really live like that? We are all aware that failure and misfortune offer incomparably better opportunity for personal growth than smooth sailing and success—but how many of us remember this in the midst of a crisis? Many of us have an inkling that our existence holds possibilities far more panoramic than the biographic summaries we're familiar with—but how much energy do we invest exploring these?

Analytical meditation holds the key. For readers who are unfamiliar with the process of meditation, I've provided a "how to" in the appendix of this book. Even those of you who already have a meditation practice may find it useful to quickly read over the suggestions provided in the appendix before you begin the analytical meditation exercises.

One positive side-effect of analytical meditation is that when we focus on a subject during meditation, it will often pop up in our thoughts later during the day. We'll find fresh relevance in a newspaper headline, or a snatch of conversation will return us to the subject again. And by focusing more and more of our thoughts on useful material, and steering them away from negative feedback loops that often dominate our inner self-talk, the balance of our preoccupations starts to shift—and with it, our behavior.

When you order your regular cappuccino or latte, your pizza, pad thai, or any other consumables to go, you are essentially taking whatever you are buying to enjoy in an environment of your own choosing—to savor it in private, on your own terms. In just the same way, *Enlightenment to Go* provides a complete package of teachings and meditations for you to study and use at a time and in a way that suits you. Within it is contained all the main teachings of the Tibetan Buddhist path, as well as the means to help penetrate the true essence of these teachings.

RANDOM READING

On a shelf in my office is a well-thumbed copy of Shantideva's *Guide* that I use in a way you may also find helpful with this book. During challenging moments, I will take the *Guide* off the shelf, flick it open, and read a few verses at random. The effect is almost always beneficial. However disturbing the subject previously occupying my thoughts, I am reminded of the much broader reality in which it is of little importance. Often, curiously, the page I open directly addresses my agitation, as though Shantideva himself were right beside me in saffron robes—usually, wagging a finger at me and telling me to get a grip!

I hope you also find this book opens at just the right place for your needs at a particular moment. Whether you find yourself having to confront a difficult situation, or are simply looking for stimulation, I have no doubt that Shantideva can also offer you a fresh perspective on whatever challenges you may face.

ENLIGHTENMENT FOR WHOM?

The objective of Buddha's teachings, as illuminated by Shantideva, was not to convert people to a particular belief system but to offer access to a set of psychological tools which, at the very least, can improve our sense of inner peace and happiness. More than this, with patient application these tools transform our whole experience of reality. The Tibetan Buddhist view is that all beings with consciousness have the potential to achieve enlightenment. Whatever our background and cultural conditioning, whatever negative states of mind we may experience or wrongdoing we have committed, like clouds passing through the sky none of this can taint the natural state of our primordial mind, which is boundless, formless, blissful, and unceasing.

In writing this book, I am assuming my readers have no prior knowledge of Buddhism, and I hope that whatever the background tradition you may come from, you will find in *Enlightenment to Go* some useful insights and practices. My own formative years were in mainstream Presbyterianism, and I was a regular Sunday school attendee until my midteens. My parents were devout in their own private way, and in retirement my father has become a lay preacher in northeast Scotland. When *Buddhism for Busy People* was first published some years ago, I think he felt a sense of paternal obligation to read it. I could picture him, the day that it arrived in the mail, sitting down in his favorite armchair, steeling himself to read the combustible contents that were likely to have steam coming out of his Calvinistic ears.

But, to his own surprise as much as mine, he actually quite enjoyed the experience—partly, I expect, because he discovered some useful observations and anecdotes. He is always on the lookout for fresh material for his next sermon, and *Buddhism for Busy People* became an unexpected source book: I suspect that in the following months a number of "Buddhist" ideas were repackaged and found their way into a variety of pulpits around Scotland!

The point is that no tradition has a monopoly on compassion. The same ethical framework underpins all the world's major traditions, along with the yearning for the wholeness that comes from a direct experience of ultimate reality, whatever we choose to call it. Compassion—exemplified in the bodhisattva way of life—is the force that is supposed to motivate the followers of all the world's great traditions.

While *Enlightenment to Go* has not been written specifically for seasoned Buddhist practitioners, I also hope that fellow students who read this book may find in it a fresh source of stimulation. When trying to penetrate the meaning of a subject, particularly subtler concepts, I've often found that a slightly different presentation of even a well-explored theme can illuminate the idea in a more accessible way. The effect can sometimes be that our understanding "clicks" into place.

It may seem audacious for a Western student to be offering even a highlight tour of Shantideva, but I would like to emphasize that I am not doing so from an assumed position of superior learning. Instead, I am offering ideas that may provide catalysts for your own inner development. It was, after all, one of the Buddha's most important teachings that enlightenment isn't something that can be given to us by others, but rather a state of being which it is our own personal responsibility to develop.

THE PRINCE WHO GAVE UP HIS KINGDOM

You may well be wondering about Shantideva himself—where did he come from, and what kind of person was he? In some ways, Shantideva's life story reflects that of the Buddha himself: although born into a royal family, he chose to reject his comfortable lifestyle of wealth and status.

Born in Gujarat, western India, from an early age Shantideva showed a strong interest in practicing the Dharma, as Buddha's teachings are collectively known. After the death of his father it was, dramatically, on the eve of his coronation that he decided to flee the palace, traveling to a highly regarded seat of learning, the great monastic University of Nalanda.

It's important to put this part of Shantideva's story into context, because to be a member of a royal family in eighth-century India was to occupy a position of immense privilege. Unlike these comparatively egalitarian times, when most of us in developed countries live in relative comfort even without the benefit of any particular social status or great wealth, in eighth-century India, if you were not part of a tiny elite, everyday life was usually nasty, brutish, and short. The gulf between rich and poor was huge. And the lifestyle of a monk demanded austerities which Shantideva would have been completely unused to. For him to give up a life of ease and privilege in pursuit of inner development would equate, in modern times, to the youthful heir to a multibillion-dollar business dynasty permanently forsaking the luxury homes, fast cars, and glamorous lifestyle to become an aid worker in Africa.

On the surface of things, such a decision may strike us as eccentric at the very least. But for someone with firsthand experience of all the pleasures of wealth and status to shrug them off perhaps tells us as much about the value of such things as it does about the person. Our own experience of life in a consumerist age confirms that despite enjoying a level of affluence far greater than our forebears ever dreamed of, our life's central challenge remains essentially the same: how to live with a sense of enduring happiness and purpose.

THE CONSPIRACY THAT BACKFIRED

Once at Nalanda Monastery Shantideva continued to be a nonconformist, but here it was monastic convention against which he rebelled. Instead of studying, meditating, and debating with his fellow monks during the day, he used to sleep, carrying out his own meditation practices at night in the strictest privacy. This unconventional behavior didn't endear him to his contemporaries, who used to refer to him sarcastically as the "Three Realizations" because they believed the only things he knew about were eating, sleeping, and defecating. Over time, some of them became determined to evict the monk they saw as a useless layabout who besmirched the fine name of Nalanda. In a scheming fashion you can't help feeling was decidedly un-Buddhist, they set up Shantideva for a very public humiliation. He was ordered to deliver a Dharma discourse to the entire monastery.

One can imagine the atmosphere in Nalanda's meditation hall when the appointed day finally arrived. How the monks would have awaited the speaker's appearance with unusual excitement. Did the plotters mask their glee behind poker faces, or were surreptitious smirks exchanged during prayers? Whatever the case, the anticipation in the hall must have been electric when Shantideva finally made his way to the teaching throne, center stage, and began to speak.

Within a few minutes, however, the schemers' plans began to unravel. Far from embarrassing himself in front of his assembled peers, Shantideva delivered teachings that immediately captured the attention of all present. His lecture was so incisive, so learned, and so eloquently expressed that it was soon recognized—however grudgingly by some—for its brilliance. Even more ironically, when transcripts of the teachings were copied some time later, they become far better known than any of the other learned teachings to have emerged from Nalanda. They are sometimes referred to as the best practical guide to achieving enlightenment.

They are the teachings that form the basis of the book you now hold in your hands.

A number of English translations of the complete *Guide* exist, but my personal favorite has always been the work by teacher and writer Stephen Batchelor. A former monk who combines impressive scholarly credentials with an incisive understanding of the Western mind, his translation is outstanding because it captures both the poetry and the power of Shantideva's language. It has an immediacy and freshness that keeps the text alive.

As the author of the bestselling *Buddhism without Beliefs*, and more recently *Confession of a Buddhist Atheist*, Stephen's ability to capture the essential wisdom of Buddha's teachings is extraordinary, and he has applied this same ability in reviewing and, as required, revising the verses presented here specifically for this book. I am sincerely grateful to him for bringing Shantideva's voice to us down through the ages with such wonderful clarity.

GOING BEYOND ORDINARY REALITY

You will have already gathered from this introduction that while knowledge and intellect are admired in Buddhism, far greater value is placed on the practical application of learning. It is significant to understand this if we are to make sense of what happened when Shantideva got to what is now known as the ninth chapter of his *Guide,* because it was at this point in his lecture that, we are told, something strange and magical—even by Himalayan standards— began to occur. Instead of remaining on the teaching throne, Shantideva began to levitate. Up and up he floated in meditation posture, a mesmerizing presence, carrying on his lecture as though nothing out of the ordinary was going on. Higher and higher he ascended until he'd disappeared from sight—but through an amazing and hitherto unsuspected power, he continued to speak, his disembodied voice carrying on quite clearly until he'd finished his teachings.

From a twenty-first-century Westerner's perspective, the idea of such a thing happening may seem altogether fanciful—another mystical tale from far, far away and long, long ago. But what Westerners would skeptically regard as claims of "psychic powers" are in Tibetan Buddhism, even today, considered to be significant but by no means exceptional manifestations of a highly experienced meditator.

It is especially relevant that the ninth chapter of Shantideva's *Guide* concerns the nature of reality, a subject that goes to the very heart of Buddha's teachings. More than two millennia before quantum scientists and neuropsychologists made their startling discoveries about the nature of reality, the inaccuracy of divisions between subject and object, and the deception of dualism, Buddha and other teachers were saying exactly the same things. Eastern mysticism and Western science have arrived at the same conclusion—summarized by physicist Sir Arthur Eddington when he said: "The concept of substance has disappeared from fundamental physics."

What if, instead of only understanding such concepts at an intellectual level, Shantideva was able to apply them to reality? Perhaps the famous story of his levitation wouldn't then seem quite so fanciful—it would, instead, merely have been an appropriate illustration of the wisdom he was conveying. And if the practical application of this wisdom wasn't unique to Shantideva, what is to stop us from doing the same? Why should we not also strive to achieve an understanding that takes us beyond our usual conception of reality—an enlightenment to go?

It is with such a motivation that we should set out on our "best of" tour of Shantideva's *Guide*, an exploration blessed by the Dalai Lama's repeated and emphatic endorsement. While grounded in the practical reality of daily life, Shantideva's teachings offer us truly awe-inspiring wisdom about a different way of being. Penetrating the meaning of this wisdom is exciting enough: *experiencing* the wisdom we taste reality in an entirely different way.

For it is the ultimate purpose of Shantideva's *Guide* to help awaken the buddha potential that dwells in each one of us: to provide step-by-step instructions on how to develop this potential; and, like Shantideva himself, to help us achieve a personal transcendence that goes beyond anything we might currently even begin to imagine.

PART I

*Developing the Compassionate Mind
of Enlightenment*

~

1

The Choice of Awakening

MANY PEOPLE AROUND the world are making the choice to awaken, beginning an inner journey that, though less easy to measure than a road or rail trip, and with a destination more difficult to define, is nevertheless just as real. For most of us it begins with a heartfelt yearning for greater purpose and contentment, the recognition that "there has to be more to life than this."

Whether our recognition builds up over time, or is thrust upon us by the crisis of a job loss, relationship break-up, serious illness, or other personal drama, the important thing is what we do *next*. Do we attribute our unhappiness to our heartless former employer, our deceitful ex-partner, the fickleness of fate? Or do we recognize that we have some say in the way we feel? Do we believe that external circumstances force us to experience certain emotions we'd much rather avoid? Or are we not the inevitable victims of circumstance?

In short, can we choose the way we feel?

As a society our answer to this question is ambivalent. So much of our behavior is based on the assumption that happiness is to be found in things that are external to ourselves—in particular, material comforts and relationships with other people. We spend a lot of our lives working to achieve or sustain a certain standard of living, a set of relationships, and sometimes the acquisition of influence or status—all the things that society seems to promote as the basis of a happy and fulfilled life. When these don't deliver the required levels of happiness, we see no paradox in turning to mood enhancers, be they alcoholic, prescription, or some other variety, which we know will do nothing for our external circumstances, but which we hope will make us feel a whole lot better about them.

Like most people, until I got quite some way into adulthood I never gave a moment's thought to whether or not I could choose the way I felt. Looking back on the major psychological landmarks of my early years—the anxieties I experienced at the start of my career in public relations, the frustrations of my work as a writer, the indignation that landlords and roommates and innumerable others could be less than scrupulous—I realize that all these feelings seemed normal, even inevitable, in the circumstances. As for the biggest landmark of them all, when my first serious girlfriend dumped me, the dark abyss of depression into which I fell seemed to me all too unavoidable. When someone pointed out the irksome truth that not all dumped ex-boyfriends reacted with quite the same dramatic intensity, I understood the point being made but—at least initially—came up with all kinds of reasons to explain why I wasn't like other dumped boyfriends.

Like a bird whose cage door is opened yet who does not fly to liberty, sometimes we find all kinds of excuses to remain in painful, familiar confinement even when the possibility of freedom is offered. It was only later that I was ready to explore the idea that I didn't actually have to live in despair.

CHANGING OUR INNER REALITY

If the starting point of our journey to awakening is dissatisfaction with the status quo of our lives, our first step only becomes possible when we choose to do something about it. The Buddhist term for this is "renunciation," which approximately translates as "turning away from the causes of our suffering."

In the West, such is our preoccupation with external reality that the word "renunciation" instantly evokes images of monastic austerities like sackcloth and ashes—in secular twenty-first-century terms perhaps, giving up our favorite high-cholesterol foods for a grim, low-calorie regime in an effort to lose weight.

Fortunately the Tibetan Buddhist view of renunciation is somewhat different. It is not the external reality that we are renouncing, but our inner reality. The whole point is that the causes of our suffering are to be found not "out there" but "in here." If we want to turn away from them, the focus of our efforts has to be on our mind.

Which brings us to the first stop on our highlights tour of Shantideva. And, perhaps appropriately, to one of the most quoted verses of the entire *Guide*. It is a verse you may have already encountered: the power of its message and economy of expression make it a perennial favorite with lamas, psychologists, and self-development teachers alike.

⌒

Where would I possibly find enough leather
With which to cover the surface of the earth?
Yet wearing leather just on the soles of my shoes
Is equivalent to covering the earth with it.

With the simplicity of genius, Shantideva explains the whole point of renunciation. In just four lines he illustrates the impossibility of trying to control everything in the world around us, contrasting it to the more manageable alternative of controlling the way we experience the world.

This explanation is based on the understanding that on our journey through life we will inevitably experience the psychological equivalent of stubbing our toes, stepping on thorns, cutting our ankles, and worse as we encounter harsh emotional terrain. Without protection we suffer pain. Just as shoes provide a defensive layer for soft feet, we should safeguard our emotions with a layer of protection—a shielding barrier of interpretations, values, and beliefs.

WHAT KIND OF SHOES?

My Dharma teacher, Les Sheehy, often teases the class that there's one subject on which most of us are expert. With decades of practice under our belt, we're all so good at it that we mostly do it without even trying. The area of expertise he's talking about is our ability to make ourselves unhappy.

The Sanskrit word *dukkha*, central in Buddhism, doesn't have a direct English translation, but it encompasses all forms of dissatisfaction, from everyday disgruntlement to the most profound suffering. Many of us are specialists in our own particular field of dissatisfaction. Some people are experts at experiencing frustration that their goals and dreams are never fully realized. Even when they do conquer a particular mountain, another, higher range looms up to meet them. Other people are grudge gurus, expert at feeling bitter resentment against political leaders who don't share their worldview, a wide range of industries—oil, financial, pharmaceutical, and the media are the usual suspects—and sometimes entire nations or races. Then there are victims, people whose lives are a woeful litany of one abusive experience after another—if ever there's a harrowing situation on offer, it seems to happen to them. And so the list goes on: they are the worried, the angry, the cheated, the depressed.

Of course, not everyone is like this. We all know people who manage to remain robustly upbeat and positive despite the most daunting personal circumstances. Indeed, they come to mind very easily because there are so few of them around!

Given that we all share the same world and many of the same

experiences, what accounts for such a variety of reactions? The answer, of course, is the layer of assumptions, beliefs, and habitual thoughts through which we mediate our experience of the world. To extend Shantideva's metaphor, some people wear sandals that constantly catch up sharp stones. Others wade through swamps wearing only canvas shoes, bitterly complaining when their feet get wet. Only a small proportion wear robust footwear.

Shantideva's *Guide* helps us all to find better shoes.

OUR INGRAINED MENTAL HABITS

One of the main challenges of this process isn't so much identifying our negative mental habits as replacing them. Like the bird that has lived in its self-imposed cage for too long to fly out the open door, we may very well be remaining in captivity for no better reason than sheer force of habit. We may share our world, perhaps even our homes, with people who have a quite different and more positive way of dealing with external reality, but still remain trapped in our routine negative patterns. In this way, we sabotage our own prospects for happiness.

Shantideva recognized the truth of our self-sabotage when he said:

Although wishing to be rid of misery,
They run toward misery itself.
Although wishing to have happiness,
Like an enemy they ignorantly destroy it.

Yes, we all agree, we do want to be happy. It's just that our ingrained mental habits—often referred to as "delusions" in Buddhism—can sometimes make this difficult to achieve.

Buddhist teachings offer a way of breaking this cycle in the form of radical methods of interpreting reality. These methods might be likened to pieces of leather with which to improve the quality of our shoes. Layers to protect us against the inevitable challenges of life.

Importantly, Buddha also recognized that we need a means by which to start applying these different methods of interpretation, a way of interrupting the old cycle of negative habitual reactions with more positive ones. The next few chapters focus on each of these radical interpretations in turn. Then, in Part II we will explore exactly how to apply them to everyday life—the reframing devices, the techniques, and the practices we can use to break out of the pattern of negativity.

I first discovered the value of these for myself as a Dharma student in Perth, Western Australia. Having met and married my Australian wife while living in London, I arrived in Perth in my midthirties at what felt like the start of an exciting new chapter in my life. I had recently signed a two-book deal with a major UK publisher and was looking forward to embarking on a life as a novelist.

Instead of the grinding commute to work through grey mornings in overcrowded train carriages, I suddenly found myself having breakfast al fresco, with only the screech of rainbow lorikeets in the palm tree to contend with. No longer was the phone jangling with imperative demands from clients and journalists as it had when I worked as a public relations consultant in London. Nor did I have to cram writing into whatever spare pockets of time I could find. Instead I had the luxury of whole working days to devote to my work.

Basking in Perth's life-enhancing Mediterranean climate, expansive white beaches, and vast blue skies, I felt that I was following in the footsteps of some of the great writers of the past. Somerset Maugham had escaped from England to the South of France, Ian

Fleming to Jamaica, Gore Vidal had abandoned America for Italy. This seemed to be the pattern in the natural order of things.

This supremely self-indulgent reverie was, however, abruptly cut short. No sooner had my first thriller been published in paperback than my publishers wrote to say they were dropping me from their catalogue. In the space of just a couple of years I'd gone from the next big up-and-comer on their thriller list to a discarded also-ran.

In the circumstances, it was hard to think of my novel-writing "career" as anything but a colossal failure. As I walked the pristine sands of Cottesloe Beach, I was no longer following in the footsteps of Ian Fleming or Somerset Maugham. Instead, I was washed up, on the wrong side of the world, far away from anywhere that mattered.

It was my very good fortune, however, to be a Dharma class regular at this time, and to be aware that a different perspective of my situation was possible. Specifically, I did have some choice in the way that I felt. I could blame my publishers, agent, or others for the chain of events that had reduced me to the status of failed novelist, or I could recognize that this interpretation of events was entirely my own. I could allow negativity and bitterness to dominate my thoughts and feelings, or I could reach for a more robust pair of shoes, a set of more accurate interpretations that would help me feel altogether more positive about my place in the world.

It was here that Buddhist classes proved invaluable. First, because I was introduced to the technique of analytical meditation along with the benefits already described; and second, because in my teacher, Les Sheehy, I found the perfect coach to challenge my usual "default mode" worldview. It didn't matter that my own particular brand of negative self-talk was different from the negativity of the Dharma student sitting next to me: the content of my depressing feedback loop wasn't really that important. In reality, all negative thinking, from which arise unhappy feelings, is based on only a handful of common assumptions, beliefs, and interpretations.

Several misconceptions in particular shape our thoughts, and Shantideva challenges each of these with masterful insight. One is our tendency to focus almost exclusively on the short-term here and now of our daily lives while habitually ignoring the bigger picture. A second is our routine overvaluing of external, material circumstances while undervaluing our internal, cognitive circumstances, which though less tangible, are much more important in their ability to make us happy. And a third is our preoccupation with narrow self-interest at the expense of a broader, other-facing worldview.

Each of these, in turn, forms the subject of the next three chapters.

Our first step, however, is the liberating recognition that the emotions that trouble us are by no means inevitable and unavoidable. Not only can we help the way we feel—the truth is that we are the ultimate creators of the world we choose to experience.

Mindfulness Exercise

This first exercise is not an analytical meditation so much as a warm-up. There's no need to go too hard, too soon—but don't underestimate the value of properly warming up. Your task is quite simple. At different times during the day, simply stop and ask yourself: *What am I thinking right now?*

▶ Stop yourself at intervals and consider the content of your thoughts and the way that you feel, and how one thing— the thought—leads to the other—the feeling. If it helps, put reminder notes where you will see them at different times of the day.

▶ Approach the exercise as though you were a researcher, trying to reach an objective assessment of your thoughts and feelings. Identify the predominant themes. Are they positive, negative, or a balance of the two? Pay particular attention to the habitual thoughts that give rise to any negative feelings.

▶ Observe how you talk to yourself during the day. What is the overall tone of your self-talk, and what messages do you send yourself?

▶ Through this exercise, try to become more aware of the assumptions, interpretations, and beliefs you have about yourself and the world around you—especially any recurring patterns and the feelings that they create.

2

The Big Picture or the Here and Now?

SOME YEARS AGO in London, a policeman was telling me about his work in a brutally dangerous part of the city. His beat was dominated by public housing estates where gang warfare and drug-fueled violence created a climate of constant fear. The policeman described how brutal gang attacks, fire-bombings, and vandalism were a daily occurrence, how most residents of the council estate locked their steel security doors at five o'clock in the afternoon and wouldn't dare venture out again till the next day, and how muggings, knifings, and other violent assaults peaked every Thursday—the day people got unemployment checks.

The world he described couldn't have been more different from the circles I moved in—even though the estate was only a twenty-minute drive from where I was living. After listening to several harrowing tales I paraded my naivety. "What do these guys think of normal people?" I asked him.

"Normal people?" He raised his eyebrows.

By "normal people," of course, I meant people who earned a living, rented or bought their own home, didn't take drugs, and generally stayed on the right side of the law.

"People like us," I said.

The policeman was quick to correct me. "So far as they're concerned," he told me bleakly, "they *are* normal."

Since that conversation I've often marveled at the huge variety of experiences that people consider to be normal—and that our own sense of normality is almost entirely dependent on our upbringing and culture. I've also come to recognize that by assuming normality is what we believe it to be—according to our highly limited, personal definition—we create most of our own unhappiness.

Recently I came across the story of an indignant high-society wife who unleashed an angry tirade on her unfortunate husband as they drove away from a dinner party at which he'd made the mistake of telling his hosts they were leaving early the next morning to catch a trans-Atlantic flight. Never had she felt so humiliated, she blazed. In front of their fellow diners, all owners of private Gulfstream jets, he'd admitted they were dependent on public transport (even if it was, one assumes, first class).

We may find it hard to feel much sympathy for someone like the society wife. We may believe that people who enjoy lives of immense affluence should be grateful for what they have, instead of whining that their privilege doesn't extend to a personal jet. But for this woman at the time, their dependence on scheduled flights was a source of genuine suffering.

WHAT EXACTLY *IS* NORMAL?

The two stories above beg the question: how "normal" is our own idea of ordinary reality? Most of us think of ourselves as leading regular lives. Some of us are aware we're privileged in certain respects. But what if I were to tell you that you are an individual endowed with exceptional abilities and privilege? Would you shrug off the idea as a little crazy? Clumsy flattery? A judgment you can't take seriously because it's based on no knowledge whatsoever of your personal circumstances?

As it happens, there are certain deductions I can make about you. For starters, in terms of intelligence and education you must be way above the average human baseline or you wouldn't be able to read and understand these words. To provide some context, this book is written at least at secondary school level, but even primary education is far from universal—right at this minute over 320 *million* school-age children worldwide have never seen the inside of a classroom. Thus in terms of intelligence and education, it's probably safe to say that you're in the top half, if not the top quartile, of the human population.

I can also deduce that you possess a certain level of self-discipline or emotional intelligence to support your reading of this book. Without it, there's very little chance you would have bought a book of this type to begin with, or if you had, you wouldn't have got this far into it without being distracted.

Self-mastery, or so-called emotional intelligence or "EQ," differs from IQ in that it reflects our ability to delay gratification in order to achieve bigger or more important goals. EQ is a more effective predictor of achievement than IQ because managing our emotions is more important than intellectual prowess in producing the sustained effort that all great accomplishment requires.

The reality is that many people, even those with an above-average IQ, don't have the EQ needed for sustained effort. As Calvin Coolidge, the thirtieth president of the United States, once noted: "Nothing in the world can take the place of persistence. Talent will not; nothing is more common than unsuccessful men with talent. Genius will not; unrewarded genius is almost a proverb. Education will not; the world is full of educated derelicts. Persistence and determination alone are omnipotent."

The fact that you enjoy not only above-average EQ and education but also understand the importance of self-discipline puts you higher up again, perhaps in the top eighth or sixteenth.

Then there's the fact that you have an interest in self-fulfillment or inner development—something that is the preserve of only a very small elite. Psychologist Abraham Maslow's famous hierarchy of needs, a pyramid-shaped model, describes how human needs evolve from the most basic essentials of food, shelter, and safety, through more developed needs for belonging and self-esteem, to reach an apex in the form of "self-actualization" or wishing to fulfill our maximum potential.

While Maslow's model was never intended to be interpreted in a fundamentalist way—the poorest among us also question the meaning of life—when we look at the vast populations of Asia, Africa, and South America, the billions of people who live at subsistence levels, we start to realize how incredibly fortunate we are not to have as our main focus the next meal we're going to eat, or a safe place to sleep tonight. Closer to home, in the developed world we don't have to look far to see how preoccupied most people are with the demands of going to work and raising families, and how their relatively few leisure hours are usually dominated by television or other distractions. They may have moved up the hierarchy from satisfying the most basic needs of food and safety, but they still haven't reached the point where realizing their own ultimate nature is of special importance to them.

ONE OF A RARE ELITE

So, while you may have believed that you're nothing special, when we look at the broader context we reveal the truth that you are among a rare elite. Does it matter whether you're in the world's top sixty-fourth, one hundred and twenty-eighth, or an even more unlikely fraction?

And we're not finished quite yet. It's also possible to deduce that you have at least some discretionary time. Whether you're reading this book on an airplane or during a quiet moment while the kids are asleep, you have access to at least some spare time. Most people's lives are a helter-skelter scramble, becoming increasingly busy as they move through adulthood. With only a finite lifespan, and the days, weeks, and years quickly slipping by, the reality is that time is our only truly finite commodity, and thus it is incredibly precious. But you clearly have at least some time available for inner development.

You may still believe that this is a modest list of attributes. You can quite possibly think of people who are much smarter, more educated, and more focused than you and who are also highly evolved and happy individuals. That may be your normality. But the society wife who chewed off her husband's head for not having a jet also knew people who were much wealthier. That didn't make her perspective any more balanced!

The fact is that any objective and dispassionate view of human life on earth will show us that what we have, in terms of our capabilities for growth, is rare. We are among a tiny percentage of the world's most privileged people. And as Shantideva says:

> Leisure and endowment are very hard to find;
> And, since they accomplish what is meaningful for humanity,
> If I do not take advantage of them now,
> How will such a perfect opportunity come about again?

By "leisure and endowment" Shantideva is referring to precisely the combination of intelligence, motivation, self-discipline, and time that are needed to effect personal transformation. And as he makes clear, these qualities provide the basis of a "perfect opportunity" that, far from being common, is actually exceptional.

For most of us, acknowledging this requires a fundamental shift in our usual perspective—one of the radical reinterpretations that Buddha suggests we adopt. Instead of thinking about ourselves as being just normal, we cultivate the more accurate view that we are incredibly privileged. Our lives, far from being humdrum, are actually extraordinarily precious. From the perspective of awakening, we already have everything we need, and in fact belong to only a very rare few who do. Shantideva asks us a very pointed question: If we don't take full advantage of this amazing confluence of factors to achieve inner transformation now, when will we?

A BROADER PERSPECTIVE OF CONSCIOUSNESS

So far, our analysis has considered things from a purely human perspective. But consciousness exists in realms besides the human. Animals also have consciousness and are what Buddhists call "sentient beings"—"sentient" meaning "having mind." As an animal lover I like to indulge my pets: currently, two very pampered cats, eight rather fat goldfish, and a family of galahs—pink and grey parrots—who treat our garden wall as their fly-through breakfast diner. For all the fondness I feel for these creatures, however, I have no means of communicating with them on anything but the most basic level. Sure, they have consciousness and we share the same basic wishes—to be safe, well-fed, and loved. But their consciousness is, of course, limited.

From this broader perspective, our immense good fortune to experience human consciousness, with leisure and endowment, becomes even more spectacular. Because unlike animals, we have the awareness and ability to self-consciously take charge of the way we experience reality; to break the cycle of conditioning—or karma—and direct our consciousness to a more positive destiny. We have the potential to move away from negative actions of body, speech, and mind to those that will be of far greater benefit to ourselves as well as others. Put simply, enlightenment becomes a possibility.

For these very reasons, the Buddha has said
That as difficult as it is for a turtle to insert its neck
Into a yoke adrift upon the vast ocean,
It is more difficult to attain the human state.

In this verse Shantideva illustrates the incredible rarity of being born as humans, invoking one of the Buddha's most striking metaphors. As the beneficiaries of such privilege, a question inevitably follows: are we making the most of our exceptional situation? The opportunity for transformation doesn't get much better. The time available to us is constantly diminishing the older we get. What exactly are we doing about it?

LATRINE-FILLERS—OR NO LONGER ORDINARY?

Leonardo da Vinci, the fifteenth-century artist, scientist, and thinker, used to disparage the majority of his fellow citizens in Florence as "latrine-fillers." A harsh judgment, no doubt, but as someone acutely aware of the possibilities of his era, he despaired that so many of those around him did so little to seize the burgeoning opportunities available.

When we occupy our time with activities purely concerned with our own short-term material well-being, from the perspective of the Dharma, or Buddha's teachings, we are also doing no more than filling latrines. But because our culture places so much emphasis on consumerism, latrine-filling feels like entirely normal behavior. Raising our sights to goals more appropriate to our exceptional status, by contrast, is somehow unusual. It's only when we truly realize the rarity of our immense good fortune that we realize we shouldn't squander it. The Dalai Lama sometimes likens the experience of human consciousness with leisure and fortune to being visitors to an island of jewels—and he implores us: Please don't leave it empty-handed!

Shantideva expresses the same idea in the following verse. When he uses the word "wholesome," I take it to mean not only "ethical" but also motivated by benevolent purpose.

If when I have the chance to live a wholesome life
My actions are not wholesome,
Then what shall I be able to do
When confused by the misery of the lower realms?

When consciousness is dominated by deprivation, fear, and hostility, the struggle for survival makes principles like ethics and benevolence difficult, if not impossible, to aspire to. Recognizing this, we can see that here and now we have the most extraordinary opportunity to develop a sense of purpose that goes well beyond narrow self-interest to an altogether more panoramic state.

Buddhist teachings tell us that the human condition is a very special one because we experience both dissatisfaction as well as pleasure but are not consumed by either. Our vantage enables us to see that neither the avoidance of suffering nor the enjoyment of pleasure can be anything but temporary. A more permanent solution demands a paradigm shift, one in which we move from the very changeable experiences of our current consciousness to the radiant and more permanent freedom offered by Buddha's teachings. Simply becoming aware of this possibility is an immense privilege.

GRATITUDE: THE ANTIDOTE TO DESPAIR

In the early days, before I had any familiarity with these sorts of ideas, I needed the regular assistance of my teacher to help me break out of negative thought patterns and widen my perspective. But over the years I've learned to apply this skill for myself, and not only when things are busy or difficult. At the start of my daily meditation session, I usually remind myself of my exceptional good fortune not only to be born human but to be a human with leisure and endowment, and one who has discovered the Dharma—and, even more unlikely, one who has the opportunity, here and now, to practice it. I find that simply reflecting on this sequence of thoughts is a cause of gratitude and inner peace. When I'm able to hold the recognition of my good fortune single-pointedly for a while, the gratitude becomes even more expansive and heartfelt. Those moments when I'm able simply to dwell on the extraordinary preciousness of my life help me to experience reality in a more accurate, panoramic way, and they're also wonderfully restorative. At odd moments during the day, the recognition of my good fortune will suddenly bubble up into my thoughts; where once I had never seriously considered this view of reality, it has now become a more regular and happiness-creating part of my mind stream.

Meditating on leisure and fortune gave me a particularly helpful point of reference in the months during which it became clear that I was not, after all, to take my place in the literary firmament. In the past, my reaction to such a devastating setback would have been to retreat into deep depression. Particularly in my twenties, I had experienced months when it was all I could do to drag myself out of bed in the mornings and through a pretense of normality each workday, returning home at night to sedatives, alcohol, and sleep—anything to help avoid the feeling that, despite the most strenuous efforts, my life was an unmitigated disaster. By my thirties I was older and wiser. To a certain extent I had toughened up. But the real difference came when I learned to challenge my most negative and deeply ingrained thought patterns. I'd find myself sinking into the familiar darkness of despair and then there'd be a new thought: "But what about the bigger picture?"

I returned to working as a public relations consultant in the finance industry, the career I had pursued while living in London. It's a stimulating occupation for someone curious about the mechanics of money—an interest I'd discovered early on. And although I'd arrived in Western Australia with no business contacts at all, events unfolded in a way that made it possible for me to find clients whose company I enjoyed and whose businesses did interesting things.

The sun still rose every morning. On long summer evenings, the chilled white wine from the Margaret River region tasted just as sweet. And even though in my early adult years I'd told myself that it was only when I was a full-time writer that my "real life" would begin, I now had the mental tools to realize what a dumb-ass way of thinking that was. There was nothing unreal about my current occupation. In fact, if there was any unreality about my life at all it was the sheer, incomprehensible good luck of it. I was enjoying a lifestyle I'd only been able to dream about while living in London, and at the same time as leading this privileged existence I was also receiving teachings from a most amazing Dharma teacher.

But negative thoughts and feelings don't just magically disappear in one fell swoop. When they've been part of our way of thinking for a long time, they will certainly continue to recur—but I've found that their frequency diminishes and their effect becomes less powerful as we learn who to work with and transform them. One way we create our own unhappiness is by focusing too much on the short-term here and now at the expense of the bigger picture—but this is only one of several habitual mental patterns through which we create more suffering. Another is our habitual overvaluing of external circumstances and undervaluing of internal circumstances in their ability to make us happy. We explore this subject in the next chapter.

Analytical Meditation

Before beginning each analytical meditation, stabilize the mind with a breath meditation exercise. Only when the mind is calm and relaxed should you begin the analytical stage of the meditation. I suggest that when you first begin meditating you aim for ten or fifteen minutes in total, with about one third of the time allocated to calming the mind through breathing meditation, as described in the appendix, before moving on to your chosen analytical subject. The appendix to this book explains the process of analytical meditation in more detail.

▶ Reflect on how reality is experienced by animals, who comprise the vast majority of conscious beings on our planet. Think how animals share our desire to avoid suffering, and to have food, safety, and happiness. Consider the lives of most animals who are merely food for other animals. Contemplate the mind states of these sentient beings on a moment-by-moment basis.

▶ Consider the rarity of being born a human being. Recollect Buddha's analogy that achieving a human rebirth is as rare as a turtle rising through the ocean and lifting up its head through a yoke that happens to be floating on the surface. Think of the statistical improbability of being born a human being.

▶ Now reflect on the scarcity of human beings who are born with leisure and endowment compared to the billions who are not. Think how the vast majority of people on our planet spend most of their days struggling for all the basics we take for granted. Recognize the rare opportunity for inner growth that you possess. Think how amazing it is that you enjoy the endowments of leisure and education. Consider how you have also encountered the Dharma, which provides a unique set of tools to help develop the full potential of your mind. How rare are these teachings, and how few people ever come to study them!

▶ Think: "I have the opportunity, here and now, to start practicing these techniques. This is a rare and precious opportunity for which I feel a deep and abiding sense of gratitude." Try to hold this thought single-pointedly—that is, keeping your focus on it with mindfulness and awareness.

3

Inner Experience or Outer Appearance?

ONE OF THE MOST intriguing aspects of the Dharma, for me, is the way it takes us on a journey of unfolding self-discovery. From my discussions with fellow students, some of whom have been practicing for decades longer than me, I know this experience is true for us all. No matter how jaded, cynical, or world-weary we may be, Buddhism has an extraordinary way of challenging our conceptions and offering fresh and quite unexpected perspectives. One such challenge struck me early on in my Dharma practice: it is the hugely important trade-off that most of us aren't even aware we're making.

We all make trade-off decisions on an ongoing basis: do I take the incoming call from someone I'm longing to speak to, or leave right away and get to my next appointment on time? Do I have that glass of wine—which may well become two—with dinner, or do I finish the work I brought home and impress my clients with my productivity when we meet tomorrow morning?

At a higher level the trade-offs are more weighty. Should I stay in a difficult relationship in the hope it can be renewed, or leave it for an unknown future? I'd like to take early retirement from the unfulfilling job to follow my dreams, but would I struggle to live on my retirement package? Would it be better to get a second job, or to spend more time with my family?

While the universal and enduring dilemmas relating to love and money have always commanded the attention of poets, psychologists, and advice columnists alike, the biggest trade-off of all is rarely, if ever, discussed. The set of issues that arguably holds the greatest consequences for our happiness is the one that our society mostly overlooks. It is the trade-off we make about how much time and energy we spend in shaping our external, material world versus the time and energy we spend in shaping our internal experience of that world.

We have already touched on this in the first chapter, with Shantideva's metaphor of covering the world with leather versus wearing a pair of shoes. But let's look in more detail at exactly what this metaphor implies.

The starting point is the goal we all share: the wish for happiness. In the secular West, our common belief is that this is to be achieved by rearranging the externals of our lives; hence the preoccupation with relationships, money, and power, and all the things that flow from them. The financial security provided by work, in particular, is one of our most dominant drivers. Most of us spend between eight and ten hours a day at work, including the commute there and back. And while it's true that the world of work has become more flexible with job-sharing, tele-working, and e-lancing, the reality for most mid- or senior-level workers is that work is still an all-consuming focus of their time and energy. The people and projects we work with become so important that they not only dominate our working day but often occupy our thoughts away from the office. We talk about them over dinner. Stew on them over the weekend. In times of stress they even keep us from sleeping. Introducing ourselves to others, we often define ourselves by our job. On losing our jobs, we not only suffer anxiety about the loss of income, but our whole sense of identity takes a hammering too.

One of my clients is a financial planning firm that advises corporate high-fliers how to invest, manage, and protect their wealth. They tell me that of every five executives they see, only one has his or her financial life in order. The other four have no clearly articulated financial goal, let alone a strategy to reach that goal. These time-scarce high-rollers often make investment decisions on an ad-hoc basis. They leave themselves and their families exposed to unrewarded risk. Despite being astute and resourceful, and earning significant incomes, they neglect their own financial interests. The reason? Here's the greatest irony of all: they're too busy pursuing the financial interests of their employers.

Many of us have been caught up in this curious paradox. Driven to achieve in a material sense, we get so absorbed in the *process* of earning a living that we not only allow it to dominate our waking lives, we also fail to effectively manage and invest the money we earn—the main reason we go to work in the first place.

As it happens, there's nothing at all new about this paradox. It's at least twelve hundred years old, judging by Shantideva's take on the subject. While in the West we sometimes talk about the work treadmill or the hamster wheel, Shantideva illustrates the trade-off between effort and reward at work in a somewhat different way:

> In the same way as animals drawing carriages
> Are only able to eat a few mouthfuls of grass,
> Likewise desirous people
> Have many disadvantages such as these, and little profit.

Like donkeys snatching the odd mouthful of greenery as we heave the corporate carriage forward, says Shantideva, if we allow material concerns to dominate our lives, the paltry benefits we enjoy are by far outweighed by the effort involved.

EXAGGERATING THE POSITIVE

The term "desirous people" deserves clarification because in our society it may seem to carry specifically sexual overtones which Shantideva didn't intend. In this instance we might replace "desirous people" with "consumerists," because in this verse Shantideva refers to a particular aspect of Buddhist psychology, which suggests that much of our unhappiness is created by attachment/desire at one end of the spectrum and its opposite, aversion/hatred, at the other.

This psychology looks at how we interact with people and objects in the world around us, and the way we tend to categorize them into positive, negative, and neutral according to our conditioning—or karma. When it comes to the positive, we have a tendency to exaggerate the degree to which certain things, people, or situations could make us happy. We may think that having a particular woman or man in our life would make us feel truly complete. Or that driving a particular car would make us feel glamorous and successful. Or that the money and recognition we'd get from landing a particular job or contract would do wonders for our self-esteem.

So we work our hearts out to get the job, the contract, the car. We try our best to impress, court, or seduce the boy or girl. We're so sure of the happiness that will come from winning this particular prize that we may be tempted to make ethical compromises, believing that the ends will most certainly justify the means.

And then it happens: *we get what we want.* How fantastic is this?! For a period of hours, months, or somewhere in between, we're absolutely thrilled. But as we get to grips with our new girl, car, or job we discover things about them that aren't entirely as we had thought. Our initial euphoria settles down. As time goes on and we adjust, we recognize that along with all the positives—which used to be the only things we could think about—there are a bunch of negatives, now impossible to ignore. The whole proposition becomes a little more complicated.

Then we're sitting at the traffic lights one day and someone pulls up beside us in a newer car than ours. We are the smooth operator no more. We read about a much younger rival who lands himself a job or contract even better than ours, and all of a sudden it feels like we're being left behind. As for the girlfriend—don't even go there!

If we learned our lesson from such experiences, they'd have a value. But most of us don't. We go on repeating the same error. If we replace the girlfriend, who turned out to be a bitch from hell, with someone more genuine, like Lucy from marketing, then things really would be different, we think. Or if we bought that up-market watch—sorry, chronograph—then we'd feel pretty special. Over and over again, contrary to so much of our experience, we keep telling ourselves that yes, we will be happy, just as soon as we rearrange the externals of our life in a particular way—the "I'll be happy when . . ." syndrome.

Daniel Gilbert, Professor of Psychology at Harvard University, has undertaken intriguing studies showing how bad we actually are at predicting our future happiness. These studies show we have a tendency to overestimate the impact of a positive event, believing that a different relationship or new career will result in permanent change rather than short-term pleasure. On the other hand, Gilbert's research shows, we underestimate our ability to bounce back from even the most traumatic events, such as the death of someone we love, bankruptcy, or a bitter divorce.

Why do we devote such an overwhelming amount of time and effort to rearranging the externals despite the mixed results we get? Possibly because we tend to confuse happiness with pleasure.

Here it's useful to distinguish between the two. Pleasure, for the purposes of this book at least, is something that we derive from an object, a place, or people. It is, by definition, circumstantial. We may get pleasure from dining in a particular restaurant or wearing elegant new clothes. But take us to that restaurant after we've just eaten a large meal, or put us in our stylish attire during a blazing row with our significant other, and chances are we will experience no pleasure at all.

If pleasure is circumstantial enjoyment, happiness refers to a deeper sense of fulfillment not dependent on circumstance, which is usually accompanied by qualities such as peacefulness, purposefulness, and benevolence. Unlike pleasure, which requires situations to be constantly renewed or upgraded, happiness is a state of mind that deepens the more we experience it.

Most of us try to achieve happiness by pursuing pleasure, which by definition is circumstantial. Because it sometimes works, perhaps we assume that this highly conditional and temporary form of good feeling is as good as it gets. But perhaps the reason we focus so much time and energy on the externals is because we don't know any better. A different way of experiencing reality has never been presented to us.

THE SUPERSTITION OF CONSUMERISM

Buddhist teachings on true causes provide a simple but radical analysis. According to this view, for something to be a true cause of something else it must always work. Just as two dry sticks rubbed together will always create friction, no matter who rubs the sticks, where they rub them, or how often they repeat the exercise, so too if something is a true cause of happiness it must have an effect no matter who applies it, where it is applied, or how often it is repeated.

Looking at all the things we usually regard as creating happiness, we realize they can't be defined as "true causes." It's an almost universal belief that a wealthy lifestyle is a cause of happiness, but if this is true why isn't there a direct relationship between wealth and happiness? And why are some wealthy people so miserable they commit suicide? Why is there so much antidepressant use in the affluent suburbs? Being recognized, well regarded, and famous is another commonly held cause of happiness. But once again, the isolation, loneliness, and pressures of being in the public eye lead to many a celebrity meltdown. On a more everyday note, not even humble ice cream can be a true cause of happiness. Sure, one cone on its own may be delicious, but how many do you need to eat before the very thought of more ice cream makes you feel nauseated?

And yet we continue to believe in the superstition of consumerism: the shared, misguided belief that the golden path of happiness is to be accessed by rearranging the externals of our lives in a particular way. We live in a society which is mesmerized by external reengineering. Look at television output on any one night and you will find the most forensic accounts of fashion design, meal preparation, home decorating, property trading, lifestyle shifting, relationship repairing, garden renovating, cosmetic surgery—you name it. But how often do we see anything about mental reengineering? Along with all the detailed advice on extreme makeovers of the body, wouldn't it also be useful to have someone guide people through extreme makeovers of the mind—like coaching people to replace habitual negative thoughts with happiness-creating ones? As well as promoting weight loss to the heavy, and sartorial elegance to the badly dressed, how about explaining the well-established benefits and *how-to*s of meditation?

The reason for this materialist bias in Western culture is our unfamiliarity with any way to engage with the world other than via its external forms. As consumerists, however, we pay a high price for the fleeting pleasure we sometimes experience.

LASTING HAPPINESS
FOR A MILLIONTH OF THE EFFORT

As Shantideva points out, it doesn't have to be like this. There is a better way. Not only happiness and inner peace but full enlightenment is possible, he says, with just a fraction of the effort involved in the struggle to earn just a few mouthfuls of grass. Apart from anything

else, the problem with material pleasures is their impermanence—
one of the main reasons they can't possibly be a true cause of lasting
happiness.

⁓

The objects of desire will certainly perish,
And then I shall fall into hellish states.
However, buddhahood itself is attained
With just one millionth of the difficulty

Involved in continually exhausting myself
For the sake of what is not very great.
Hence the desirous experience greater misery
   than those following the Awakening way of life—
But for them there is no Awakening.

The implications of these lines are truly remarkable. Full enlightenment or buddhahood is understood to be a state of unceasing and
unimaginable bliss, formless and boundless, without beginning or
end. It's a state of consciousness so wonderful that it is quite beyond
our ordinary comprehension and certainly beyond expression. For
a Buddhist, enlightenment parallels the way a Christian might
describe the experience of the love of God, or a Jew might speak of
invoking Yahweh: it is ineffable—too great for description.

Long before attaining this state, however, there are milestones
along the way. Buddhahood isn't a way of being that comes to us in
a blinding flash of light; rather, it evolves gradually as we develop our
minds. Even in our early steps toward our distant objective we enjoy
life-changing benefits from shifting our attention to include inner
transformation, instead of a purely external focus.

What form does this inner transformation take? The practice
of meditation is a fundamental part of the process, scientifically

established to heighten activity in that part of the brain associated with happiness and relaxation. Our outer conditions may not have changed, but we can still feel a whole lot happier about them. When we meditate we also improve our concentration and generate gamma-wave brain activity patterns—the state in which higher-level thinking and insight occurs. We enhance our awareness of everything around us and our capacity to more consciously engage in our lives on a moment-by-moment basis. We increase our sense of gratitude, well-being, and interconnectedness with the world around us.

Outside of formal meditation, the application of mindfulness in daily life is another foundation practice. Through it we gradually calm and redirect the ceaseless flow of agitated mental chatter into a deeper appreciation of each moment that we live—especially the positive ones, which, ironically, we're often in too much of a hurry to notice. We are also better able to reengineer our inner experience of the outside world. For example, by reminding ourselves of our immense privilege to be leading lives of leisure and fortune, we inevitably appreciate these good conditions we enjoy—we *feel* wealthier. Making a conscious attempt to practice giving happiness to others is a further aspect of this process, paradoxically expanding our own capacity to enjoy happiness and inner peace at the most profound level. All of these and many other aspects of the inner pathway are fully described in Part II of this book, which sets out how to cultivate an enlightened way of life.

Following the path of inner development does not require us to stop engaging with the external world. Rather, we engage with the world differently. We still do our jobs, pay the mortgage, and bring up the kids. When we do this more mindfully, from the perspective of a more awakened state, we are likely to be more effective performers than otherwise. But perhaps we can also address the trade-off so that instead of investing 100 percent of our time trying to rearrange the externals, we can now spend 5 percent on inner activities instead. Finding time to meditate each morning, for example, even if only for ten or fifteen minutes, is a subtle shift that can nonetheless have the most life-altering effect.

From the perspective of this lifetime alone, the path of inner development offers incomparably greater happiness than pure consumerism. And if we embrace the possibility that consciousness continues from one lifetime to another, the implications are greater still, because any advances we make in evolving our consciousness in one particular lifetime create the causes for more positive experiences in the future. Viewed through this wider angle lens, we see the benefits of what we're doing as part of a much bigger story—one in which, like the energy from a stone cast into a tranquil lake, the impact of our actions expands in ever-widening circles, with consequences way beyond the immediate here and now, rippling out across future lifetimes to infinity.

Who is to say that, in accepting the need for inner transformation, we are not simply returning to a path we have already begun in previous lives? Taking up where we left off in an earlier existence? We may feel that we're just at the beginning, but like the athlete returning to his gym routine after a long break, we may find that all our previous training didn't go entirely to waste. Perhaps even in reading this book you are being drawn back to a path along which you have already trodden?

OUT OF TOUCH WITH REALITY?—A CASE STUDY

A concern I've heard expressed is that too much time spent meditating, or developing other inner practices, could result in people losing touch with reality. No doubt the glassy-eyed tree-huggers of some New Age communes have contributed to the view that if you're not careful you'll get so caught up contemplating your own navel that you'll forget to pay the phone bill.

My observation is the opposite of this. In Buddhism the impact of inner development makes people operate more effectively in the everyday world. In fact, it seems to provide them with skills and resources they wouldn't otherwise be able to draw on.

Early on during my days as an Australian-based PR man, I was asked to help arrange some media coverage for the Buddhist nun Tenzin Palmo, who would soon be visiting Perth. The request was a long way from the mortgages and investments that are my standard work fare, but I was so intrigued by the prospect I couldn't possibly say no. I had read about the amazing life of Tenzin Palmo in the biography *Cave in the Snow*. An Englishwoman who had been drawn to Buddhism for as long as she could remember, Tenzin Palmo had left England for India when she was only twenty and became one of the first Westerners to be ordained as a Buddhist nun. But she was probably best known for the fact that she'd spent twelve years on a solitary meditation retreat in a remote cave in the Himalayas. It seemed such an extraordinary experience for anyone to have gone through, an English-speaking Westerner in particular, that I jumped at the chance to meet her.

The opportunity came one morning at the local ABC radio studios where she was being interviewed. Greeting the diminutive figure in her red and saffron robes for the first time, I received an immediate impression of her as someone who knew exactly what was going on. Astute, alert, articulate, it was instantly evident that she had a penetrating intelligence. This was someone who could sum up the true nature of things in a flash. But balancing her otherwise intimidating perceptiveness was a touching warmth. When she smiled, she beamed from ear to ear, her whole face lighting up and blue eyes dazzling.

If, during her twelve years in retreat, Tenzin Palmo had focused on the ultimate nature of reality, this clearly hadn't created some sort of handicap to her work in the conventional world. If anything, it seemed only to have enhanced her effectiveness. Starting by teaching a handful of girls in just one room, step by step she has built a nunnery to help address the traditionally huge gender imbalance in Tibetan Buddhist training. Dongyu Gatsal Ling is now a substantial center with forty-five resident nuns, a study center, a retreat center, and a traditional temple currently under construction. Ultimately, the plan is to accommodate one hundred women at the nunnery. Tenzin Palmo has raised funds to meet the significant costs of land and buildings by traveling extensively each year and giving teachings in many countries. She has written an inspiring Dharma book, *Reflections on a Mountain Lake*. And along with her formal role at the nunnery, she has also played an equally important informal role as carer, guardian, and "mother" to the many young girls who travel from all over India, Tibet, and Bhutan to study the Dharma.

Her contribution has been so great that in February 2008 she was awarded the prestigious title of Jetsunma, which means Venerable Master, by His Holiness the twelfth Gyalwang Drukpa, head of the Drukpa Kagyu lineage, in recognition of her achievements as a nun and her efforts in promoting the status of female practitioners in Tibetan Buddhism.

Tenzin Palmo has no training or qualifications as an architect, fundraiser, or project manager. Nor is she a professional public speaker. She did not spend her life helping to manage a nunnery before establishing Dongyu Gatsal Ling. And yet her achievements in all these areas have been exemplary. From all the collective evidence, it would be hard to conclude that her twelve years of intensive inner development somehow made her less capable—indeed, quite the opposite.

As my teacher often says, when we shift our focus from external to inner development, paradoxically we find the external world easier to deal with. When we abandon the limited preoccupations of what he calls "the sesame seed mind," with its narrow, external, here-and-now concerns, not only are we happier but we also become more effective operators.

Evolving in this way not only requires a more appropriate balance between external appearance and inner experience, it also includes a shift in the focus of our consciousness. This shift is the subject of our next chapter.

Analytical Meditation

Before beginning the analytical meditation, stabilize your mind with a breath meditation exercise.

▶ Consider the concept of "true causes." Can you think of any object, person, or situation that is unfailingly a true cause of happiness?

▶ Reflect on the external circumstances of your own life. Have the times you've been wealthiest and most successful led to your greatest experience of happiness?

▶ Think of the wealthiest people you know. As far as you can tell, are they also the happiest people you know? Then think of your poorest friends or acquaintances—as far as you can tell, are they all the most unhappy?

▶ Consider how much time and energy you invest in rearranging the external circumstances of your life. By contrast, how much time and energy do you invest in inner activities such as meditation and mindfulness practice?

▶ Cultivate single-pointedly the wish to develop greater happiness and fulfillment through balancing outer activities with inner development.

4

Shifting the Focus from Self to Other

In May 2001 at the University of Wisconsin, a breakthrough scientific observation was made by neuroscientist Richard Davidson. Davidson had long been interested in the relationship between thought and feeling. His extensive work using fMRI equipment, involving hundreds of subjects, had shown that when people are happy, energized, or upbeat there is greater activity in the left prefrontal cortex. By contrast, when we are emotionally distressed—anxious, angry, or depressed—the brain's circuits in the right prefrontal cortex are more active.

It was when Davidson studied the brain activity of a Buddhist monk—a highly experienced meditator—that he made his amazing observation. The monk meditated on several different predetermined subjects, but it was when he focused on compassion for others that his left prefrontal cortex indicated the greatest activity. Feedback showed he was enjoying an *extremely* pleasant mood.

What made this study so remarkable was that it provided the first scientific evidence to support what is one of the core experiences of Buddhists: that focusing benevolent thoughts on the well-being of others is a true cause of happiness.

It's one of the paradoxes of our lives in the developed world that, for all our technological sophistication, we have such a poor understanding of what makes us happy. As discussed in the previous chapter, social consensus seems to suggest we should put our own material well-being at the front and center of our lives, despite all the evidence that it's no guarantee of happiness. Meanwhile, we see effort focused on the welfare of others as an optional extra, a feel-good add-on which we'll get to once we've taken care of looking after number one.

Of course, not all our behavior is self-serving. Most parents, for example, are wholeheartedly dedicated to the well-being of their children. All of us have feelings of affection, love, and compassion toward family, partners, friends, and pets. For the most part, though, the group of beings for whom we have such feelings is relatively small, and our interest in their welfare is often conditional on their showing care and friendship to us. But Shantideva illustrates a quite different approach.

First of all, I should make an effort
To meditate upon the equality between self and others.
I should protect all beings as I do myself
Because we are all equal in wanting pleasure and not
    wanting pain.

When both myself and others
Are similar in that we wish to be happy,
What is so special about me?
Why do I strive for my happiness alone?

And when both myself and others
Are similar in that we do not wish to suffer,
What is so special about me?
Why do I protect myself and not others?

LOVE AND COMPASSION DEFINED

One of the distinguishing features of Tibetan Buddhism is that it provides us with precise definitions. Two of the most useful are the definitions of *love* and *compassion*, which Shantideva refers to in the verses above. *Love* is defined as the wish to give other beings happiness, while *compassion* is the wish to help free them from suffering. If we try to give happiness to others, or help them avoid suffering, without the expectation of anything in return, these are pure motivations of love and compassion. When the Dalai Lama says, "My religion is kindness," or that love and compassion are at the heart of Buddhism, this is specifically what he is referring to.

It is certainly worth reflecting on the implications of unconditional love or, as Buddhists would say, love that is not "attachment-based." Attachment-based love is when we want something or someone because of what that thing or person can do for us. When we say we "love" chocolate cake, everyone knows we're using the attachment-based concept of the word, rather than the Buddhist definition: we don't love chocolate cake because of what we can do for it!

Interestingly, the concept of romantic love, endlessly presented as an idealized human experience, often looks less transcendent when we consider the motivations of those involved. Do I always wish for the happiness of the other person, without conditions, or only if the other person behaves in a particular way toward me? I may like to think of myself as a loving person who only wants my partner to be happy, but how many conditions and expectations do I load onto that person? If he or she does something trivial that annoys me, do I immediately withdraw my affection and get the sulks? If so, is "love" really the most accurate way to define our relationship?

In his *Guide*, Shantideva provides several different reasons to practice love and compassion in the Buddhist sense. The verses above form part of his appeal to reason, providing the coolly objective analysis that all of us are equal in wanting to enjoy pleasure and avoid pain. A simple argument, but it nevertheless comes as a startling challenge when he asks: "What is so special about me? Why do I strive for my happiness alone?"

Why do we? Our overwhelming sense of self is no doubt at the heart of it, not to mention deeply ingrained habit. Perhaps also an innate competitive instinct, which makes us frequently view situations as "us versus them." Sociologists might argue that the increasing emphasis on individual rights also promotes the belief that "it's all about me." Whatever the reasons, the result is that our usual worldview is emphatically dualistic. We make a big distinction between self and other. We focus so much attention on ourselves that we don't often enter the worlds of others, sincerely trying to see things through their eyes or understand their feelings. Sometimes we actively avoid any feeling of empathy, because acknowledging the hardships others face would make us feel bad about ourselves.

The driver who crosses the congested intersection on an amber light, fully aware that he will be blocking off a lane, but thinking, "They can wait"; the businessman who uses deceptive methods to gain the financial advantage on the basis that "they'd do the same to me"; the pet owner who neglects or abandons his or her dog or cat with the justification that "it's just an animal": these are all examples of people deliberately avoiding empathy with those they are abusing. People trying to fabricate reasons to avoid the simple truth that the other beings they're making unhappy are just like them in wishing for happiness and the avoidance of suffering.

A TRUE CAUSE OF HAPPINESS

But Shantideva also understood that our instinctive inclination toward self versus other is so powerful that love and compassion are unlikely to result from appeals to reason alone. This is why he also appeals to our emotions. The following verse is one of his most powerful and challenging: powerful because in trademark Shantideva style he takes no prisoners—there are no *ifs*, *buts*, or *maybes* about it—and challenging because it runs so contrary to our usual assumptions.

Whatever joy there is in this world
All comes from desiring others to be happy,
And whatever suffering there is in this world
All comes from desiring myself to be happy.

When I first encountered this verse my reaction was: *Whoa! Back up a bit. Isn't this a little extreme?* Wondering whether I agreed with it or not, I found it pretty easy to come up with exceptions to Shantideva's rule. Like the regular pleasure I get from the coffee and muffins down at my local café—I can't pretend that my motivation to enjoy them arises from any great desire to make others happy. Trips to the movies, holidays, a bottle of my favorite wine: all of these can be sources of delight, and there isn't a trace of altruism to be found in any of them.

But thinking about the difference between happiness and pleasure, I realized that Shantideva wasn't talking about the pleasure that is dependent on circumstance and necessarily transient. He was focusing on happiness—more enduring and deeply felt. And when I reflected on events in my life that have touched me at the most profound level, I realized that these are the feelings Shantideva is talking about.

Like the time I gave my ill mother a relaxation tape I'd made and watched her begin to listen to it, sinking back into her pillow with a peaceful expression. She had been fighting a gruelling war against cancer, during which I'd felt helpless to do much more than offer words of consolation. But recently we had discussed hypnotherapy, which I was studying at the time, and she surprised me by expressing an interest. Being able to make her a tape to help her let go of all her concerns, if only temporarily, was a cause of the most profound happiness for me. In fact, "happiness" seems an altogether too superficial term. It was more an abiding and heart-warming feeling of connection, a sense that in that moment, despite all that my mother was going through, everything was as it should be.

In my time I've eaten innumerable delicious meals, drunk countless glasses of delicious wine, and consumed numberless cakes, biscuits, and chocolates. How much of all that do I remember? I can't say for certain. But I'll never forget that moment I was able to help my mother—the deep sense of fulfillment that comes from helping others to be happy.

ME, MYSELF, AND I

If you think of your own most profoundly happy moments, the ones that have really moved you at the deepest level, I have no doubt you'll find similar examples. Usually they are the times when you have practiced compassion or been able to give happiness to others. Yes, career success and financial wins are usually exciting, but the "high" they give has a different quality. And our instinctive reaction to such an event is to celebrate it with someone we care about—in other words, to share the happiness with someone else.

Conversely, as for the true cause of suffering, most of us have no difficulty at all recalling our darkest moments. On the surface of things, the causes may have seemed many and varied—difficult relationships, financial disaster, and health crises are often among the main offenders. But at the heart of them is the feeling that the happiness we wish for, and perhaps feel to be our due, is being sabotaged by people or events beyond our control.

In an earlier chapter I mentioned the deep despair I felt when my first girlfriend ended our relationship. With the objectivity of distance, it's interesting to reflect how none of the thoughts that created my unhappy feelings were actually about my now ex-girlfriend. She had already taken off for pastures new and I was far less concerned with what happened to her next than with what happened to me. No, the thoughts that created such pain were very much along the lines of that anguished pop anthem "What About Me?," with all its heart-rending angst and complaints of abandonment. Similarly, when my publishers pulled the plug on my novels, it wasn't their future commercial well-being that occupied my thoughts, but my own.

What about me? The simple truth is that we're conditioned to think about ourselves all the time. Thoughts about me, myself, and I dominate our mind stream from the moment we become conscious in the morning to the last flickers of mental activity before we fall asleep. What I want. How I feel. What I will do. Me, me, me, me, me!

It's striking how the most effective and direct antidote to our self-obsession is the one that occurs to us most seldom: that is, instead of thinking about ourselves, to deliberately think about others. We don't usually need to look far to find opportunities to practice love or compassion. Other beings are no different from us in wanting happiness, and most are less likely or able than us to experience it. Whatever the cause of our distress, taking a broader view usually puts our own position swiftly into perspective.

As the Dalai Lama puts it so well, "There is something about the dynamics of self-absorption, or worrying about ourselves too much, that tends to magnify our suffering. Conversely, when we come to see it in relation to others' suffering, we begin to recognize that, relatively speaking, it is not all that unbearable. This enables us to maintain our peace of mind much more easily than if we concentrate on our problems to the exclusion of all else."

EQUALIZING SELF WITH OTHERS

When we develop greater empathy and compassion for others, our life begins to change, often in unexpected ways. We come to accept the idea that all beings are just like us, not least in placing the highest value of all on their own lives. For example, where my wife once saw cockroaches as loathsome carriers of filth and disease to be sprayed to death as fast as possible, she has since overcome her conditioned revulsion toward them: when the occasional roach finds its way into our house, she now catches it in a large matchbox and releases it outside.

Not so long ago, she was waiting with some other class-goers for the gym doors to open early one morning when a snail made its silvery path onto the pavement. Realizing it would be trampled underfoot in the impending stampede, she quickly picked it up and released it into a nearby garden, accompanied by the horrified squeals of her fellow gym ladies. When one of them challenged her, my wife said: "The snail's life is as important to the snail as your life is to you." The other woman seemed initially taken aback by this bizarre and unexpected 6 a.m. perspective, but the inherent truth in it obviously struck her, because some weeks later she told my wife that she had stopped using snail bait in her garden and instead used to drop all her unwanted visitors over the garden fence.

Sometimes even the smallest of acts can spark the most unexpected changes in the people around us.

MOTHERS, LOVERS, AND FRIENDS FROM PREVIOUS LIFETIMES

Equalizing self with others is one method to cultivate empathy and compassion. Another, available to those who believe in the possibility of rebirth, is the notion that we have had close relationships with every single living being, during one lifetime or another, since beginningless time. Buddhists sometimes talk of "all mother sentient beings," reinforcing the idea of encountering every living being as if that being has been our mother during a previous lifetime. Invoking the mother relationship may work more powerfully for some people than for others. If it is more helpful, you can instead think that all living beings have been your best friend, brother, sister, or lover in a previous lifetime.

This concept can also be a quite potent way of undermining the prejudices many of us feel toward various groups of people. It doesn't matter whether you dislike conservatives, revolutionaries, gays, Muslims, spiders, or rich people, instead of getting irate next time another one of them gets in your face, rather consider the disturbing probability that you were almost certainly one of them in a previous lifetime!

EXCHANGING SELF FOR OTHERS

Once the idea takes root that others are just the same as ourselves in seeking happiness and wishing to avoid dissatisfaction, it becomes easier to take the next step—what Shantideva calls a "holy secret."

Thus whoever wishes to quickly afford protection
To both the self and other beings
Should practice that holy secret:
The exchanging of self for others.

The more we are able to shift our preoccupation from self to others, the happier we will be. Like so much Buddhist wisdom, this is simple to understand but far from easy to put into practice. The seasoned Buddhist monk whom Richard Davidson observed in his laboratory obviously had this practice down to a fine art, but what about the rest of us? How do we set about making it a living reality?

Initially, it's useful to explore for ourselves the concepts Shantideva illustrates in this chapter at a deeper, experiential level: to become familiar with concepts that might seem obvious but may nevertheless be quite novel—the idea that all beings are equal to us in wanting to enjoy happiness and avoid suffering, and that our most profound joys arise from focusing on creating exactly these experiences in others. Science confirms the ancient wisdom of the Dharma: that the more we're able to shift the balance of our mental activity from self to other, the happier, more balanced, and resilient we will be. The Dalai Lama often refers to this as being "wisely selfish," emphasizing the paradox that it is in our own best interests to think less about our own situation and more about others. Our challenge, at least initially, is to develop our awareness and confidence in this approach and, with a good conceptual understanding, to work toward making it a direct, experiential reality.

THE EFFECTS OF SHIFTING FOCUS

It's interesting to observe how the motives, goals, and behavior of people change as they integrate Buddhist psychology into their lives. This is usually a gradual process that occurs as confidence in the teachings develops. Little by little our understanding deepens through meditation and we see the benefits of the practices both for ourselves and for others.

After several years of going to Dharma classes, I had become increasingly aware of how entirely self-serving my own preoccupations were—I had also realized this was no recipe for happiness. This had been particularly true of my writing ambitions, where my motivation for writing mainstream thrillers had been the unashamed pursuit of commercial success. For all the initial promise, this materialistic approach hadn't got me very far. But like most writers I still had an unstoppable urge for self-expression. I enjoyed the creative process, the opportunity to create a rapport with readers, to open the door to new, unexplored worlds. From my developing understanding of the Dharma, I began to wonder how I might use my creative instincts to be of greater benefit to others.

As it happened, it didn't take very long for a new idea to emerge. For quite some time before "officially" becoming a Buddhist I had been interested in the tradition. I'd bought a variety of books on the subject over the years, and while some of them had really captured my interest, there wasn't one that pulled together all the main concepts into a single, easy-to-read summary, presenting the Dharma in the same inspiring way as my own teacher. Wouldn't it be wonderful, I thought, if I could provide other people with the same access to the teachings that I enjoyed? The challenge was to write an introductory book that normal, busy Westerners would find as relevant, stimulating, and practical as the classes I attended each week.

I was also aware of a trend in publishing for ordinary people to write about their experiences doing extraordinary things—like moving to the south of France to restore an ancient olive farm, or heading for the Himalayas in search of rare, exotic plants. Books such as these gave readers the opportunity to share in the experiences vicariously without having to leave the comfort of their armchair. I wondered if it might be possible to do the same thing but involving an inner adventure rather than an outer one; to combine the story of how I encountered the Dharma with the accessible introduction I felt was missing from bookstore shelves.

Within a short while I was busy working on the first draft of *Buddhism for Busy People*, a book that, in almost every way, couldn't have been more different from anything I'd written before. In terms of self versus other, I was making a conscious attempt to invest my time in work that would be of value and benefit to others, and for that reason alone I felt I was doing the right thing. Whether or not the book would appeal to readers in the hugely competitive book market was something I had to wait many months after finishing the work to find out. Whatever the outcome, the exercise itself provided a sense of fulfillment and purpose I had never experienced in my writing before.

Analytical Meditation

Before beginning the analytical meditation, stabilize your mind as usual with a breath meditation exercise.

▶ Consider the extent to which your own actions are dominated by the wish to enjoy happiness and avoid dissatisfaction or suffering. Think about all the things you typically do from waking up in the morning to going to bed at night: what are the motivations behind all these activities?

▶ Now consider friends, family, and others you care about, and how, in their own way, they also strive for happiness and to avoid dissatisfaction. Reflect that complete strangers are motivated by just the same things. Ask yourself: what is so special about me that I am the only one deserving of happiness? Why am I the only one who should be protected from suffering?

▶ Try to identify the deepest moments of joy and fulfillment in your life. Who was the focus of your thoughts during these peak experiences?

▶ What have been your darkest times of anguish, despair, or fear? Who was the focus of your thoughts then?

▶ Try to penetrate the paradoxical truth that our most profoundly happy moments are usually when we are focusing on giving others happiness or relieving their suffering.

▶ Cultivate a determination that for the sake of your own happiness you will shift your thoughts toward others, focusing less on yourself. Hold this thought single-pointedly.

5

Bodhichitta: The Compassionate Mind of Enlightenment

OUR ENCOUNTER WITH *bodhichitta*, a Sanskrit word meaning "the mind of enlightenment" or "the awakening mind," marks an extraordinary milestone in our journey of self-development. It introduces us to a new purpose with the potential to transform the way we think of everything we do, so that even our most mundane experiences can be used to support an audaciously panoramic and positive interpretation of reality.

In the last chapter we discussed the Buddhist definitions of love (the wish to give happiness to others) and of compassion (the wish to free others from suffering). We looked at the benefits of shifting our thoughts away from our constant preoccupation with self toward a state of being in which we open our mind and heart to others.

The Buddha encouraged us to go even further. He also spoke of "great love" and "great compassion," which are different from the ordinary kind because they include the happiness of all beings *without exception.* "Great" means that we expand the scope of our concern from the family, friends, and colleagues who form the typically quite narrow focus of our love and compassion, to include every sentient being, every mind-possessor, in universal space.

A tough ask? An impossible objective? It's important to be clear about what is being suggested. In cultivating an attitude of great love, or the wish for all living beings to be happy, the Buddha is not suggesting that our attitudinal change will be complete only when we succeed in making all living beings happy. Given the level of dissatisfaction and suffering that persists in the world, this would imply that all existing buddhas have failed miserably in their efforts.

It's not what's out there we're trying to change but what's in here. We succeed in developing an attitude of great love when we cease categorizing those around us as "friends," "strangers," and "difficult people" and wishing only for the happiness of the first category while remaining indifferent to the suffering of the second, and secretly pleased when the third do it tough. Great love and great compassion require us to develop equanimity, seeing all beings as exactly the same as us in wishing for happiness and the avoidance of dissatisfaction.

BODHICHITTA: THE JEWEL OF THE MIND

Whether we develop equanimity based simply on the acceptance that all other beings are just like us in wanting to be happy, or from a recognition that the web of relationships connecting us to one another may be more profound than we generally assume, Buddha suggests that instead of wishing only for their mundane happiness we should set our sights very much higher. Just as we might aspire to achieve enlightenment ourselves, we should develop the same aspiration for others. More than this, we should make it the central purpose of our lives. This is the true meaning of bodhichitta.

⁓

If the thought to relieve
Living creatures of merely a headache
Is a beneficial intention
Endowed with infinite goodness,

Then what need is there to mention
The wish to dispel their inconceivable misery,
Wishing every single one of them
To realize boundless good qualities?

The intention to benefit all beings
Which does not arise in others even for their own sake,
Is an extraordinary jewel of the mind,
And its birth is an unprecedented wonder.

I love Shantideva's phrase "jewel of the mind," which underlines the extraordinary preciousness of bodhichitta, as well as his emphasis on the fact that bodhichitta is "an unprecedented wonder." Later on in his *Guide*, he expresses the same idea with a different image:

Just like a blind man
Discovering a jewel in a heap of rubbish,
Likewise, by some coincidence,
An Awakening Mind has been born within me.

This verse emphasizes the mind-blowing improbability of our discovery of bodhichitta—how unlikely would it be for a blind man to discover a jewel in a heap of rubbish? In just the same way, the discovery of bodhichitta motivation is as amazingly unlikely, almost random.

The literal definition of bodhichitta, provided in one text, *Ornament of Clear Realization*, is: "For the sake of others, wishing to attain complete, perfect enlightenment." It is significant that "for the sake of others" comes first in the definition, as it reminds us where to place the focus of our attention. Bodhichitta motivation is so powerful in part because it encapsulates the several different agents of transformation already explored in this book within a single motivation. If, for the sake of others, we wish to attain enlightenment, our thoughts are, by definition, directed more to a big picture perspective than to the here and now, more toward working on inner processes than rearranging our external world, and more toward a compassionate focus on other beings than on ourselves.

Equanimity is also implicit in bodhichitta—we are not seeking enlightenment only for the sake of those we feel close to, but for all beings equally, wherever in the universe they reside and whatever level of sentience they experience. There is no place for partiality in bodhichitta.

My teacher likens bodhichitta to the fuel in a car or airplane—it is the means by which our inner growth is propelled. To extend his metaphor, an intellectual understanding of the Dharma may be likened to the vehicle itself—and the more deeply realized that understanding, the better. But without the heartfelt purpose of bodhichitta—without the urgent need to put great love and great compassion into action—no vehicle, no matter how many extras and special features it may have, is going to get us very far. In Tibetan Buddhist texts on this subject, the Dalai Lama says, "We find that compassion is not only highly praised, but the authors also repeatedly emphasize its importance in the sense that it really lies at the root of all spiritual endeavor."

In a formal sense, the point at which people officially become Buddhists is when they take refuge in the Buddha, Dharma, and Sangha (the last is our community of fellow practitioners). It is a simple process in which we commit to abandoning up to five harmful behaviors, namely killing, stealing, sexual misconduct, lying, and taking intoxicants (only the first is an absolute requirement). In Tibetan Buddhism, when we take refuge we usually also take bodhichitta vows. These include eighteen root vows and forty-six branch vows, providing the guidelines through which the motivation of bodhichitta is translated into action. Cultivating bodhichitta, the compassionate mind of enlightenment, is therefore central to

Tibetan Buddhism, and is what distinguishes it from other Buddhist traditions.

People's reactions when presented with bodhichitta for the first time vary greatly: some want to take a good, hard look at it from all angles, while the response of others is intuitive and heartfelt, a sense of discovering—at last!—the basis of a meaningful life. In my own case, the idea of it instantly caught my imagination and I quickly realized that I couldn't think of a motivation more altruistic, noble, or worthwhile. When it comes to thinking big, it is impossible to think bigger than bodhichitta.

But this recognition was accompanied by a dispiriting thought: who was I to start telling myself I was working to achieve enlightenment for the sake of all beings, when the reality was so very different? I am too small-hearted, too self-centered to convincingly make bodhichitta my central motivation, and it would be hypocritical of me to pretend otherwise.

WISHING AND VENTURING BODHICHITTA

The Dharma recognizes that it takes time to develop confidence in the goal of bodhichitta and to develop the practice of bodhichitta itself. For this reason a distinction is made between "wishing" and "venturing" bodhichitta. We need to become familiar with bodhichitta, to hear about it, think about it, and meditate on it, until the point at which we develop a heartfelt conviction in it.

The Dalai Lama tells us, "Our bodhichitta may not yet be spontaneous. It is still something we have to fabricate. Nevertheless, once we have embraced and begun to develop this extraordinary attitude, whatever positive actions we do...while not appearing any different, will bring greatly increased results."

Initially you may feel like a fraud when you recollect bodhichitta motivation—but even at this stage, simply becoming mindful of the motivation is extremely beneficial. What starts out as nothing more than a thought can—little by little—become our defining purpose. As Buddha explains in the Dhammapada: "The thought manifests as the word; The word manifests as the deed; The deed develops into habit; And habit hardens into character... As the shadow follows the body, as we think so we become."

Buddhists a lot further down the Dharma path than me have explained how bodhichitta can gradually evolve from just a superficial idea to a very genuine motivation—how we get to the point where we no longer question the wisdom of thinking of others because we know, from familiarity, that this is the true source of indestructible happiness. A shift occurs at the core of our being.

THE INCALCULABLE BENEFITS OF BODHICHITTA

And with this profound shift comes incalculable benefits. When the Dalai Lama refers to "greatly increased results" he is alluding to the karmic results of bodhichitta, which Shantideva describes with the following metaphor:

All other virtues are like plantain trees;
For after bearing fruit, they simply perish.
Yet the perennial tree of the Awakening Mind
Unceasingly bears fruit and thereby flourishes without end.

This verse highlights the specific, extraordinary benefit of bodhichitta—that its karmic results are limitless. At the most basic level, the law of karma, or cause and effect, explains that doing something positive for others will result in the enjoyment of positive experience oneself at some stage, not necessarily immediately or even soon. When we undertake the same positive action with bodhichitta motivation, instead of benefiting from the positive experience only once, our action "unceasingly bears fruit and thereby flourishes without end."

How is such a thing possible? Enjoyment is a positive mental experience and when we practice bodhichitta we are consciously reengineering our thought processes so that they are more conducive to the future enjoyment of positive experience. If we maintain our focus on the mundane, our rewards will be mundane. By focusing on the extraordinary, we create results that are extraordinary.

Part of what gives karma its power is our motivation. If we give someone a gift because of what we hope they'll do for us in the future, our state of mind is very different from giving a gift with no expectation. We are conditioning our mind differently. As for receiving a gift as a karmic result of the previously created cause, this is also an area fraught with complexity. The gift we give is merely the means by which the recipient may have a positive experience. The gift itself has no significance apart from what we attribute to it. (We all know that, as recipients of gifts, we sometimes attribute very different qualities to those same gifts than the giver does, even when the person is well-intentioned!) So on what basis do we identify which positive experiences arise from any specific act of giving?

My own understanding of karma is that it's best to see it as a process of psychological conditioning. As the Buddha said, thoughts become words, then actions, then habits. Our experience of reality is ultimately defined by the way we think. If we wish to change the experience, we begin with our thoughts. And if we wish to open ourselves to the experience of a radiant and ongoing happiness beyond ordinary conception, then we should identify the most supremely positive thought possible—bodhichitta—and, step by step, incorporate it into our every action of body, speech, and mind.

THE PERSONAL RESPONSIBILITY OF BODHICHITTA

The definition of bodhichitta—for the sake of others, the wish to attain enlightenment—is based on the understanding that, having realized our own ultimate nature, we will be in a better position to help others achieve this too. Born from the wish for all beings, equally and without exception, to be happy and free from suffering, bodhichitta could be regarded as the ultimate expression of compassion. Or as the Dalai Lama says: "Everyone has at least some unselfish tendencies, however limited. To develop these until the wish to help others becomes limitless is what is called bodhichitta."

Thinking of the bigger picture, as we did in Chapter 2, it doesn't take long to recognize the incredible rarity of our opportunity for realization and inner growth. Even though our minds remain subject to negative conditioning and habitual reactions, at least we have the ability to recognize what is happening, and to begin to take action— to follow the bodhisattva path. Gradually, as we become increasingly acquainted with bodhichitta motivation, we see it more and more as our personal responsibility. In relative terms there are so few of us in a position to help, and thus we need to pursue inner growth as quickly as possible for the sake of others.

One of the most well-known analogies in Buddhism is that of a burning house in which all beings are trapped because of their negative conditioning and ignorance about the true nature of reality. If you or I were to find ourselves in a house on fire, we wouldn't hesitate to make a run for it, taking with us anyone else still inside and grabbing the family terrier and birdcage on our way out. We should apply much the same sense of urgency in our Dharma practice, recognizing the suffering being experienced at this moment around the world. As members of an elite minority with leisure and good fortune, including access to transformational psychology, it's up to us to do something about the dire situation, not only for ourselves but also for the sake of those who can't do it on their own. This is not some messianic ego trip, because we recognize, with humility, that in our current state of mental agitation we need to do a lot of work on our own minds first. Nor is it any reason to thrust our Buddhist views on others—there is no tradition of evangelism in Buddhism, because we are working to change our own way of experiencing reality, not other people's. Nevertheless, the sense of personal responsibility bound up in bodhichitta provides an energy and direction to our Dharma practice. As my teacher often reminds us: "This is our real job. It is the main purpose of our existence."

Where do we begin? Part II of this book provides the detail of how we put bodhichitta, the compassionate mind of enlightenment, into practice on a day-to-day basis. For the moment it is sufficient to explore the development of bodhichitta motivation both as an idea and as a meditation practice.

Perhaps the most common stumbling block for embarking on bodhichitta is the fact that while we may have little difficulty wishing to achieve enlightenment for the benefit of people we care for, and even strangers who we may perhaps conceive of in an idealized way, there are almost certain to be people for whom we find it very hard to entertain positive feelings. Former flames; business associates who have deceived us, or who constantly try to undermine our position; once best friends who have become sworn enemies; and perhaps those who are ideologically opposed to our point of view.

While I am fortunate to have no one I regard as a personal enemy, the idea of cultivating heartfelt love and compassion toward certain world leaders is not easy, given the vicious and venal destruction of the countries over which they have presided. But this is where it gets interesting. If we wish to take away the suffering of our enemies, it is the true causes of their suffering we need to eliminate. And those true causes are their attachment/desire on the one hand, and their hatred/aversion on the other. If we want to give them happiness, once again it is the true causes they must be given. Those are love, or the wish to give happiness to others, together with compassion, the wish to free others from dissatisfaction and suffering. Imagine our enemies stripped of all their hostility, jealousy, pride, or greed, and filled instead with compassion and a single-minded purpose to give happiness to everyone. With "enemies" like these, who needs friends?!

Tonglen Meditation

Taking bodhichitta beyond merely an interesting idea to a compassionate motivation that occurs spontaneously to us is the journey of a lifetime. Given the level of self-obsession we all need to battle against, learning to focus our thoughts on others rather than on ourselves is not something we can just decide to do, even if we want to. Instead, having convinced ourselves of the value and benefits of bodhichitta at an intellectual level, we need to begin to realize it directly in meditation. And there is a specific meditation practice designed to help us do exactly this. *Tonglen*, or "giving and taking," is one of the most widely practiced Tibetan Buddhist meditations that has come down to us through the millennia. Practiced correctly over time it is one of the most profoundly transformational meditations, one which helps develop the innate love and compassion that we already possess to some degree.

Instructions for tonglen are as follows:

▸ Adopt the meditation posture of your choice. Once you are sitting comfortably, remind yourself of your bodhichitta motivation. Think: "For the sake of others, may I achieve complete and perfect enlightenment."

▸ To help intensify this feeling, imagine beaming down from the sky in front of and around you rays of light from all existing teachers, buddhas, and bodhisattvas. This light is in the nature of love, compassion, and wisdom. As the light penetrates you, it dissolves away all your self-cherishing thoughts, all your anger and attachment, to reveal your true buddha nature—that is, your perspective is now that of a mind and heart radiant, spacious, and infused with love and compassion toward all beings. Playfully imagine you are a buddha.

▶ Visualize on your left-hand side an important female presence in your life for whom you find it easy to experience feelings of love and compassion, for example your mother, another female relative, or your wife or partner. Allow yourself to feel connected to that person. Open yourself to any feelings of anxiety, stress, fear, depression, or loneliness she may be experiencing. Cultivate the motivation: "I will free this person from whatever suffering she may be experiencing as well as the true causes of her suffering."

▶ Holding that person in your mind as vividly as possible, with your next inhalation visualize breathing in her suffering in the form of a dark-colored cloud that comes from her body into your heart, where it dissolves away instantly, taking with it any final traces of your own self-grasping. This process can't hurt you—but it does help counter the innate self-cherishing habit from which we all suffer.

▶ As you exhale, imagine that you are beaming out toward her a brilliant white light, which contains healing love, happiness, peace, and whatever other specific qualities she needs. Visualize the impact of this on her as you continue to inhale all her suffering, and suffuse her with radiant love and great bliss.

▶ Then move on to do the same for other important women in your life, visualizing them on your left-hand side, each time giving and receiving for as long as you like.

▶ Repeat the same exercise for important male presences in your life—your father, brothers, husband, or partner—

but this time visualizing each one in turn on your right-hand side.

▸ When you are ready, turn your attention to the people you find difficult. Visualize these people directly in front of you. Whether they are sworn enemies, irritating neighbors, work colleagues, or politicians you abhor, the process is exactly the same. Recognize that in taking away all their suffering, and filling them with love and compassion, you have completely transformed them—they are no longer recognizable as enemies.

▸ Next, practice tonglen on your friends, individually visualizing each one behind you and repeating the same process.

▸ Last of all, imagine all human living beings, strangers who are gathered in limitless numbers around you, beyond the inner circle of those you know. Once again, breathe in their collective suffering and radiate the light of your compassion.

▸ When you first begin tonglen you may find it easier to practice visualizing only one person in front of you—someone you feel close to, and for whom you experience feelings of love and compassion. If that person is experiencing difficulties of some kind, your tonglen practice will feel very natural. You may want to spend entire sessions focusing on just one person, or a handful of people, before expanding your practice to include more distant friends, relatives, strangers, and even enemies, as described above.

▸ You may decide to allocate a set number of breaths to each individual and over time build up a familiar visualization involving many different beings. I personally allocate four breaths to around a hundred beings, both alive and passed away, human and much-loved pets—a visualization I've built up over some years. In the case of those who have passed away, it is their reborn forms for whom one wishes to take away suffering and give happiness.

▸ As your tonglen practice becomes stronger, develop the conviction that your bodhichitta is purifying all traces of others' suffering and negativity and transforming their experience of reality to a joyful one. Allow the profound happiness of this conviction to permeate your consciousness at the deepest level.

▸ When you are ready to finish, dissolve the visualization and rest in silence for a few moments.

▸ Conclude your tonglen session with this dedication, which you can recite mentally or aloud: "By this virtue may all beings, quickly, quickly, achieve complete and perfect enlightenment."

PART II
The Compassionate Mind of Enlightenment in Practice

~

6

Open Heart, Open Hand:
The Perfection of Generosity

WELCOME TO PART II of *Enlightenment to Go*! Having explored the benefits of cultivating a mind of enlightenment, or bodhichitta, in Part I, this is where we look at putting theory into practice.

If you're anything like I was, you may have become curious about how bodhichitta provides a transcendent purpose for life that engages both heart and mind. But like the blind man making his amazing find in the rubbish heap, you may still be trying to make sense of what the discovery of this "jewel of the mind" means to you.

In response to just this question, Buddha outlined six *paramitas*, or perfections, to provide the basis for enlightened living. These are the perfections of generosity, ethics, patience, joyous perseverance, meditation, and wisdom. We will look at each of these in turn, beginning in this chapter with the first paramita: the perfection of generosity.

In true Tibetan Buddhist style, to avoid any confusion, let's start with a definition of the perfection of generosity from my teacher, Geshe Acharya Thubten Loden: "Generosity is those actions of body, speech, and mind motivated by the virtuous thought to give. Any generosity motivated by bodhichitta becomes a perfection of generosity. Thus the determinant of the perfection of generosity is not the physical action of giving, nor the gift itself. Rather, it is the virtuous mind of generosity, motivated by bodhichitta, that precedes and accompanies the action of giving."

Buddhism teaches that generosity comes in four different forms. We can give materially, such as money. We can be generous with love by giving happiness to others. We give generosity of protection when we save other beings—even cockroaches and snails—from injury or death. And we can also practice generosity of the Dharma by sharing whatever understanding we have with those who sincerely ask for it, or by supporting others in their Dharma practice—for example by sponsoring nuns or monks.

The emphasis of any perfection is on what motivates the action. When we give, are we doing this out of generosity—itself a virtue—or because of generosity motivated by bodhichitta, an incomparably more powerful motivation?

Even before we discover the Dharma, when we give, we usually do so from the heart. Whether it's something as trivial as slowing down while driving to let another motorist into the line in front of us, or as significant as donating a large sum of money to charity, our kindness is usually inspired by love and compassion, even though we might not express it in such terms.

When we learn about bodhichitta, however, we can take these already virtuous acts and transform them into something even more extraordinary by thinking: "By this act of generosity, for the sake of all living beings may I achieve enlightenment."

Just as the Dalai Lama suggests in the previous chapter, when we first begin the practice of bodhichitta we have to fabricate. The very first time you slow down to let in another driver and self-consciously think, "By this act of generosity, for the sake of all living beings may I achieve enlightenment," you will most probably have the sense that you are artificially sticking a motivation onto something you would have done anyway. But you shouldn't underestimate the importance of what you have just started. Not only have you exercised mindfulness in recognizing an opportunity to practice the perfection of generosity, you have also begun a habit of wishing for the ultimate welfare of all living beings. This habit, once started, increasingly permeates our thoughts, speech, and actions until it moves from being an artificially contrived exercise to a genuinely heartfelt wish—from being a motivation we attach to acts of generosity we would have done anyway, to a true cause of giving. And practiced regularly alongside the other perfections, it has the effect of gradually shifting our internal monologue away from constant thoughts about me, myself, and I to an expanding and benevolent awareness of others.

THE PRIVILEGE OF GENEROSITY

As human beings with leisure and fortune, it is our privilege to enjoy a multitude of opportunities to practice the perfection of generosity on a daily basis. Our everyday interactions offer limitless possibilities to help someone else, whether that's cooking a meal for them, playing taxi driver for the kids, feeding the pets and showing them affection, staying late to help a colleague, sending a service provider a "thank you" email, putting out seeds for wild birds, or dropping a coin into a collector's tin.

We shouldn't take these opportunities for granted. My two pet cats seem to lead an idyllic existence even when they're not being fed their favorite food—basking in the sun, or curled up inside in a quiet spot. But what opportunity do they have to practice simple generosity, let alone the perfection of generosity? The truth is that they have very little scope to break out of their individual cocoons of self-absorption. The more than 1.4 billion people living in extreme poverty on planet Earth similarly have vastly reduced opportunities, compared to a minority of us, to practice material generosity. We don't often think about generosity as a privilege, but when we look objectively around us, we discover that it is.

Of all the perfections the Buddha could have picked, why did he choose to teach about generosity first? One reason could be that when we give we usually feel good about ourselves—not in the me-centerd way of feeling good that we experience when we enjoy a delicious meal, favorite wine, or other sensual gratification, but rather a sensation of contentment. I'm sure that every reader of this book has experienced the happiness that comes from giving. But if, like me, you tend to doubt the subjectivity of your own experience, you will be pleased to learn that there is powerful scientific proof that giving makes you happy!

Dr. Michael Norton, Assistant Professor of Business Administration at Harvard Business School, and his colleagues Elizabeth Dunn and Lara Aknin conducted a series of studies at the University of British Columbia. Together they showed that people are happier when they spend money on others than when they spend it on themselves. The results were published in *Science* magazine in 2008.

The work included a national survey in which researchers asked 632 American men and women how much money they earned each year; how much they spent each month on living expenses; and how much they spent on others, including donations. They also asked them to rate how happy they felt.

The survey showed that people who spent more on others also reported a higher level of happiness, while how much they spent on themselves had no impact on happiness.

A different test monitored how sixteen employees at a Boston-based company spent a profit-sharing bonus. Employees were asked to rate their own happiness before and after receiving a bonus, as well as report how they spent the money. Those who spent more of their bonus on others registered a higher level of happiness than those who spent it on themselves. Furthermore, "the dollar amount of the bonus had no impact on happiness over time," said

Dr. Norton. "People were just as happy whether they received $3000 or $8000. All that mattered was the percent [of the bonus] spent on other people."

In a third experiment, researchers gave out envelopes of money to university students with the instruction to spend it however they liked. The results mirrored those from their other studies. "We found that people who spent the money on themselves that day weren't happier that evening," said Dr. Norton, "but people who spent it on others were. The amount of money . . . didn't matter at all. It was only how people spent it that made them happier."

The research has far-reaching implications, said Dr. Norton: "Instead of thinking about winning the lottery and making other large life changes, our research suggests that encouraging people to do small things on a frequent basis might get them to be happier over time."

Other studies, quoted in *The Happiness Hypothesis* by Jonathan Haidt, provide evidence that practicing generosity gives people a sense of both purpose and well-being. Whether giving money, as in the studies quoted above, or practicing generosity in other ways, like giving blood or volunteering for a charity, we are happier when we give. This impact is greatest of all among older people, where there is even evidence that volunteering helps improve health and longevity.

THE ETHICAL BASIS OF GIVING

Part of the reason that giving feels good is perhaps because we recognize, at some level, that it's the right thing to do. This ethical basis for giving is one shared by all the great traditions. The Hebrew word for "charity" is *tzedakah*, meaning "justice," suggesting that far from being an act of exceptional kindness, being generous is simply part of a just life. Islam demands its adherents give generously to those in need—specifically 2.5 percent of their total net wealth each year.

The Bible makes more than three thousand references to alleviating poverty: generosity is a central moral issue for Christians too. The reason for this strong consensus is no doubt the shared view that if it is easy to help people who are in real need through no fault of their own, it cannot be right to ignore them.

In his book *The Life You Can Save*, philosopher and ethicist Peter Singer delivers a tour de force argument that there has never been a more urgent—or rewarding—basis for giving than right now. He points out that the proportion of people unable to meet their basic physical needs is smaller than at any time in recent history, while the proportion of people with far more than they need is also unprecedented. We have never had such a great opportunity to do so much for so many. More importantly, rich and poor are now linked in ways they never were before. The twenty-four-hour news media and online world open up networks that simply didn't exist as recently as twenty years ago.

Right now, 1.4 billion people in the world live in extreme poverty—that is, on less than US$1.25 a day. Many of us in the West spend more than this amount every day on things we don't need—a soft drink, a coffee, or a glass of wine, even though we could quench our thirst with water from the tap at only a tiny fraction of the cost. Yes, we may have earned the money, and it's ours to spend, but to a larger extent than we might usually consider, it is our social circumstances as much as our own efforts that enable us to enjoy the level of affluence that we do. As Warren Buffett, one of the world's richest people, has said: "If you stick me down in the middle of Bangladesh or Peru, you'll find out how much this talent is going to produce in the wrong kind of soil."

Taking action to redress this balance is the ethical basis for generosity. Whatever charitable organization we choose to support, and however we can best support it, the important thing is to cultivate the habit of giving on a regular and meaningful basis. To quote Peter Singer:

The problem is that we are living in the midst of an emergency in which 27,000 children die from avoidable causes every day. That's more than 1,000 every hour. And millions of women are living with repairable fistulas, and millions of people are blind who could see again. We can do something about these things. That crucial fact ought to affect the choices we make. To buy good stereo equipment in order to further my worthwhile goal, or life-enhancing experience, of listening to music, is to place more value on these enhancements to my life than on whether others live or die. Can it be ethical to live that way? Doesn't it make a mockery of any claim to believe in the equal value of human life?

GENEROSITY AS A CAUSE OF WEALTH

For those who have some acceptance of karma and rebirth, the Dharma provides a further reason to practice generosity. This is summarized in a verse by the seventh-century Indian Buddhist teacher Chandrakirti from his *Engaging in the Middle Way*:

All these beings want happiness,
But human happiness does not arise without wealth.
Knowing that wealth arises from giving
The Subduer first taught generosity.

This appeal to generosity is made on the basis of long-term self-interest. If we wish to receive, we first must give. Just as Maslow's hierarchy of needs explains that self-actualization is a need we turn to only after we have satisfied more basic requirements, the message here is that our future happiness depends on a certain level of material well-being. It's up to us to create its karmic causes.

Although this reason for generosity is emphasized in traditional teachings on generosity, I hesitated about including it in this book, because karma is so misunderstood in the West. So a word of caution about practicing giving in order to receive: there is no defined timeline between cause and effect. I've heard stories of New Agers in the first flush of devotional fervor who have been unstinting in clearing their savings accounts, selling off their belongings, and giving it all away to good causes in the expectation that "the universe" would reward their kindness in magical and hitherto unexpected ways. Unfortunately, "the universe" didn't come to the party.

Generosity is not an obvious method of instant wealth-creation: if it were, even the most miserly among us would be doing it. When we give, we shouldn't do so with any expectation of receiving some sort of literal, external payback next week, next year, or even in this particular lifetime. In the context of beginningless time, a single life is like an instant in the journey of our mind stream. Is it realistic to expect the effects of karmic causes to manifest in that same instant?

Much better to think of the karmic result of our generosity as the good feeling we enjoy when we give. The giving of money or other material things makes us *feel* more fulfilled and connected, and more aware of our material well-being and philanthropic purpose as we focus on the needs of those to whom we are giving. And surely it's better by far to experience these profound and life-enhancing feelings than to achieve some entirely random and hypothetical net worth figure on an asset register?

GENEROSITY AS A STATE OF MIND

Whether we choose to give because it makes us feel good, because it's the right thing to do, or to enjoy the karmic benefits, the important thing is to recollect our motivation. It is not what we give or who we give to that counts so much as the thoughts that motivate and accompany our giving. We are, of course, trying to improve the external reality of the person or animal we are giving to. But also important is the inner transformation we are seeking to perfect. Generosity isn't measured by the amount of money or time donated. One of the many curious parallels between Jesus's teachings on ethics and the Buddha's is the example of the widow's mite—how the few, low-value coins given by a poor woman to the church represented a far greater sacrifice to her than the much larger sums given by the wealthy. In relative terms, she is far more generous than they. As Shantideva notes:

> The perfection of generosity is said to be
> The thought to give all beings everything;
> Together with the fruit of such a thought;
> Hence it is simply a state of mind.

When we practice the perfection of generosity, our main area of focus is our mind. Do we recollect our bodhichitta motivation, initially as a contrived thought, but more and more out of habit? And how genuinely heartfelt and spontaneous is our giving? For me, quite a useful barometer is when charity collectors come door-knocking or when I encounter a collector on the street corner. What is my first instinct? Is it to avoid having to deal with the request out of miserliness—sometimes cunningly disguised as being in too much of a hurry? Is it to check the charity being collected for? (In which case I am not practicing equanimity.) Or do I sincerely think, "Great! An opportunity to practice the perfection of generosity!"?

> "If I give this, what shall I have left to enjoy?"
> Such selfish thinking is the way of ghosts;
> "If I enjoy this, what shall I have to give?"
> Such selfless thinking is a quality of the gods.

Some people seem to find it a lot more difficult to give than others, despite being in a similar situation. If our formative years were spent in straitened circumstances or we come from a family with a "poverty mentality," where resources are considered hard to come by and must be held on to tightly at all costs, then we're pushing uphill against a huge weight of conditioning.

HOW TO OVERCOME GRASPING

The Dharma recognizes that our innate grasping is often hard to overcome, so suggests a helpful way to start softening our attitudes. Instead of giving away real money or material things, we begin by visualizing this. Shantideva had no money or belongings to give away, and to this day monastic Buddhists generally live very frugally. This is why the practice of visualized offerings is so important among Tibetan Buddhist monks and nuns. One might say that they have turned it into an art form. In Shantideva's case, some of the most lyrical verses of his *Guide* describe his imagined offerings; in my view, these match the most soaring passages to be found in Shakespeare. Here he strives to visualize the most superlative offerings presented to an imagined host of the buddhas:

> Fragrances of the celestial realms,
> Incense, wishing trees and jewel trees,
> Uncultivated harvests, and all ornaments
> That are worthy of being offered...

And later:

> I offer them jewelled lamps
> Arranged on golden lotus buds;

Upon land sprinkled with scented water
I scatter delicate flower petals.

Creating these things in my mind, I offer them
To the supreme beings, the buddhas, as well as their children,
O Compassionate Ones, think kindly of me
And accept these offerings of mine.

Tibetan Buddhism encourages us to become masters of visualization. As we saw in the last chapter, the Buddha suggested that "as we think, so we become," and this idea is powerfully manifest in the practice of visualization, where we imagine an end result as vividly as possible.

We are not talking here about daydreaming or fanciful make-believe. Instead, we're talking about the kind of visualization practiced by elite sportspeople, business professionals, musicians, ballet dancers, and others who know that mental rehearsal has a hugely positive impact on actual performance.

Step by step we can build up our own visualized offerings, using the power of whichever senses are appropriate—sight, sound, fragrance, taste, and touch—as we practice the perfection of generosity in visualized form.

GENEROSITY: ITS OWN REWARD?

When it came to the publication of *Buddhism for Busy People*, I decided to donate the advance I received for the book to the Tibetan Buddhist Society, the Dharma group I belong to, which at the time was raising funds to build a temple. While the advance wasn't a huge sum of money and didn't match the greater generosity of other members of the group, it felt right to me. It was only thanks to my teacher that I was able to attempt even writing such a book. And donating the advance helped reinforce in my mind the fact that I wasn't writing this book for the money, but to share the Dharma. It was wonderfully satisfying for me when the book made its first appearance in bookstores in November 2004. What neither I nor my publishers could tell was whether it would be of interest to the mainstream non-Buddhists for whom it had been written.

So in early 2005 I was very pleasantly surprised to be told that a number of bookstores were reordering, and the publishers had decided to do a reprint. When publishers distribute books to retailers, they do so on a sale-or-return basis. Most shops will keep copies of a book for up to two months and, depending on what kind of book it is, if it hasn't sold by then, it will be returned to the publisher. This means you have only a relatively small window of time to appeal to readers before you make way for the next author. Reorders are the first tangible sign that a book is moving, at least in certain stores, so it was a promising development. *Buddhism for Busy People* hadn't stormed up the bestseller charts, but nor had anyone expected it to. It seemed, however, to have found a readership, and further sales were being supported by word-of-mouth recommendation—the best form of marketing.

In subsequent months, the book was reprinted several more times, and over the years it has been published in a second edition. It has become what's known in the trade as a "slow burner," never selling sufficient copies in any one week or month to attract great attention, but steadily, over a period of time, outselling other, higher profile titles which burst into public attention before being replaced by the next big thing.

Writing and publishing *Buddhism for Busy People* was in almost every respect a qualitatively different experience from my previous commercial thrillers. But without question, the most profoundly satisfying aspect was the emails I receive from readers via my website. I was, and remain, both stunned and humbled by the impact the book has had on people's lives. Even though nowhere in *Buddhism for Busy People* did I suggest you should pick up the phone to an estranged sibling and attempt a family reconciliation, I heard from one reader who, as a result of reading it, felt compelled to do exactly that. Another email was from a mother who had finally drawn a line under years of guilty resentment and established a positive new relationship with her handicapped child.

Along with these extraordinary cases, there were many more from ordinary, busy people who had found in the book a concept, a practice, a fresh perspective that had helped make their lives happier and more enjoyable. Their gratitude was more than I could ever have hoped for. And for me this is the true wonder of the perfection of generosity. When we connect with others and help bring about positive change in their lives, the effect is powerful and profound, for both giver and receiver. Generosity truly is its own reward.

Exercise: The Perfection of Generosity

Identify three things you do regularly to help others. Ideally these will be everyday activities like making someone coffee or a meal, taking the dog for a walk, or slowing down to allow a stranger to step into a train or supermarket line ahead of you.

▶ From now on, whenever you do these things, recall your bodhichitta motivation. Both before and while you undertake the activity, think: "By this act of generosity may I achieve enlightenment for the benefit of all living beings without exception."

▶ If time permits, follow this thought with the reminder that the being you are helping is just like you in that he or she only wants happiness and to avoid dissatisfaction.

▶ If you have further time, recollect the four immeasurables: four powerful lines recollecting in turn love, compassion, sympathetic joy, and equanimity, the "sublime attitudes" taught by the Buddha as the basis of the enlightened mind. They are:

May all beings have happiness and the causes of happiness.
May all beings be free from suffering
and the causes of suffering.
May all beings never be parted from the happiness that is
without suffering—great nirvana, liberation.
May all beings abide in peace and equanimity,
their minds free from attachment,
aversion, and indifference.

7

A Practical Approach to Ethics

I'D LIKE TO BEGIN this chapter with an admission: I find ethics a difficult subject to write about. For starters, there are few things less appealing than self-righteousness and I've done too many unpraiseworthy things in my life to present myself as some sort of high moral authority. Also, all too often the subject of ethics is—and there's no nice way to put this, so I might as well just come out with it—boring. Dull. A long list of "thou shalt nots" that are all very worthy, but, you can't help asking, where is the upside?

It's also the case that as a Dharma practitioner I find the perfection of ethics—the gradual ripening of our capacity for ethical action—presents quite subtle challenges, because it's more difficult to be mindful of the bad things we're not doing than of the good things that we are.

With these reservations in mind, I'll try to provide a brief outline of Shantideva's approach to this subject, trying to avoid all sanctimony and tedium, while also providing some practical suggestions on how to integrate the perfection of ethics into daily life. Perhaps the best starting point is a reminder that the perfection of ethics, like other perfections, is based on bodhichitta motivation: the wish to achieve enlightenment for the sake of others. It is, more than anything else, a state of mind.

THE TEN NONVIRTUES

Just as other traditions have codified ethics into rules like the ten commandments, Buddhism has ten nonvirtues, otherwise known as the ten precepts or negative actions, of which three are nonvirtues of body, four are nonvirtues of speech, and another three are nonvirtues of mind (see below).

THE TEN NONVIRTUES

Nonvirtues of body: killing, stealing, sexual misconduct

Nonvirtues of speech: lying, divisive speech, harsh speech, idle gossip

Nonvirtues of mind: covetousness, malice, wrong view

The ten *virtuous* actions are abandoning these same activities.

While some of these are self-explanatory, a few words of clarification may be useful about those that are different from mainstream Western ethics. "Killing" means causing the death of any sentient being, not only the "murder" of humans. "Sexual misconduct" means sexual activity that may cause others unhappiness—usually infidelity, whether inside or outside of marriage. "Divisive speech" is when we say things to make other people dislike one another. "Harsh speech" is pretty obvious but surprises some people coming to Buddhism for the first time, as does "idle gossip." These three nonvirtuous actions of speech aren't regarded as particularly heinous in Western culture. On the contrary, turn on the television any night of the week and we are subjected to an endless stream of divisive speech, harsh speech, and idle gossip, especially on reality TV and chat shows. An entire genre of magazines seems devoted almost entirely to idle gossip. The all-pervasive nature of this media can only have the collective effect of normalizing these particular nonvirtues, with unhelpful consequences for our collective well-being. Shantideva could well have been describing twenty-first-century media when he used his famous lightning metaphor:

Just as a flash of lightning on a dark, cloudy night
For an instant brightly illuminates all,
Likewise in this world, through the might of the buddhas,
A wholesome thought rarely and briefly appears.

Turning to nonvirtues of mind, while "covetousness" and "malice" are well understood, "wrong view" refers specifically to holding the view that key Dharma teachings are incorrect.

ETHICS AS A CAUSE OF HAPPINESS

When Les Sheehy talks about ethics, he often directly addresses the perception some people have that ethical frameworks are restrictive sets of rules put in place merely to ensure civil order—that is, to control people. Is Buddhism the same as other traditions in this respect? While a more harmonious society may arise from ethical behavior, this is not the primary motivation of an individual practitioner. Again we are working on what is in here, rather than out there. As the Dalai Lama himself points out, "those individuals whose conduct is ethically positive are happier and more satisfied than those who neglect ethics."

So, a good first reason to practice ethics is to be happy ourselves. If we have no underlying sense of guilt or regret, if we are not constantly having to cover our tracks, if we don't have to worry what we said to whom and when, life gets a whole lot easier. I've known people who have gone to elaborate lengths to conceal from their partner the fact that they were having an affair. The sense of excitement and high drama, together with the thrill of the dangerous liaison itself, seems usually to be accompanied by an acute sense of guilt that what they're doing is wrong and makes them a bad person, along with fear of how their partner would react if he or she found out, not to mention worry that the end result will be the loss of both lovers and, often, collateral damage to their children. When the affair is discovered, the painful consequences can seriously undermine any sense of inner peace and well-being for a very long time.

Then there are those who engage the best legal and accounting brains to set up intricate off-shore structures so they can avoid having to pay tax, or who have to constantly monitor how much legitimate money they spend to hide the fact that the tax man doesn't know about all the undeclared cash they're earning. I once shared a literary agent with a well-known author who took tax-avoidance measures to extreme lengths via a convoluted web of off-shore trusts. According to the agent, despite all the author's considerable wealth and success, her obsession with being ripped off by tax departments, accountants, lawyers, and agents made her the most miserable person to deal with.

Why do we make life so complicated for ourselves? It's not that we set out to be unethical. It's more that our drive for romantic intimacy, sexual passion, or material advancement causes us to override our scruples. Of course, we can always justify our behavior. Most of us are remarkably inventive at coming up with reasons why the ethical principles we say we believe in don't, in this particular instance, fully apply to us. But after the sexual passion has lost its intensity, or we've taken our material toys out of the box for the umpteenth time and found we're bored with them, we're forced to confront the reality of what we've gained and what we've lost. And we may well conclude that ethical restraint, while a less exciting and/or more difficult option, is, as the Dalai Lama suggests, more conducive to an overall sense of happiness and inner peace. We may confirm that, as Shantideva put it:

Although wishing to be rid of misery,
They run toward misery itself.
Although wishing to have happiness,
Like an enemy they ignorantly destroy it.

I was recently reading the diary of Samuel Pepys, famous for providing a tantalizing glimpse of everyday life in seventeenth-century London. In it, I came across a passage where he describes the emotional upheavals following his wife's discovery of his affair with her attractive young maidservant—a liaison that had been causing him sleepless nights for nearly three weeks. Having tried to patch things up with his furious wife, he wrote on November 19, 1668: "and so with some rest [I] spent the night in bed, being most absolutely resolved...never to give [my wife] occasion while I live of more trouble of this or any other kind, there being no curse in the world so great as this of the difference between myself and her... This night the upholsters [*sic*] did finish the hanging of my best chamber, but my sorrow and trouble is so great about this business, that put me out of all joy in looking upon it or minding how it was."

How little human nature has changed in the last three hundred and forty years!

ETHICS AS A CAUSE OF ATTRACTIVENESS

Ethical people are nicer to be around. When you know someone is on the level and, far from wanting to take advantage of you in any way, just wants you to be happy, you can relax. As Geshe Loden points out in *Path to Enlightenment*: "As a fragrant perfume delights and attracts others, people are drawn to the person with pure ethics like bees drawn to honey. His pleasant appearance, relaxed and open behavior, and lack of malice make others feel very comfortable.

They feel safe because of his lack of harmfulness. His presence and ambience are attractive and comforting."

A good way of testing this point is to think of its opposite. How do we feel spending time with people we suspect may not be entirely above board?

GOING BEYOND "THOU SHALT NOT"

Restraining ourselves from negative actions of body, speech, and mind is one aspect of ethical practice, but by no means the only one. In Buddhism, as in other traditions, good ethics means going beyond not doing bad things to include doing good things too. Or, as the Dalai Lama emphasizes in his book *Ethics for the New Millennium*: "It is worth saying again that ethical discipline entails more than just restraint. It also entails the cultivation of virtue. Love and compassion, patience, tolerance, forgiveness and so on are essential qualities."

In the last chapter, I quoted philosopher Peter Singer arguing that it is wrong to remain in a self-absorbed bubble, ignoring the sickness, poverty, and neglect in which others are so helplessly trapped and which we can so easily do something about. He approaches the subject from the viewpoint of what is fair and just. Buddhism approaches it from the perspective of improving our sense of well-being, but both approaches come to the same conclusion.

Ethics and generosity are so inextricably linked that in the Dharma they're sometimes compared to the two wings of a bird—both are needed if we wish to achieve inner peace. In terms of karma, while generosity is a cause of experiencing wealth, the main cause to be born human is virtue. Interestingly, generosity without ethics is considered to create situations where we experience wealth but only temporarily, before having it taken away from us. Alternatively, we may be wealthy but lack the ability to enjoy our wealth—and many of us know grizzled old curmudgeons who fit *that* category!

Ethics are also implied in the perfection of patience, explored in the next chapter. By way of brief illustration, instead of responding to provocation with a tirade of invective, if we were to remain calm we would avoid the nonvirtues of harsh or divisive speech. Indeed, the need for ethical behavior is so fundamental to our Dharma practice that as humans with lives of immense privilege, not to practice ethics doesn't make any sense. Or as Shantideva puts it:

> So if, when having found leisure such as this,
> I do not attune myself to what is wholesome,
> There could be no greater deception,
> And there could be no greater folly.

Exercise: The Perfection of Ethics

We have already looked at the process by which we can begin to apply the perfection to daily life. But what about some tangible cases? The following are a few examples I personally find useful. Perhaps they may spark a thought about similar situations in which you can regularly and consciously go about putting the perfection of ethics into practice.

▶ **Killing:** When I pick up used dishes of cat food from the verandah, they are often crawling with ants. It would be very easy to dunk the bowls, ants included, into a sink of hot, soapy water. Instead, I move the dishes around, which gets the ants leaping off, and I'll brush off the remaining stragglers. As I do so, I think: "By this action of protecting life and avoiding killing, may I quickly attain enlightenment for the benefit of all living beings." (Technically, this is a "double perfection" because giving protection is one of the four kinds of generosity, and avoiding killing is an ethical practice.) I also recollect that, to each individual ant, its life is as important as my life is to me.

▶ **Nonvirtues of speech:** There are some groups of people I socialize with who are far more likely than others to prompt me into harsh speech, divisive speech, or idle gossip. I find it useful in these situations to visualize myself as a buddha with a gold body in the nature of light—that is, like a hologram. From my heart I visualize gold light radiating out to each one of these people, transforming them into buddhas as well. To make this a perfection of ethics, I think: "By avoiding nonvirtues of speech, may I quickly attain enlightenment for the benefit of all living beings." (Another method to help with nonvirtues of speech is to imagine that any person being discussed is physically present. This may help curb the negative things we say, or how we say them.)

▶ **Covetousness:** If an attractive person or object catches your eye and gives rise to inappropriate thoughts, the buddha-visualization practice described above for non-virtues of speech also works very well. When visualizing oneself as a hologram-like buddha, concerned with giving others the true causes of happiness, it's not so easy to have desirous feelings for another hologram-like buddha or thing!

▶ **Jealousy:** Although jealousy isn't specifically listed under the ten nonvirtues, it may be regarded as a sub-category of malice (or of covetousness). One technique I've found helpful in dealing with jealous thoughts is a version of the buddha-visualization above, where instead of sending out gold light rays, you send the person of whom you are jealous the very things you're most jealous of, be they wealth, success, or a happy relationship. While you're at it, you can give them the true causes of happiness as well—love and compassion. You become the imagined source of all their good fortune and happiness. It is *you* who is making them happy! You can do this whether they're physically present or simply imagined. Once again, this antidote practice is a powerful way of countering the negative feelings that might otherwise trouble us. Accompanied by bodhichitta motivation, jealousy can even be transformed from a debilitating cause of unhappiness to a source of love and compassion of which you are the first beneficiary.

8

Thank Buddha for Aggravation! The Perfection of Patience

SOME OF SHANTIDEVA'S most frequently quoted verses are on the subject of the third paramita—the perfection of patience. In Tibetan Buddhism, patience is practiced as an antidote to three different challenges, namely, provocation by others, hardships of all varieties, and practicing Dharma. We will consider the second and third challenges in Chapter 11 when we consider the four laws of spiritual success—in particular, self-discipline. The focus of this chapter is on patience as the antidote to our number-one psychological challenge, the greatest threat to our happiness and inner peace: anger.

There is no transgression like anger,
And no fortitude like patience.
Thus I should strive in various ways
To meditate on patience.

Shantideva begins his chapter on patience with these uncompromising words. On the surface of things, his elevation of anger to the worst of offenses may seem a bit extreme. Just as in the last chapter we saw how harsh speech and idle gossip rank among the ten nonvirtues, saying that there is no transgression like anger may appear unduly hardline. In our culture, anger is not considered to be so dreadful. There are plenty of commonplace situations in which many people would consider an angry reaction to be perfectly justifiable—poor customer service, banking errors, unreliable colleagues, and displays of selfishness by family members, to name but a few. Some people may even see anger as an energy that can be harnessed to positive effect. Many forms of activism—political, environmental, or social—are fueled by a burning sense of injustice and resentment toward those upholding the status quo, as well as the passionate wish to see a new order come into being.

So what's the big deal about losing your cool?

THE EFFECTS OF ANGER

Because as Dharma practitioners we're in the business of mind transformation, the main problem with anger is the profoundly negative effect it has on our own inner peace. Or as Shantideva very simply puts it:

...there is nobody
Who lives happily with anger.

The moment we become angry, any feeling of peacefulness we may have been experiencing instantly evaporates. The two can't coexist. To invert the Buddhist practice of antidotes, we might say that the practice of anger is the most effective antidote to inner peace.

The immediate consequence of disturbing our own mental equilibrium is only the start of the negativity. When we are angered by people or situations, we also reinforce the likelihood that we will be angered by them again in future—we create the karmic cause for a later effect. Many of us can bring to mind situations where we have a tendency to get angry: why is it that so many otherwise calm, rational people turn into raging monsters the moment they sit behind a steering wheel? There may be one person in particular at work or home who knows exactly which buttons to push to drive you crazy. But every time you get angry you reinforce your conditioning or likelihood to experience future unhappiness.

While the immediate impact of anger and the negative conditioning it creates are bad enough, the external repercussions often go way beyond this. Full-blown anger can be like a form of temporary insanity in which we say and do things that we would never normally contemplate, setting off a whole chain of negative repercussions that can't be undone, and which we may very well come to sincerely regret. When I look at my own family, it's easy to see the deep wounds caused by anger, leading to estrangement, misery, and self-recrimination that in some cases have gone on for many years.

Most of us don't have to look too far to see how anger has often been the turning point in business relationships too. I recently lost a significant investment in a property development project because the company's two business partners had such a bitter falling out that they became more focused on destroying each other than completing the project, which eventually went into liquidation. Anger not only consumed both men, it inflicted devastating losses on the investors who had trusted them with their money and the contractors whose substantial work went unpaid.

Geshe Loden writes that "anger creates the karma to experience malice, fear, increased ignorance, as well as loneliness and a lack of resources." When I think about the two partners involved in the failed property company, or family members who have become alienated, evidence of each of those effects can hardly be overlooked.

You may be wondering what is meant by "increased ignorance." This is not a reference to someone's IQ deteriorating or memory fading, but to the specific form of ignorance that is explored in more detail in Chapters 14 and 15. Briefly here we might say it points to the way anger makes us see people and situations as inherently negative—the world around us becomes a darker and unhappier place. Many of us can think of people whose anger is never far from the surface and who feel they are constantly being ripped off or persecuted by service providers, tax departments, ex-partners, relatives, and other "enemies." It is this tendency to concretize a "world versus me" dualism that is implied by "increased ignorance" and that opposes our most profound yearning to experience wholeness and nonduality.

Still on the subject of the effects of anger, while the list provided by Geshe Loden is already a pretty daunting line-up, it goes on to include mental agitation, sleeplessness, and an upset digestive system. The Dalai Lama writes: "In the Tibetan medical system, anger is a primary source of many illnesses, including those associated with high blood pressure, sleeplessness, and degenerative disorders—a view which seems increasingly accepted in allopathic medicine."

Part of the reason that anger is regarded as particularly dangerous is because it arises instantly and without forethought, as Shantideva describes:

Without thinking, "I shall be angry,"
People become angry with no resistance,
And without thinking, "I shall produce myself,"
Likewise anger itself is produced.

We never set out to get angry. It just happens. Someone does or says something and . . . ka-boom! The whole destructive chain of psychological and physical responses is triggered.

Here it may be useful to distinguish between "wrathfulness"—where we appear to be angry even though we aren't—and the anger that is a spontaneous expression of the emotion we truly feel. Parents use wrathfulness to discourage their children from activities that may harm them. Motivated by compassion, the anger they express is only a surface appearance, not something they're truly feeling at the time.

Incidentally, if you have ever wondered about the ferocious-looking buddhas depicted in pictures and wall-hangings in temples, they are also known as "wrathful." These multiheaded, multilimbed monsters, breathing fire and brandishing a lethal arsenal of weapons, are actually manifestations of compassion, having only the appearance of fury. They symbolize the psychological truth that our most threatening delusions can be overcome by the even more powerful forces of love and compassion.

WHEN ANGER IS INTERNALIZED: DEPRESSION

Many of us have to deal with the internalized version of anger, where instead of other people being the focus of our resentment, we turn it on ourselves. We hate ourselves for our inadequacies—the way we look or talk, our habitual responses to people or situations, the fact that we haven't succeeded in achieving our goals, or if we have succeeded, that the price we paid was so high. We hate ourselves for not doing as well as someone else, not having a home as nice as theirs, failing in relationships, or lacking qualities like self-discipline, self-confidence, or good humor.

Depression is the biggest mental problem of our time, the fourth most common reason people in the developed world visit doctors, and every bit as damaging and dangerous as its externally focused counterpart. While it is contemporary psychology, rather than Buddhism, that describes depression as an internalized expression of the same dynamic which causes anger, Shantideva could just as easily have written, "there is nobody who lives happily with *depression*," and "without thinking, 'I shall be *depressed*,' people become *depressed* with no resistance."

As someone who has been deeply depressed in the past, and knows how easy it is to slip into that dark abyss, I am something of an expert at interpreting any given situation in such a way that I come out of it badly. Although the target of delusional interpretation is different—self rather than other—the process is much the same for depression as it is for anger (this does not refer to depression caused by chemical imbalances within the body).

Fortunately, I have discovered in Buddhism an extremely powerful methodology that pulls the rug from under the feet of my depressed feelings. And I'm far from alone in this experience. The proliferation of mindfulness meditation programs focusing on exactly this technique is evidence of the transformative power of this psychology. I provide specific instructions for antidepression meditation in Chapter 15, which should be read in conjunction with Chapter 14.

The subject of this chapter is the perfection of patience, but so far we have only discussed its opposites. The reason for this is simple: most of us can more easily relate to the experience of anger or depression than we can to the experience of practicing patience. When the Buddha gave his first teachings in the deer park at Sarnath, before he began describing enlightenment and its causes, he spoke about dissatisfaction. He spoke about what people could relate to before moving on to more positive possibilities. Having identified the specific mind states we wish to avoid, let's now turn to the opponent practices that are recommended to help us climb out of our habitual reactions and attain a more enlightened mind state.

ANGER AND DEPRESSION AS "NOT PART OF ME"

As a preliminary to the various reframing options illustrated by Shantideva, it's important to first counter the view that some of us are irredeemably bad-tempered grumble-bums who will fly off the handle at the least provocation. While it's true that some people are more prone to anger than others, it's not true that this state can't be changed. Ditto the notion that we are condemned to suffer depression for the rest of our lives. (I am referring here to exogenous depression rather than endogenous, which arises from a biochemical imbalance that can usually be pharmacologically treated.) We can blame our genes, our upbringing, or other external circumstances all we like, but the reality is that anger and depression, like all other emotions, arise, abide, and pass. They are not part of me. They are not who I am. To think, "I'm just an angry/depressive person and I can't help the way I am," is not only profoundly self-limiting, it is simply untrue.

In her commentary on Shantideva's *Guide*, Pema Chödrön mentions a person who used to be a very angry man but who changed after the onset of Alzheimer's disease. Losing his memory, he no longer had the fuel for his previous bitterness. "Without his story lines," she says, "the causes for anger dissolve." It's fascinating to think that one can forget why to become angry. I also know a man who has Alzheimer's and for whom exactly the same thing occurred. I feared for his petite and gentle wife when I first heard about the Alzheimer's, wondering if his anger would bubble over into violent and dangerous rages. But just the opposite happened: the more that he forgot, the more mild and even-tempered he became.

It may seem extreme to use a degenerative disease to suggest that anger isn't a permanent aspect of personality, but it's only one illustration. Some of my fellow Dharma practitioners had serious anger management problems in the past but are now the most easygoing of people. For my own part, the depression that used to hang like a deep fog over my every waking moment for weeks at a time may still arise, but without the irrational thoughts and beliefs to sustain it, it has no basis to remain for very long.

MINDFULNESS OF ANGER-CREATING SITUATIONS

Another preliminary to the anger reframing devices described by Shantideva is the importance of mindfulness. Just as it provides the foundation for our practice of the perfection of generosity and ethics, it is also essential to our practice of the perfection of patience. If anything, our mindfulness needs to be even more acute when trying to counter anger, which, as Shantideva illustrates, arises so quickly and without forethought. Given that we're dealing with a mind state that is so habitual and destructive to our inner peace, we need to be on our guard even more than usual.

If you are regularly vexed by certain situations or people, you may like to mentally assign these as periods in which to ensure your mindfulness is switched to high alert. If you're usually driven crazy by driving to work, dealing with a particular client/subcontractor, or another everyday situation perhaps involving a family member, you may like to assign these situations, right now, as times during which you have a tailor-made opportunity to practice the perfection of patience. From now on, think of these as research opportunities for a new cognitive experiment, one in which you will attempt to identify and replace a habitual negative reaction with an alternative that is immeasurably more positive.

You may very well feel a resistance to this suggestion on the basis that you're not going to allow such-and-such to walk all over you: he or she is such a bully and requires firm handling if you're to get any attention or respect. Practicing patience is not about being a door-mat, however, or agreeing to actions or accepting attitudes that you wouldn't otherwise put up with. You can still stand your ground, if that is what's required, but without the anger. In fact, calmly reasoned logic, stripped of emotion, is more likely to command respect than is emotionally charged ranting.

That said, we all need to get real. If we are prone to angry outbursts behind the steering wheel, perhaps we need to accept that this is an area requiring particular attention. Like a specialist surgeon about to focus on a specific operating site, perhaps we can come to view this activity as the main focus of operation for our own practice of the perfection of patience.

REFRAMING I: TAKING OWNERSHIP—
IT'S NOT OUT THERE, IT'S IN HERE

One of our biggest misconceptions when feeling angry is that the cause is external. In the moment we experience it, we are absolutely convinced that people and circumstances outside of us are entirely to blame. The selfish driver. The sullen child. The phone company's so-called customer care department. We were perfectly content before our contact with those people, we reason. So, obviously, our anger has been caused by them.

But as Shantideva so graphically illustrates:

> If I become angry with the wielder,
> Although I am actually harmed by the stick,
> Then since the perpetrator, too, is secondary, being in
>   turn incited by hatred,
> I should be angry with the hatred instead.
>
> Both the weapon and my body
> Are the causes of my suffering.
> Since the other gave rise to the weapon, and I
>   to the body,
> With whom should I be angry?

While most of us are hopefully not on the receiving end of physical beatings by others, we can see the application of this metaphor to everyday life. When an attractive and self-obsessed young man pushes his way into the supermarket checkout line ahead of us, Shantideva would reason, he may be doing the pushing in, but we're the ones getting upset—don't imagine it's a one-sided business. If we're going to be angry about anything, shouldn't we be angry with the self-obsession that afflicts him?

Another person standing in the queue may not share our anger, thus proving that it is not an inevitable emotion. Someone else standing in the line may be amused by his chutzpah and enjoy the eye candy while waiting in line. So where exactly is the anger coming from?

The interesting thing about taking ownership of angry feelings is that, as soon as we do so, we introduce the possibility that they are unnecessary as well as inappropriate. As soon as we think, "I am the cocreator of this anger," we start to take responsibility for it. We can't pretend it's all somebody else's fault. If we have a tendency to get angry quite often, we may also begin to realize how revealing this is of our own state of mind. As Carl Jung once observed: "Everything that irritates us about others can lead us to a better understanding of ourselves."

Taking responsibility for our own anger also empowers us to do something about it. As long as we feel ourselves to be the hapless victims of external events, there's little we can do to stop other people "making" us angry apart from avoidance. But in the moment that anger arises, if we are able to remind ourselves that we have the choice to practice patience, we interrupt a negative pattern. If we are also able to recollect our bodhichitta motivation in this moment, we create the most profound circuitbreaker in our negative conditioning. When we think, "By the practice of patience, in this moment now, may I attain enlightenment for the benefit of all living beings," we are switching ourselves off the well-worn tracks of an entirely negative emotional journey and onto a trajectory of infinitely positive potential.

In the early days of this practice you will probably feel completely fake while doing it. "For the benefit of all living beings" may be a phrase you repeat in your mind through metaphorically gritted teeth. Restraining your urge to lash out, you may feel that the practice of patience is nothing more than suppression. And isn't bottling up anger supposed to be bad for you?

Buddhism isn't about suppressing or repressing anger. When we begin the perfection of patience, in the moment we take action it may very well feel like it is suppression. But the more we think and meditate about anger, the better we understand its true nature. How, like every other emotion, it arises, abides, and passes. How there's actually nothing to bottle up or concretize in any way—unless that's how we choose to think of it.

As we see in the next reframing method, we may even get to the stage where, instead of being apprehensive about difficult people or infuriating situations, we come to welcome them.

REFRAMING 2:
THANK BUDDHA FOR DIFFICULT PEOPLE!

There is a wonderful story about Atisha, the revered meditation master famous for reintroducing Buddhism to Tibet in the tenth century. When traveling, Atisha was usually accompanied by a student who would act as his general factotum. His choice of student surprised many, because instead of one of the pleasantly compliant disciples he could so easily have picked, he chose a belligerent Bengali. His reason for this was simple if unconventional: having to deal with an ill-tempered staff member made it difficult for him to deceive himself about his own attainment of equanimity.

When things are going well, it's easy to think of ourselves as masters of our particular universe. Embarked on a journey of inner development including the perfection of patience, if we never run into any serious resistance we may believe we have graduated to a more enlightened state of being, even though the reality may be a lot less flattering.

Patrul Rinpoche, an illustrious nineteenth-century spiritual teacher, is said to have visited a yogi who had been on meditation retreat for many years with his main focus on the perfection of patience. Arriving unexpectedly, from the outset Rinpoche needled the meditator, questioning his practices and suggesting he probably hadn't made any real progress. The jibes and teasing went on only so long before the yogi cracked, losing his temper and demanding that Rinpoche should leave. Rinpoche readily agreed, though as he was going he turned to explain that he had only come visiting to test the yogi's perfection of patience.

Most of us have no shortage of Rinpoches in our lives—not that we see them like that. We may sometimes wish we could get far away from the frenetic busyness of our lives and enjoy a slower and more laid-back lifestyle. There may be particular individuals at home or work who are an ongoing source of frustration. A different way to reframe our encounters with such people is to see them as opportunities to practice patience.

The Dharma tells us that while it's wonderful to be surrounded by congenial friends, they very rarely give us the opportunity to practice patience. What we need for that are people who will provoke, chafe, stir up, and aggravate. In our spirit of experimentation, only such people provide the opportunity to identify habitual negative patterns of thinking and replace them with more life-enhancing alternatives. Or as Shantideva puts it:

> Thus, since patient acceptance is produced
> In dependence upon one with a very hateful mind,
> That person should be worthy of veneration just like the
>   sacred Dharma,
> Because that one is a cause of patience.
>
> Therefore, just like treasure appearing in my house
> Without any effort on my part to obtain it,
> I should be happy to have enemies
> For they assist me in my conduct of Awakening.

We set up an extraordinary but wonderful dynamic in our minds when we take the conscious decision to earmark certain people or situations as opportunities to practice the perfection of patience. Instead of experiencing stress, fear, or anxiety in our next encounter with that person, we adopt a more clinical approach. When the familiar provocation begins, we deliberately take the view: "This is a fantastic opportunity—thank you! None of my close friends provide me with such fertile ground for the practice of patience. By practicing patience, here and now, may I achieve enlightenment for the benefit of all beings."

Just as in the earlier reframing example, this practice will feel entirely contrived to begin with. Chances are you will react with your customary irritation and only remember your bodhichitta motivation halfway through an angry outburst; even after recollecting yourself, you won't really feel thankful at all. But once a habit has been broken a new possibility is created. You shouldn't underestimate the power of what you have achieved.

Even in the short term, your new attitude may have a curious effect on the people who irk you. They may detect a change in your approach and wonder what's going on. This could lead to even more intense or frequent provocation. But when you still don't take the bait, the other people may have to rethink their strategy. Their view of you may change. You may even find you've taken the first step to putting those relationships onto a different and improved footing.

THE EQUIVALENT TO VANQUISHING ALL FOES

Whatever method we choose to use in perfecting the practice of patience, Dharma teachers traditionally suggest that we begin with our family and our partner. After all, they really know how to irritate us! Some of them can do it with nothing more than a roll of the eyes at just the wrong moment. Once we're able to perfect patience with friends and relatives, then we're better able to broaden our scope.

The reality is that the frontline of our anger is not out there, but in here. If we can learn to perfect patience when those in our immediate circle throw their worst at us, chances are we're doing quite well. One of Shantideva's most popular verses on this subject reads:

Unruly beings are as unlimited as space:
They cannot possibly all be overcome.
However, if I overcome thoughts of anger alone,
This will be equivalent to vanquishing all foes.

In this verse he echoes one of the most famous sayings of the Buddha: "Though one man conquers a thousand men, a thousand times, in battle, he who conquers himself is the greatest warrior."

Exercise: The Perfection of Patience

Identify one or two situations or people you encounter regularly who irritate you. Even if you usually conceal your anger toward them, it's still an opportunity for practice. From now on, whenever you encounter these situations or individuals, put yourself on "perfection-of-patience alert." This isn't easy. Our conditioned responses are so powerful that, before even realizing it, we slip into habitual patterns of behavior. If it helps, create some external cue as a reminder—for example, if you suffer from road rage, put a post-it note on the dashboard of your car. Try to be aware before the encounter occurs that you are entering a psychological danger zone, potentially harmful to your inner peace.

▶ As you make contact with the anger-creating person or situation, try to be mindful that you now have a fantastic opportunity to practice patience. While interacting, as much as possible think, "By practicing patience may I achieve enlightenment for the benefit of all beings."

► If time permits, you can follow your bodhichitta thought with the reminder that the person or people who cause you aggravation, or who are behind the aggravating situation, are just like you in wanting happiness and wishing to avoid dissatisfaction.

► If you have further time, you can recollect the four immeasurables listed in Chapter 6, four powerful lines in which we recall the true causes of happiness and of suffering. Repeating them here, they are:

May all beings have happiness and the causes of happiness.
May all beings be free from suffering and the causes of suffering.
May all beings never be parted from the happiness that is without suffering—great nirvana, liberation.
May all beings abide in peace and equanimity, their minds free from attachment, aversion, and indifference.

If you succeed in not feeling as angry as usual, congratulate yourself and recollect how fortunate you are to have this treasure of a person or situation to offer you an opportunity for the perfection of patience. If you don't succeed, perhaps reflect on the advantages of practicing patience, and the disadvantages of not practicing patience, to strengthen your resolve for the next encounter.

9

Mindfulness and the Yoga of Coffee Drinking

MINDFULNESS IS the founding practice of spiritual transformation. Wherever we are in our personal journey and whatever our circumstances, mindfulness is the basis on which we effect positive change. Meditators understand the importance of this life-changing practice, though it's a tool too powerful to be confined to the meditation cushion. As Dharma practitioners we aim to make it a 24/7 activity.

What is mindfulness, exactly? We may define it as moment-to-moment, nonjudgmental awareness of every action of body, speech, and mind. It is being fully present to each unfolding experience. When we're mindful, we are completely awake to the here and now.

All of which may seem deceptively straightforward: are we not, to a large extent, doing it already? Most of us lead busy lives juggling a variety of personal, work, family, and other responsibilities. If we weren't aware of what we were doing, how would we be able to function?

While that much is true, it's surprising the extent to which our inner life is disconnected from what we are actually experiencing at any particular moment. Sure, we may have a good overview of what we're doing, but the truth for most of us is that we zoom into a high-resolution focus on the here and now for only brief moments, and quite rarely, before retreating to our usual low-resolution state. For evidence of this we need look no further than the last cup of coffee we bought.

Many of us are prepared to pay for the pleasure of drinking a latte, cappuccino, or espresso rather than drink the instant coffee we can make at home for a tiny fraction of the price. But think back to your last cup of premium coffee and ask yourself, in all honesty, how much of it did you actually savor and enjoy? If you were texting on your mobile, busy at your workstation, or talking to friends, there's every chance that for most of your coffee-drinking time you weren't tuned in to your taste buds at all. More likely you were focusing on social arrangements, contemplating your share portfolio, or thinking about a subject that had nothing to do with the treat you had bought to enjoy.

Next time you buy a coffee, practice the yoga of drinking it mindfully. Yoking together body and mind, implied in the word "yoga," focus your attention on every forensic detail of the experience. The aroma as you raise the coffee to your mouth. The taste as it runs over your tongue. The warm sensation as it glides down your throat. Truly experience that coffee—not just the first mouthful, which we're usually pretty good at noticing, but every mouthful. You didn't spend three or four dollars for just one mouthful of coffee. Make sure you get full value for your money!

BRIDGING THE DISCONNECT THROUGH MINDFULNESS

In many ways, the drinking of premium coffee is a metaphor for so much of our lives. If Shantideva had been around today, perhaps he would have worked it into one of his verses. Because even when we do get the externals of our lives the way we want them to be— even when we're clutching our cappuccino *grande* and have found the perfect spot to enjoy it—how much of our own good fortune do we actually savor? How much of the time are we too distracted to notice it?

This principle applies not only to coffee drinking, but to so many aspects of the external world that we spend so much time and energy trying to get right—and then, the moment we do, promptly ignore and start thinking about something completely different. What is the point of indulging in a restaurant meal, heading down to the beach, or going away for a weekend break if we're hardly even aware of where we are for most of the time or, worse, are dwelling on less than happy thoughts? As we've seen, Shantideva likened the material rewards of our working lives to mouthfuls of grass snatched by beasts of burden as they drag carriages. It's bad enough that these snatches of grass are small reward for all our effort: we make it even worse when we're not able to fully enjoy even these fleeting experiences.

If an improved standard of living was the recipe for happiness, wouldn't we expect to see nothing but happiness in wealthy nations and the wealthiest suburbs? But of course, we know this is not the case.

Never has the disconnect between out there and in here been so striking. Helping bridge that disconnect, though, is the practice of mindfulness. If we were able to shift our attention, even slightly, away from our customary self-obsessive wish for more to an appreciation of the truly amazing life we already possess, what a positive impact that could have!

THE SCIENCE OF MINDFULNESS

Like so many of the other Buddhist teachings described in previous chapters, the practice of mindfulness has been powerfully endorsed by contemporary science. Since the 1970s, dozens of research studies have been conducted to test the application of mindfulness, finding it to have surprisingly dramatic effects on a wide variety of medical conditions. Mindfulness is now a foundation subject at the growing number of mind/body institutes, and the University of

Massachusetts has a dedicated Center for Mindfulness in Medicine, Health Care, and Society, established in 1995 by Jon Kabat-Zinn, a pioneer in the area and founder of the acclaimed Stress Reduction Clinic at the university's medical school.

Over the past thirty years the center's work—mindfulness training for patients across a wide range of medical diagnoses including many different chronic pain conditions, as well as those with secondary diagnoses of anxiety and/or panic—has shown consistent, reliable, and reproducible demonstration of major reductions in symptoms. When practicing mindfulness, patients are better able to manage chronic pain and stress, and they also benefit from what researchers term "enhanced psychological hardiness" and "a greater sense of coherence." It is revealing that mindfulness can be of benefit to people experiencing such a wide variety of conditions.

Mindfulness is so powerful because it gives us the ability to take charge of our thoughts and feelings. If we do not fully attend to these—if we live our lives in a state of constant distraction—we are condemned to keep experiencing whatever thoughts, interpretations, and emotions habitually recur.

The content of those thoughts may be very different. We may have habitually stress-creating thoughts: "The deadlines I have to deliver against are endless and overwhelming." Or depression-creating: "I'm never going to succeed and/or no one will ever love me for who I am." They may create anxiety: "What if we fall behind on our mortgage payments and lose the house?" Or induce fear: "Things are completely out of our control—we're done for!" Whatever our personal brand of negativity, the simple but critically important first step in eliminating it is to recognize it when it happens. Or as Shantideva so vividly puts it:

If someone dropped a sword during a battle,
They would immediately pick it up out of fear.
Likewise, if I lose the weapon of mindfulness,
I should quickly retrieve it, being afraid of hell.

As a former warrior prince, Shantideva often used military imagery, which seems incongruous to those who think of Buddhist monks as gentle, peace-loving types. But as Shantideva framed it, each one of us is engaged in his or her own inner war with "enemies" who threaten our sense of well-being and have the potential to make us deeply unhappy. Terms like "stress" and "depression" weren't used in Shantideva's day, but he did talk about "hellish states," by which he meant the same thing. We might insert our own "enemy" into the last line of that verse: "I should quickly retrieve it, being afraid of *stress/anxiety/depression*" (or any other mental affliction that we habitually experience).

What he illuminates in this verse with such dramatic power is the importance of practicing mindfulness on a moment-by-moment basis. His choice of martial imagery was deliberate: there could be few places where human awareness is more heightened than on the battlefield, in hand-to-hand combat with numberless enemies whose sole purpose is to kill you. Losing one's sword in such a situation would soon be followed by death. We should attach the same urgent sense of purpose to our practice of mindfulness in daily life, he tells us, because without it our sense of well-being is at serious risk.

THE DANGERS OF MINDLESSNESS

Allowing negative thoughts to gain a toehold in our consciousness is the first step of our descent into "hellish states." The Buddha taught that negative thoughts lead to negative feelings, and that if such feelings are allowed to continue they quickly become habitual.

If we are to make the switch in thought content from negative to positive, we must first be aware of the negativity that is arising. For if we are not mindful:

> Just as poison spreads throughout the body
> In dependence upon the circulation of blood,
> Likewise, if a disturbing conception finds an opportunity,
> Unwholesomeness will permeate my mind.

Shantideva's use of the word "poison" can be understood in the context of "the three poisons"—Buddhist shorthand for attachment/desire, anger/hatred and ignorance. These three poisons are identified as the underlying cause of all our unhappiness. The analogy of poison is deliberately used to make the point that even a very small amount of it can be lethal. All it takes is a single unpleasant idea for one's mind to quickly become "permeated" with negativity.

To validate the importance of mindfulness as a key tool in overcoming habitual negativity we need look no further than the research studies conducted by Dr. John Teasdale of the UK Medical Research Council's Cognition and Brain Sciences Unit in Cambridge, Dr. Mark Williams of the University of Wales, and Dr. Zindel Segal of the University of Toronto and the Clarke Institute of Psychiatry in conjunction with the Center for Mindfulness. This team focused specifically on depression—surely one of the most hellish of states—and how even in people who had recovered from previous depressive episodes, "periods of mild depressed mood could reactivate old patterns of negative ruminative thought, setting up vicious spirals that could intensify depression and lead to relapse."

The researchers taught patients how to become mindful of negative thoughts in a treatment called mindfulness-based cognitive therapy (MBCT). Specifically, "MBCT teaches patients how to switch out of an automatic, habitual, ruminative mode of mind in which they identify with their negative thoughts and feelings, to a more mindful, intentional mode, in which thoughts and feelings are seen from a wider perspective as simply events passing through the mind."

This perspective of seeing thoughts as merely "events passing through the mind" is identical in approach to the well-established Buddhist meditation of "mind watching mind" (see Chapter 15). And the broader notion of combining mindfulness with the reframing of inner experience is also exactly in accord with Dharma teachings. But most significant of all were the results. "A multicenter clinical trial evaluating MBCT in a group of 145 recovered depressed patients showed that, for patients with three or more previous episodes of depression, MBCT approximately halved relapse rates (37% vs. 66%) compared to treatment-as-usual." A separate clinical trial confirmed this finding.

Once again, Buddhist and contemporary psychology converge at the same point. The poetry of Shantideva and the statistics of clinical research come to the same powerful conclusion: that mindfulness is a highly effective weapon in combating self-harming thought patterns, even when these are deeply engrained.

APPLYING BODHICHITTA MINDFULLY

While the focus of Western psychology has traditionally been on helping distressed people feel more normal, Buddhist psychology has always had the much more ambitious purpose of encouraging us toward states of transcendental happiness far beyond everyday experience. Just as a person who isn't suffering any physical ailment may not be particularly fit and healthy, so too merely coping well enough with daily life doesn't make us especially happy, fulfilled, or realized individuals. If we want that we need to work at it, in the same way as a regular exercise and diet regime can do wonders for our physical well-being. Being extraordinary takes effort.

As trainee bodhisattvas seeking to realize our buddha nature, mindfulness is our most powerful tool. In the past few chapters where we discussed the perfection of generosity, ethics, and patience, in each case the practice of mindfulness was a prerequisite. Unless we are mindful of an act of generosity, how can we perfect it with bodhichitta motivation? If we don't recognize we're at risk of participating in idle gossip or ill will, on what basis do we practice the perfection of ethics?

Combining mindfulness with bodhichitta motivation is at the heart of the bodhisattva path. If we wish to transform an ordinary experience of the world into an extraordinary one, we make it part of our bodhichitta practice. Our motivation need not be restricted to acts of generosity, ethics, or patience. There is actually no activity to which the transformational alchemy of bodhichitta cannot be applied.

Returning to "the yoga of coffee drinking": at the beginning of this chapter we looked at how "tuned out" we usually are when drinking coffee, even when we've gone out of our way to enjoy our favorite brew, and considered how we might relish the same experience more intensely by being mindful of every aspect of the coffee-drinking experience.

Now let's take things to the next level: before and during your mindful coffee-drinking experience, recollect your bodhichitta motivation by thinking: "By the act of drinking this coffee mindfully may I achieve enlightenment for the benefit of all beings." If you have time, also reflect on your good fortune to enjoy a life of leisure and fortune that includes drinking great coffee, unlike the vast majority of our fellow humans. In so doing, you will reaffirm a sense of gratitude about your enormous good fortune, instead of regarding coffee drinking as just another everyday experience. Through mindfulness we transform the mundane act of coffee drinking into one that not only enhances our sense of gratitude and well-being but that is also a cause to become enlightened for the benefit of all living beings.

You may well be wondering how drinking coffee could possibly be a cause for enlightenment. Some of the biggest consumers of coffee I know are among the most bad-tempered misanthropes I've ever had the misfortune to encounter. The liter of caffeine they drink each week has had no evident impact on their spiritual evolution.

Drinking coffee in itself is not a cause for enlightenment, but we transform it by recollecting our bodhichitta motivation. By recollecting bodhichitta more and more frequently each day, by making the practice of love, compassion, and equanimity part of our mental landscape, we systematically set our thoughts on a more positive trajectory. And, by necessity, we systematically eliminate negative or mindless mental activity.

When we begin our practice, the process is deliberate and contrived. But as we continue, the mask becomes the person. The habit is ingrained and our bodhichitta becomes more spontaneous. This is especially helped if our off-cushion Dharma practice is supported by on-cushion analytical meditation, when we integrate the meaning and value of what we do at a deeper level. By conjoining external practice with direct, nonconceptual experience, our entire experience of reality begins to shift.

BEGINNING, CONTINUING, AND ENDING EACH DAY WITH MINDFUL BODHICHITTA

Don't stop at drinking coffee. Because Dharma practice is a 24/7 activity, we have countless opportunities to recollect bodhichitta motivation each day—if we are mindful of them. My teacher sometimes asks the class: "What are the first things you think about when you wake up each day? Where is the focus of your attention?" If your mind is dominated by an overwhelming sense of all the things you have to do—perhaps activities you don't want to do and encounters you can't avoid—or memories about how you used to wake up to a better time and place, none of these thoughts serves any purpose except to make you unhappy. They don't improve your mood or performance. They certainly don't contribute to a state of relaxed, creative capability. And if they set the tone for the inner monologue that continues for the rest of the day, how unfortunate is that? Wouldn't it be better to wake up thinking, "May each of my activities today be a direct cause for me to become enlightened for the benefit of all living beings"? If possible, also cultivate a sense of gratitude that your own life, in relative terms, is so privileged.

Then as you shower, shave, and shampoo you are presented with an opportunity to be mindful of purification and rejuvenation, accompanying this external process with an inner purification by thinking: "By this act of purification, may I remove all my unhappiness-causing thoughts and habits, and create only positive ones, so that I can become enlightened for the benefit of all beings."

Approach bodhichitta with a creative, playful feeling. That way, through mindfulness, every meal you eat and beverage you drink becomes a source of bodhichitta, as does every journey to work, every meeting you attend, each social encounter, and even every TV show you watch.

Sitting with work colleagues in a meeting, or with friends relaxing, take a moment to visualize yourself as a buddha, radiating golden light to them all while reflecting: "May I attain enlightenment not only for this circle of colleagues, but for all living beings without exception."

Similarly, last thing at night, recollect your bodhichitta motivation through mindfulness as you lie in bed. Reviewing your day's activities from a Dharma perspective may be useful, as long as this doesn't stop you falling asleep. You may recognize missed opportunities to practice patience, generosity, or ethics, and resolve not to miss them again. You may take satisfaction in your positively motivated activities. Especially, cultivate the thought: "By sleeping soundly tonight and waking reenergized tomorrow may I sustain my physical good health so that I can create further causes of enlightenment for the benefit of all beings."

Mindfulness Exercise

Choose an activity you do every day, ideally several times a day, such as eating, drinking, washing your hands, or walking to and from the office. Set yourself the objective of using that activity for mindfulness practice.

▶ Next time you begin the activity, cultivate bodhichitta motivation with the thought: "By this practice of mindfulness may all living beings achieve enlightenment." Now carry out the activity mindfully, as described in this chapter. Apply a forensic focus, studying the tiniest details of every aspect of the activity. Be completely present to the experience of it.

▶ If you forget your plan to practice mindfulness until you're partway through the activity, begin it then. It can take a while to develop this habit.

▶ If everyday thoughts intrude into your mindfulness practice, recollect that you've given yourself permission not to dwell on these. Place your attention back on the object of your practice.

▶ If possible, close your mindfulness activity by reflecting on your bodhichitta motivation.

▶ As you begin to enjoy the benefits of mindfulness accompanied by bodhichitta, try expanding the activities to which you apply it until it becomes the ongoing theme of your mental life throughout each day.

10

Breaking the Cycle of Dissatisfaction

I RECENTLY CAME across a Buddhist parable about two calves and a piglet who lived in a country household. The calves weren't very old before they were pressed into service, dragging plow through the rocky fields—hard work, for which they were only provided with hay. No such labors were demanded of the piglet, however, who quickly grew to maturity, becoming fat on a rich diet which included rice pudding topped with brown sugar. So pampered was the pig's life that among the other animals he earned the nickname "No Squeal," because it seemed that he didn't even have to make a noise for his every wish to be manifest—usually in the form of a trough full of food.

In time, the younger of the two calves—Little Red—complained to Big Red about the injustice of the situation. "Here we are helping the family make a living, and we're fed only the bare minimum," he said, "while No Squeal lounges about all day doing nothing and is rewarded with the most huge and delicious meals."

Big Red, wise beyond his years, cautioned Little Red. "Don't envy anyone till you know the full facts of their situation," he said.

As it happened, the calves didn't have long to wait before the facts of No Squeal's situation became brutally clear. When the daughter of the family got married soon afterward, a wedding reception was held, and No Squeal was dragged away unceremoniously by the legs and his throat cut. His next appearance was in the center of the dining table, roasted, glazed, and with an apple in his mouth.

The moral of the story is this: Don't envy the rich until you know the price they pay for their wealth.

For most of us, life doesn't conform to the morally ordered world of the two calves, where idle pigs are inevitably roasted. But the story is a useful caution, nevertheless, against becoming jealous of those of whose situation we have only a limited perspective.

Little Red in this tale was experiencing jealousy, one of five core delusions identified in Tibetan Buddhism: the others are attachment, anger, pride, and wrong view. Already in this book we have looked at the delusion of attachment (Chapter 3) and our tendency to idealize certain things, people, and situations, leading to the powerful wish to possess them. We've also looked at the opposite delusion, anger (Chapter 8), and our tendency to exaggerate the negatives about certain things, people, and situations, leading to the powerful wish to avoid or destroy them. In this chapter we look at all delusions from the perspective of Buddhist psychology: understanding how they operate is critical if we are to break the cycle of dissatisfaction in which they entrap us and instead cultivate a mind of enlightenment.

What do we mean by "delusion"? We usually talk about people being "delusional" when their attitudes are out of kilter with what we regard as the norm. This is a quite different take on the word from Tibetan Buddhism, where delusions are "mental factors that, when generated, cause the mental continuum to be very unpeaceful." Common synonyms for delusions in the Tibetan tradition are "negative minds," "afflictions," and "obstructions to liberation."

In the West, if we say someone is suffering from a delusion, unless we are being provocative—for example, "delusions of grandeur"—the implication is that the person has a fairly serious psychological condition. In Buddhist terms, being delusional is also a fairly serious psychological condition—but we all suffer from it! If we have ever had a disturbed—"unpeaceful"—state of mind, we have experienced a delusion. If we are ever anything other than happy and peaceful, the cause of our discontent can be defined as a delusion.

The immediate impact of delusions is bad enough. When Little Red returned to the stack of hay on the cowshed floor at the end of another day's exertions, how galling it must have been to look over to the pigsty to see No Squeal wallowing in an indulgent swill of creamy rice pudding. What a burning sense of injustice he must have felt! How resentful he must have been toward his owners for maintaining such an inequitable regime. Similarly, if we experience frustration that we don't have the apartment, partner, or success we want in our life—or that we want for our loved ones—and envy those who do enjoy such things, or resent the system or people who deny us personal fulfillment, we too are suffering from delusion. But, even worse than this, every time we experience a delusion we ensure that we will experience it again in the future.

THE LONG-TERM IMPACT OF DELUSIONS

This longer term impact of delusions can be understood within the context of *samsara*. Samsara is a concept shared by several Eastern traditions to describe the cycle of birth, aging, sickness, death, and rebirth. More specifically, however, we can define samsara as a "mind afflicted by karma and delusion." This is because the experience of cyclic existence, or samsara, is a mind afflicted in such a way—a mind without such afflictions is not subject to cyclic existence.

I prefer the more specific definition of samsara because it goes to the heart of the matter. And the relationship between delusion and karma is described with wonderful clarity by Geshe Loden:

> The source of cyclic existence is karma and delusion. Of these, delusion is the principal cause. If there were no

delusion, even though you may have countless previously-created karmas, suffering would not be produced. Just as a seed cannot sprout without the cooperative causes of soil, heat, and water, karma cannot ripen without the cooperative cause of the delusions. Having a deluded state of mind is like pouring water on a dry field in which lie the unripened seeds of previous negative karma. If delusions are present, even were there no previously created karma, it would immediately be created and establish future contaminated aggregates. For this reason it is important to apply antidotes to the delusions, and to do so you must become knowledgeable regarding them.

The hugely destructive power of delusions therefore arises not just from the delusions themselves but also from the negative karma they activate and the future "contamination" they create. In terms of Western psychology, we might regard this as similar to an explanation of the workings of operant conditioning, when the experience of an event—in this case a delusion—reinforces the likelihood of a similar future experience.

A recurring theme in Shantideva's *Guide* is his personification of delusions. It is an attention-grabbing technique, and through it he turns what might otherwise be a fairly cerebral subject into a much more colorful account of our ongoing conditioning. By personifying a variety of mental activities, Shantideva not only brings the whole subject more vividly to life, he also reframes our experience of reality in two important ways. First, he counters our knee-jerk response to dissatisfaction, which is to blame all our woes on external factors. Second, he provides a tangible object on which to focus our attention. One of the most famous verses of his *Guide* applies exactly this technique to the subject of delusions, presenting our "true" enemies in such a way that we cannot mistake them.

Although enemies such as hatred and craving
Have neither any arms nor legs,
And are neither courageous nor wise,
How have I, like a slave, been used by them?

I love this verse, even though I never fail to feel like an idiot whenever I read it, because it's so true! There is no wisdom in a delusion, nor does it have any capability beyond what we give it. So why *are* we used by our delusions "like a slave"?

The unfortunate answer has to be that we're all too tolerant and forgiving when it comes to our own delusions and sometimes even experience an undercurrent of satisfaction alongside them. This may seem an extraordinary statement, given that the definition of a delusion is something that disturbs our own inner peace. But when we focus more closely on dynamics like desire, anger, pride, and envy, we discover that their effect is not as singular or straightforward as we may assume.

WHY WE TOLERATE DELUSIONS

In the case of desire or attachment, along with the urgency of our wish to have something or someone, and the possible frustration that we don't already have them, we may also experience an anticipatory thrill as we imagine what it would be like to be the possessor. Whether we fantasize about a situation that we know will never happen, or one that may come within our grasp, attachment can bring with it an alluring, pleasurable energy, even though its ultimate result for us is destructive.

This is not to say it is wrong to establish goals and work toward achieving them. On the contrary, the Dharma encourages us to live purposeful and materially rewarding lives. Rather, the point is that when the achievement of our goals or wishes disturbs our inner peace then it becomes a problem. When we become fixated on something or someone, believing that we will only be happy when we have that thing or person, we reinforce a delusion.

Interestingly, this is a dynamic that successful salespeople will confirm. It's one thing to try to close a deal when you are confident in yourself and your product and are genuinely unconcerned about which way the sale goes. Sure, you know what you want, but you are relaxed about whether or not you get it. You know that your inner peace—and sales target—doesn't depend on it. But if you're strongly attached to a positive outcome and your desperation shows through, not only do you find yourself in a much less powerful position, you're also less likely to close the deal. Even on a worldly level, attachment creates problems for us.

Nostalgia can also easily become an attachment-based delusion. If we live in the past, during a time and place that no longer exists, we may feel a heart-warming glow as we reminisce, but this can become dysfunctional when our equanimity is disturbed by thoughts about how our current situation doesn't live up to the former life we recollect so fondly. I encounter this particular delusion very often when meeting fellow expatriates from Zimbabwe, and it's one I share myself: we yearn for a time and place we recollect through decidedly rose-tinted glasses. Sadly, this attachment to a mythical past can be a real hindrance to getting on with one's life in the here and now.

Turning to anger, the undertow of positive energy we experience alongside our fury at the driver in front of us is the confirmation of our superiority. He or she is, all too obviously, a much less competent driver than ourselves—perhaps even morally defective, judging from the selfishness displayed. It is rare for us to feel hostility toward others without also experiencing a sense of self-righteousness.

When you look at the behavior of some supposedly cause-driven activists, you can't help wondering if environmental, racial, or economic injustices really are the issues that drive them, or if these are merely the outlets through which they can vent their anger in a form of socially sanctioned moral indignation.

The power felt by an angry person in full flight can also provide positive reinforcement. The assertion of self over other can be quite gratifying, especially when a person feels generally frustrated by his or her lack of authority or importance. Aren't petty tyrants always the most vehement in their tyranny?

The delusion of jealousy is often accompanied by the cheering anticipation of one's enemy getting his or her comeuppance. Yes, we may resent what such people have, the recognition they enjoy or triumphs that seem to make their position unassailable; they may be on top of the world now, but just you wait...

The worst of mass-market media is driven by exactly such sentiment. "Build them up to break them down" is the established pattern, with idealized tales of heart-sweeping romances and perfect Hollywood weddings quickly followed by stories of tragic estrangements and gut-wrenching betrayal, all reported with lip-smacking relish.

Pride is not a delusion we have explored so far, but it can be subtle if pernicious in its workings. Pride in our good looks, social status, wealth, family, intelligence, knowledge, or erudition may make us feel important, but it is isolating, breeds resentment, and ultimately creates tension in our relations with others that seriously compromises our chances of happiness and inner peace.

Pride is a particular danger in our Dharma practice because it stops us from evolving. One Dharma analogy talks about the three pots, or three attitudes, that prevent us from developing as practitioners. The pot with the crack in the bottom is the distracted mind, so agitated that it can't focus or retain information. The pot containing poison is the cynical mind, so critical and judgmental that it doesn't matter what new substance is poured into the pot, it will be contaminated. The third pot—the proud pot—is already full. It contains so many preconceptions and ideas that new information, however valuable, simply overflows down the sides.

Whatever our particular delusion—and we all tend to have one or two that are dominant—it is useful to identify how we experience them and what positive side-effects encourage us to tolerate them. The more we analyze them, the more we realize how entirely misplaced our tolerance really is. Wryly alluding to his teachings on patience, Shantideva says of delusions:

For while they dwell within my mind
At their pleasure, they cause me harm,
Yet I patiently endure them without any anger;
But this is an inappropriate and shameful time
*   for patience.*

Identifying one's own delusions is an uncomfortable exercise. In the descriptions given so far you may have already recognized your pet delusion(s). In my own case, I'd no sooner heard about the five poisons than I recognized myself as an attachment-based person. However, it has taken me several years to understand the workings of this in more depth—exactly how my attachment operates, how it affects my thoughts and feelings, and what emotional gratification accompanies it. Even though I have a much deeper knowledge of it now, I certainly couldn't claim to have cracked the problem. That is the journey of at least one lifetime. In my discussions with other Dharma practitioners, it seems to be a common experience that we repeatedly come up against the same problems in different guises, the same psychological challenges in our lives, even though our response to them may become more evolved. We are dealing with deeply ingrained psychological patterns and conditioning. It would be unrealistic to expect them to disappear in a matter of months or even years, purely on the basis of our recognition and insight, however profound.

But facing up to our delusions does help us cope with them, because the initial recognition of our main challenges, through the application of thought and meditation, moves from an intellectual conception to the much deeper understanding that's needed to free ourselves from the myths on which our delusions are based. In other words, to destroy our samsara.

For just as we may describe someone as being "delusional" who believed, for example, that snipers on surrounding rooftops were constantly aiming at them, or who thought that running naked through the park would be a source of immeasurable bliss, our own delusions also have no basis in reality. They are based on myths— even though these myths, like the Emperor's new clothes, may not be recognized as such by the society in which we live.

Take attachment, one of the most universal of delusions. The wish to have or experience something is based on the delusion that the thing or experience itself is a cause of happiness. Have I ever discerned this to be true? Does it really work all the time and for everybody? If not, where did I get the idea that it will work for me?

Stated like that it seems easy to understand and all so obvious. And delusions are always easier to see in others. But when it comes to our own delusions, even if we recognize the myths on which they're based and the suffering they cause, even if we decide that we're not going to be a victim of our limbless enemy any longer, without clarity, understanding, and vigilance it's all too easy for our habitual, delusional thinking to sneak back up on us.

HOW DELUSIONS SNEAK BACK UP ON US: TWO CAUTIONARY TALES

As an attachment-based person, one of my own greatest delusions is that writing and publishing novels is a cause of personal fulfillment and happiness. Uncovering why that particular delusion has arisen would probably take hundreds of hours on the psychiatrist's couch, but it may have something to do with my childhood years, during which I remember my father, then a teacher and writer, hammering away at the Olympus typewriter in his study. Perhaps another influence was the veneration given to writers in the family and society in which I grew up, and my own youthful hero-worship of my favorite writers. Whatever the reason, as I have described earlier, fulfillment of this ambition became an obsession from my teenage years until the publication of my first novel in my thirties.

Recollecting the definition of a delusion as something that causes the mind to be "very unpeaceful," there can be absolutely no doubting that I suffered from a particularly serious delusion. By way of contrast, had I pursued my dreams without attachment—that is, without making any great emotional investment in the outcome of a particular project or allowing my mind to be disturbed by it—that wouldn't have been delusional; it would probably also have been a whole lot more effective. But so urgent was my ambition that my limbless enemies within made me very unhappy indeed. My whole sense of purpose, of who I was and what I thought made my life worthwhile, was bound up in the fulfillment of an ambition within a notoriously fickle industry.

As it happened, I did get to realize my ambition and, predictably, to discover that despite all my expectations, my whole world didn't change overnight. Yes, there was a great sense of satisfaction, but there were also a number of unexpected negative side-effects. Like the isolation of being a writer after having worked for years in the busy world of public relations. Like finding my career suddenly dependent on the whims and balance sheets of people with whom I had little contact, and who were under no obligation to communicate with me. Most of all, discovering when I woke up in the mornings that I didn't feel any different from the way I'd felt before.

You'd think I'd have learned my lesson from this, and that my personal experience of the joys and trials of being a novelist would have given me a much more balanced view in future. Having discovered the myths of my own delusion, surely I could no longer succumb? Alas, no.

Soon after publishing *Buddhism for Busy People* I decided to try my hand at novel-writing again. Drafting the first few chapters and the summary of a novel called *The Magician of Lhasa*, I contacted an agent who expressed an interest in the book and said she was keen to read the material and get back to me.

The habits of book buyers had been unknown to me before my contact with publishers, but I'd come to learn that people who buy novels rarely buy nonfiction books such as this one, and vice versa. As someone who enjoys reading both, I'd always imagined everyone else was the same as me, but apparently not. In writing *The Magician of Lhasa*, apart from the sheer creative fun of writing a novel, I hoped to impart some of the life-changing wisdom I'd discovered in a format that would appeal to people who never strayed to the self-help section of a bookstore.

While the interested agent was reading the first few chapters, I wrote a few more. She came back to me with an enthusiastic response, as well as some suggested improvements, which I implemented in the material I'd written. The expanded, revised draft took her longer to read, during which time I had become so absorbed by the story that I continued to write. And write.

Somewhere along the line, without my even noticing it, my age-old adversary snuck up on me and I began getting very attached to the outcome of the project. Even though I'd promised myself not to commit too much to any new novel until I had a commitment from a publisher, I broke my own promise. I kept on writing because, after all, the novel *was sure to be snapped up for a hearty advance and published to great acclaim.*

Before I knew it, and with the passage of a few months, I'd written most of the book. Because the novel was so far advanced, my agent encouraged me to complete it, on the basis that publishers would be more interested in a full, polished draft. By now I was completely hooked. I kept on writing, committing myself more and more with every word that I wrote.

The submission process that followed was lengthy and tortuous, interjected with numerous revisions and rewrites. Commissioning editors seemed to take forever to come back with their decisions. And phrases like "borderline decision" and "we loved it but the sales team didn't know where it would go in the bookstore" came back as reasons for the rejections that followed.

While one part of me was naturally disappointed, another part, watching my mind, was aware of the all-too-familiar dynamics at work—the emotional soap opera that seemed to be the story of my life. The rising hopes with each successive round of submissions. The frustration that accumulated on receiving each new set of refusals. The growing realization that I had just wasted an entire year of precious spare time writing a book that would never be read. The wily new self-sabotaging belief that, as writing the book had been part of my Buddhist path, I hadn't only failed as a writer, I was obviously a hopeless practitioner too.

It would be misleading to suggest that my attachment-based delusion was as troubling as it had been in the past. Simply having an awareness of it helped contain its effects. Contemplating one of the many proposed rounds of revisions, I remember discussing with some of my fellow meditators on retreat whether I should continue with it, or whether this would only reinforce my attachment—and therefore potential unhappiness if things didn't work out later. Wisely, they counselled me that it wasn't what was going on out there that mattered, it was what was going on in here. The real question wasn't whether or not I should undertake further revisions so much as the attitude I had toward them. Could I undertake them without getting further emotionally caught up in the outcome?

THE INSIDIOUS NATURE OF DELUSIONS

I offer this story to illustrate the insidious nature of our delusions. Attachment, in particular, is said to be the most difficult of all delusions to eliminate. Anger or hatred are sometimes compared to a dark patch of mud on a white cloth, while attachment or desire is like a grease stain on the same cloth: the mud patch is far more obvious and unsightly, but in a relative sense is easier to get rid of. By contrast, the subtle stain of attachment presents us with a much greater challenge.

Comparing our pernicious inner enemies with those we may usually think of as being our opponents, or at least difficult people in our life, Shantideva says:

—

All other enemies are incapable
Of remaining for such a length of time
As can my disturbing conceptions;
The enduring enemy has neither beginning nor end.

For most of us, relationships with unpleasant colleagues or bosses come to an end, as do once intimate romances that have soured, or commercial partnerships that wind up in court. Our "enemies" in the mundane world may be a cause of intractable difficulty and unhappiness. But generally speaking, our contact with them comes to an end at some stage, and we're able to get on with our lives without further interference. Regrettably, the same can't be said of our delusions, which are capable of enduring much longer.

Analytical Meditation: Attachment Versus Love

There are two reasons to practice the following meditation. The first is to truly realize the difference between attachment and love. The second is to recognize the destructive nature of attachment, in order to strengthen our resolve to abandon it. (This meditative approach can be applied to any delusion, but we are focusing here on attachment.)

Before beginning the analytical meditation, stabilize your mind as usual with a breath meditation exercise.

► First, consider a situation in which your attachment to a person, thing, ambition, or idea has become a source of unhappiness to you—that is, a delusion. What thoughts do you have/have you had about the object of your attachment? (For example, "I'll only be happy when I have him or her or that.")

► Reflect on the negative emotions created by these thoughts (for example, despair that you don't have him or her or that and therefore can't be happy; frustration that you haven't achieved a goal and that you feel thwarted).

► Consider how unbalanced and inaccurate your perspective of the object is by thinking of all the people who already have what you would like. Are they all permanently happy as a result?

► Recognize that attachment is a true cause of suffering. Develop a strong determination to abandon the attachment-based thoughts that create unhappiness. Hold on to this conviction single-pointedly.

► Next, consider love: the wish to give happiness to others. What thoughts do you have/have you had about situations when you have given profound happiness to others? Recollect the emotions you experienced. Identify that another person is/was at the center of your wish to give happiness.

► Recognize that love, the wish to give happiness to others, is a true cause of happiness. Develop a strong determination to practice love more often. Hold on to this conviction single-pointedly.

11

The Four Laws of Spiritual Success

BUDDHISM IS AMONG the most optimistic and self-confident of all spiritual traditions. It is no coincidence that one of the images most powerfully associated with Buddhism is the lotus, a plant that, though rooted in the filth of the swamps, rises to the surface to flower with the most extraordinary beauty. The lotus symbolizes our ability not only to transcend the challenges of samsara, but to use these—much as a lotus plant thrives on the decay of the swamp—to manifest with such radiant beauty that the ultimate result appears to have little connection to the swamp-bound root system from which it emerged.

As Buddhists, this is something we do on our own. We do not expect the external agency of a god, savior, guardian angel, or other force to help us. The reason for our focus on self-reliance is quite simple: if benign and powerful beings were in a position to help us, would they not have done so already?

While there is a logic, simplicity, and power to the practices of transformation, including those described in previous chapters, they're certainly not easy. Replacing deeply ingrained, self-destructive mental habits and setting ourselves on a dramatically more positive and panoramic trajectory requires sustained effort. Practicing mindfulness, the perfection of patience and nonattachment is hard work. Buddhism isn't for wimps.

Which is why Shantideva devoted a whole chapter to the subject of "enthusiasm." Shantideva knew as well as anyone the attitude needed to made real progress on the Dharma path. Before demonstrating his own advanced powers by levitating out of sight while reciting Chapter 9 of his *Guide*, he revealed the specific combination of mental factors required to achieve exactly such spiritual attainments—the four traits needed if we are to succeed in achieving genuine transformation. We might regard these as providing the psychological profile of a buddha-in-training.

Not surprisingly, these four attributes are frequently mentioned by high achievers in other disciplines—Olympic athletes, classical musicians, entrepreneurs, and others who aim to be the best of the best. Shantideva lists them as aspiration, firmness, joy, and moderation; in modern parlance they might be translated as goal-setting, self-discipline, finding happiness in what we do, and achieving balance.

GOAL-SETTING

Goal setting is adhered to by most well-run organizations, as well as by individuals with a passion to achieve their objectives. The main premise of goal-setting is the self-evident but often overlooked notion that unless we know what we want, we can never achieve it. Without a defined destination, it really doesn't matter what we do or where we go—our activity essentially lacks purpose.

As Tibetan Buddhists, we are fortunate to have a ready-made ultimate goal: to become enlightened for the sake of all living beings. This goal might be compared to that of an eight-year-old pianist who sets her heart on playing in the Royal Albert Hall, or a twelve-year-old swimmer who decides that one day he is going to win gold for his country at the Olympics: a clear direction is set, an overall purpose provided.

Between now and our ultimate goal, however, it's also useful to have shorter-term objectives, relating to various parts of our practice—for example, our commitment to meditation, mindfulness, generosity, or ethics. I personally find it useful to set goals for the next six and/or twelve months. These typically include reading or rereading a core Dharma text, going to weekly classes, attending a meditation retreat, learning a particular text or definition by heart, maintaining or expanding on my regular meditation practice, and focusing on a particular aspect of practice in daily life.

This approach tackles my larger goal in bite-sized chunks, and as such is unspectacular. But these modest interim goals provide a focus for Dharma practice that is more achievable and realistic in the short term than achieving buddhahood for the state of all beings— an ultimate goal I can probably imagine less well than an eight-year-old pianist might be able to conceive of performing onstage with a full symphony orchestra.

Shantideva highlights the importance of goal-setting. His whole *Guide* is redolent with the purpose of freeing living beings from dissatisfaction and suffering, and in his chapter on enthusiasm he is explicit about this.

First of all, I should examine well what is to be done,
To see whether I can pursue it or cannot undertake it.
If I am unable, it is best to leave it,
But once I have started I must not withdraw.

Here Shantideva tells us to do our homework before signing up to anything, and is open about our option to not even start on something if we don't believe we can see it through. This is an important attribute of success in any field of endeavor, Dharma or otherwise. We should choose for ourselves only those goals to which we have a genuine, well-informed commitment: goals of the head as well as the heart.

I have a friend who would regard himself as a committed Buddhist practitioner. He has made a number of trips to India and Nepal over the years, has received initiations from several high-ranking lamas, and is an active member at a center that does helpful work in the community. He's always up for the next big Buddhist thing, whether that's fundraising for a new *stupa* or monument, sponsoring school-children in Tibet, or flying halfway round the world to receive teachings from His Holiness the Dalai Lama.

From the outside he seems to be a highly engaged and active member of the Dharma community. But he recently told me, with genuine sadness, how he realized that despite the many years he's been a Buddhist, he doesn't feel he has evolved as a practitioner to nearly the degree he could have. He has switched through a variety of different practices and trainings but never stayed long enough with any one of them to experience the full benefit. He feels like the same person he was when he started, albeit with a wide general knowledge of the Dharma. Rather than sticking to a single set of goals, by allowing himself to be distracted by the many intriguing practices, he has short-changed himself.

SELF-DISCIPLINE

Buddhism has many stories extolling the importance of what Shantideva called "firmness." One of the best known is the legend of Asanga, who became one of the most revered practitioners, teachers, and authors in the Tibetan Buddhist lineage. The story goes that, having achieved an excellent intellectual understanding of the Dharma, Asanga retreated to a cave for a three-year meditation retreat, to meditate on Maitreya Buddha. Three years is a typical length of time for an extensive meditation retreat, and Asanga hoped to emerge from it with a transformed nonconceptual understanding of the ideas he already understood at an intellectual level—in short, having achieved realizations directly from Maitreya.

Regrettably, he didn't. In his three long years meditating he achieved no realizations of any kind. Emerging from the cave feeling disappointed, he happened to look up to where birds nested in a rock face, noticing how the rough rock had been worn smooth by the birds' wings as they flew in and out of their nesting places. If the repeated application of something as soft and gentle as a bird's feather could make such an impact on hard rock, he decided, perhaps this was a lesson on the importance of perseverance.

He returned for a second three-year retreat, but once again failed to achieve any realizations. This time he was making his way from the cave, again deeply disappointed by his lack of progress, when he noticed a pool that had formed underneath a hanging rock. The sustained drip of water from the overhang had, over a very long time, created a deep, smooth bowl in the stone beneath. Once again, Asanga saw this consequence of persistence and decided to return to retreat.

Contemporary stories and jokes always go in threes—the Scotsman, the Englishman, and the Irishman went into the pub, etcetera—so we might expect that after Asanga's third retreat in the cave he would emerge as a fully realized bodhisattva. Unfortunately, he had no such good fortune. Now deeply dejected, this time after he emerged from his meditation cave he encountered a man using rocks to grind down strips of iron into needles. Asanga thought about how much time and effort the man was putting into such a mundane achievement. Surely full enlightenment, buddhahood, deserved further effort?

Asanga did achieve enlightenment—but only after his fourth long retreat in the cave, and not in the way he imagined. Leaving his cave having spent twelve years meditating, still without any realizations, he came across a dog writhing in pain from a maggot-infested wound in its abdomen. Feeling great compassion, he immediately wanted to help the dog—but realized that the maggots would die unless he gave them something to feed on. He decided he'd cut off some of his own flesh for the maggots, and he was about to reach over to begin removing them when he realized that by picking them up between his fingers he might inadvertently kill them. The only safe way he could think of removing them was by licking them off with his tongue, one by one.

Closing his eyes, about to begin this disgusting task, as he extended his tongue the dog dissolved into light—and appeared as Maitreya, the Buddha who had been the focus of his meditation for so many years. Overcome with emotion, Asanga asked Maitreya why he had appeared now, after he'd left his retreat and given up on attaining any realizations. Maitreya replied that he had been with him all along in his meditation cave. It was only Asanga's obscurations that had prevented him from seeing him. But Asanga's great compassion had purified his remaining negativities, enabling him to see what had previously been hidden.

Asanga's is a great lesson not only in persistence, but also in managing expectations. As busy Westerners, most of us are unlikely ever to become nuns or monks, much less embark on even one three-year retreat! So we shouldn't beat ourselves up when our more modest meditation practice fails to deliver dramatic short-term results.

Shantideva identifies a number of obstacles to self-discipline, one of which is particularly appropriate to many Westerners: "despising oneself out of despondency." Like so much of his writing, this expression sits uncomfortably in these politically correct times, when we talk politely about "self-esteem issues"—but it describes, rather more accurately, how we feel about ourselves when we are down.

There's no place for depression, self-loathing, or giving up in our practice of the Dharma. Yes, we may sometimes take it easy, enjoy a break, or find a balance if we've been through an intense time, as described later in this chapter. But feeling bad about ourselves can create real obstacles to our progress, as Shantideva describes in one of his oft-quoted metaphors:

> When crows encounter a dying snake,
> They will act as though they were eagles.
> Likewise, if my self-confidence is weak,
> I shall be injured by the slightest downfall.

Using his technique of giving form to our negative self-talk, here the negative thoughts—crows—are emboldened by the weakness of the snake—our poor self-belief.

When we wake up on a cold winter's morning and decide that, because our meditation session yesterday was so bad, we're better off snuggling up in bed for another half an hour, that's when a crow has just turned into a much more dangerous eagle. When we think that practicing mindfulness is all too hard and we might just as well bump through the day on nonengaged autopilot, that crow-turned-eagle has us in its beak. When we decide to avoid the charity collector knocking on the front door, because we're just settling into a nice glass of shiraz and giving him a dollar isn't going to make much difference anyway, that crow-turned-eagle is about to drop us from a dizzying height!

Using the crow-to-eagle metaphor, Shantideva correctly identifies how quickly negativity can get a grip on us, with more and more self-defeating thoughts reducing us to depressed lethargy. A psychotherapist once told me that "assertive behavior acts immediately against depressed feelings." This is Shantideva's advice too, which he conveys in a verse of wonderfully upbeat self-empowerment:

> Self-confidence should be applied to wholesome actions,
> The overcoming of disturbing conceptions and my ability
>   to do this.
> Thinking "I alone shall do it"
> Is the self-confidence of action.

My teacher Les often cites the huge sacrifice that many people make to achieve worldly goals. Consider for example the gruelling training undergone by those looking to be picked for a professional sports team. They typically have to get up early in the morning to fit in a training session. Everything they eat and drink is monitored to assist peak performance. There are gym visits, coaching, trials, matches, and constant effort—all to become part of a team, to win a medal, or to secure a championship. Without in any way belittling these achievements, from a Dharma perspective they are necessarily short term and impermanent. Today's winner becomes tomorrow's former champ, and in a few years' time, just a name engraved on a silver cup. In seeking to achieve enlightenment, a state of permanent bliss from which we can act to help limitless beings, how pathetic is it to complain about sore knees after a long meditation session? To stay at home instead of going to Dharma class because the weather is bad?

What we need instead is an attitude called "joyous perseverance," which is considered so important in the Dharma that it is the fourth perfection—along with generosity, ethics, and patience. As with previous perfections, the perfection of joyous perseverance means bringing bodhichitta to our practice. So when we really don't feel like meditating because we're agitated, depressed, or bored, and we sit down on our meditation cushion anyway, we can begin with this simple but powerful motivator: "By practicing joyous perseverance, may I achieve enlightenment for the benefit of all beings."

If we're finding Dharma practice especially hard-going, but we recollect the perfection of joyous perseverance, we go beyond simply not empowering crows into eagles: we make the future appearance of crows themselves less likely.

In this context, terms like persistence, self-discipline, joyous perseverance, self-confidence, commitment, or firmness all point to the same essential attitude—one founded on bodhichitta. This attitude means, having set a goal, we will not be deterred from its achievement: "I alone shall do it."

FINDING HAPPINESS IN WHAT WE DO

In my early days as a practitioner, I once went to see Geshe Loden to ask him what my main meditation practice should be. There are so many options, some of which I'd already tried and quite enjoyed, and others which I didn't like the sound of at all. I felt the need for clear direction, and while I was sure he would put me on the right track, I was nevertheless apprehensive about asking him. What if he told me to take up one of the practices I didn't like? If I wasn't prepared to follow his advice, should I even ask him?

Given my mounting tension and anxiety, I felt very relieved and also somewhat foolish when, after I had asked the question, Geshe-la looked at me as though the answer were blindingly obvious. "Do whichever practice you enjoy the most," he said.

After all the talk so far about goal setting and perseverance, the third quality Shantideva identifies is that our Dharma practice should be fulfilling. We should aim to take pleasure in it. We may even find it more fun than fun.

As we've already seen, Dharma practice isn't only about meditating and studying the texts, but is to be applied to every moment of our lives, so long as we are mindful. At the Dharma center I go to we have a wide variety of students. Some are reserved by nature and happiest on their own doing practical tasks. The center really needs people like them as there's always a list of things that need to be done, from fixing the reticulation in the gardens to devising a way of discouraging the kangaroos from eating the garden plants. We have some wonderful cooks in the team—the backbone of any retreat—as well as graphic designers who help with newsletters, admin enthusiasts who are spreadsheet wizards, and people with other specialist skills who seem to appear at exactly the moment needed—like the steel fabrication expert who started coming to class just when we needed a throne to be constructed for the huge Buddha in our temple.

Outside the Dharma center, each of these students applies his or her practice to a wide range of careers and activities in ways that bring that person happiness and fulfillment. The idea that Tibetan Buddhists are all keen meditators of an ascetic disposition with strongly intellectual inclinations simply isn't accurate. It's not so much what we do, but the way we do it that counts.

In her commentary on Shantideva's *Guide*, Pema Chödrön writes about finding joy in what we do: "I can tell you from experience that when there's a shift toward eagerness, life takes on a whole new meaning. Not the meaning that comes from careers or relationships, but the meaning that comes from using everything that happens as an opportunity to wake up."

She makes an important distinction when she notes that the meaningfulness we find in our Dharma practice is of a different quality from that we find in other activities. It is a point Shantideva makes himself. One of the most memorable images of his *Guide*, and one which makes my tongue curl no matter how many times I read it, is the following:

> If I feel that I never have enough sensual objects,
> Which are like honey smeared upon a razor's edge,
> Then why should I ever feel that I have enough
> Merit that ripens in happiness and peace?

Here he is talking about the pleasure we find in ordinary material activities, which he likens to honey on a razor's edge because whatever sweetness we enjoy is inevitably followed or accompanied by pain. By way of contrast, in the next verse he describes the joy we seek in our Dharma practice. Wishing to escape the suffering of samsara, which in this image he likens to the torment of the midday sun, he describes our approach to Dharma:

Thus in order to complete this task,
I shall venture into it
Just as an elephant tormented by the midday sun
Plunges into a cool, refreshing lake.

The image of an elephant plunging into a refreshing lake would have been more familiar to Shantideva and the monks of Nalanda Monastery than to many readers. But having grown up in Africa, and watched these wonderful creatures at the watering hole, I can vouch for the zest and playfulness that comes over them when they have a good wallow. There is nothing contrived or half-hearted about an elephant hosing itself down or frolicking in the water. It's that feeling of complete absorption and happiness which Shantideva illustrates. A joy that, unlike licking honey from a blade, is entirely relaxed, spontaneous, and natural.

ACHIEVING BALANCE

Not long ago I received an email from someone who'd read my book *Hurry Up and Meditate*. Prior to reading my book, she had for some time been attempting a breathing meditation practice, counting twenty-one breaths in a cycle, but to her increasing frustration she seldom managed to complete the full count without becoming distracted, despite the investment of a lot of time and focused attention. In my book I suggest counting four breaths in a cycle to begin with, and only when comfortable with four to increase this to seven, ten, and so on (see the appendix for more detail).

In her email the reader said what a relief she had found it, reducing her target to just seven breaths, as suggested in my book. Her concentration had immediately improved. For the first time she was actually enjoying her meditation. She felt she was getting somewhere. And she was already thinking of increasing her target.

Finding a balance, or in Shantideva's terminology, "moderation," means setting ourselves realistic goals, and taking a break when we need to. This may seem obvious, even unnecessary, advice, but you don't have to be around meditation centers long to hear stories of people who push themselves too hard, and as a result suffer from conditions like insomnia, hallucinations, flashbacks, agitation, and other psychosomatic problems for which Tibetans have a generic term—*lung*. There is a point at which enthusiasm and seriousness of intent can tip over from being a force that energizes our practice, to becoming a real obstacle. When teaching meditation to the player of a *vina*, kind of like guitar, the Buddha once suggested that one's concentration needed to be like a guitar string—neither too lax nor too taut; advice that applies equally well to our Dharma practice in general.

This "middle way" should also apply to taking breaks when we need to:

> When my strength declines, I should leave whatever
>   I am doing
> In order to be able to continue with it later.
> Having done something well, I should put it aside
> With the wish to accomplish what will follow.

In so many ways, mental development is similar to getting physically fit. In the early stages of gym training, we feel exhausted after just ten minutes on the cross-trainer, or half an hour of a resistance class. The idea of running for an entire hour or increasing our weights threefold feels like an impossibility. If we try to go too hard, too fast, not only do we run the risk of injury, we may also get dejected by our poor progress and give up.

But if we approach our exercise regime with a more relaxed, longer term perspective, not expecting too much of ourselves too soon, but maintaining a steady discipline, it's amazing how, bit by bit, our ten minutes on the cross-trainer becomes fifteen minutes, and then twenty. How quickly our muscles build up and we can increase our weights without waking up the next morning feeling like we've been run over by a truck.

In his commentary on Shantideva's *Guide*, the Dalai Lama summarizes this subject very neatly: "Spiritual practice is difficult in the beginning. You wonder how on earth you can ever do it. But as you get used to it, the practice gradually becomes easier. Do not be too stubborn or push yourself too hard. If you practice in accord with your individual capacity, little by little you will find more pleasure and joy in it. As you gain inner strength, your positive actions will gain in profundity and scope."

In summary, the guidelines for spiritual success, as outlined by Shantideva, tell us that our practice requires structure. While our overarching goal may be to achieve enlightenment for the benefit of all living beings, within this our shorter term goals will determine the structure we adopt. Our on-cushion and off-cushion objectives are necessarily individual, and may change over time as we develop in our practice. Once we have set our objectives, though, to fulfill our true potential we should practice with rigorous self-discipline, finding happiness in what we do, and also seeking to maintain balance. These are the simple but profound guidelines that lead to our personal transformation.

Analytical Meditation

Before beginning the analytical meditation, stabilize your mind as usual with a breath meditation exercise.

▶ Begin by considering the importance of having goals in different aspects of your life—career, finances, family, and other areas. Reflect how all elite achievers set their goals high. The wish to attain enlightenment for the sake of all beings is an unsurpassable goal; spend a short while exploring its meaning. While an appropriate overall spiritual goal is the wish to attain enlightenment for the benefit of all living beings, are there any shorter-term goals for your Dharma practice that would be meaningful to you?

▶ Consider the value of self-discipline—how even ordinary people can achieve extraordinary things by simple persistence. Identify examples of such behavior in yourself. Think of ways in which your own self-discipline could be improved in your approach to putting the Dharma into practice. Cultivate a determination to apply self-discipline from now on.

▶ Reflect on how Dharma practice can be a source of joy—like an elephant at the watering hole. Consider what Dharma practices you have been exposed to in this book and elsewhere. Are there any that particularly appeal to you, which you could practice more often?

▶ Think of the need for balance in your Dharma practice. Are there areas in which you are experiencing frustration and could perhaps benefit from better balance (for example, shorter meditation sessions or fewer counts to a breath cycle)?

▶ Reflect how even though your progress may be unnoticeable from one day to the next, by applying yourself to your chosen goals with self-discipline, joy, and balance, just like the other great practitioners, you acknowledge the truth that "I alone shall do it." Focus on this thought single-pointedly.

12

Our Greatest Teacher

WHETHER WE'RE RELIGIOUS or not, there's nothing like being brought face to face with our own mortality to make us wake up to the true value of life.

Many of us, reluctantly stirring from bed each morning, don't reflect that we're being presented with an extraordinary opportunity in simply opening our eyes to another day. Instead, we take utterly for granted the facts of being alive, healthy, and benefiting from circumstances denied to well over 90 percent of our fellow humans. So accustomed are we to our rare good fortune that we generally hold the unexplored assumption that our current experience of reality will continue indefinitely. Sure, we know intellectually that we'll die one day. But unless we come close to death through illness, accident, war, or other misadventure, our own death isn't something we contemplate except as a distant abstraction. It isn't real to us.

Sociologists observe that death is the last taboo in Western society. While the hospice movement has done much to transform the *process* of dying, the secular world still largely discourages us from thinking about death, except for the purposes of selling life and funeral insurance or estate planning services. Even though death is our only certainty, seriously contemplating it is usually considered to be morbid or irrelevant. Thinking about death won't stop it, so why make yourself depressed?

With trademark flair, Shantideva describes what he sees as the bovine complacency of such a view:

—

Do I not see
That death is systematically slaughtering my species?
Whoever remains soundly asleep
Surely behaves like a buffalo with a butcher.

Shantideva's use of the word "asleep" is no coincidence. It is the opposite of the ancient Pali word for "one who is awake"—that is, *buddha*. We may behave as though death is remote and hypothetical, but in so doing we are like a herd of buffalo grazing in the field outside the slaughterhouse while the butcher removes us methodically, one by one.

VALUES AND PRIORITIES

One of the main reasons why Buddhism challenges the "buffalo with a butcher" approach to death is because it prevents us from experiencing the full value of life. Our attitude to a commodity that is scarce and irreplaceable is markedly different from the way we view something of which there's an endless supply.

I'm often struck by the unintended tragedy when people tell me that they like being busy because "it makes the day go faster." Struggling through eight or nine hours each day just so we can enjoy the few that follow seems like a pretty poor trade-off. But how many of us spend much of our lives doing exactly that? How much time and energy do we devote to activities which don't reflect our true interests?

We do these things, perhaps, because what we *really* want to do doesn't pay the bills. Because we haven't worked out a purpose for our lives. Or because we assume we can always get around to being authentic some time later.

Many of us are never shaken out of what Shantideva refers to as this "sleep." But those whose life is suddenly threatened often adopt a dramatically different perspective. At the moment we face our mortality, what we usually take for granted becomes suddenly extraordinarily precious. We'd give anything for it to continue.

People who work in elder care report how even those with a quality of life we might regard as not worth having still struggle for survival; stripped of most of the elements that we think make life worthwhile, they retain an instinct to survive, to see just one more day. This is a force of instinct to which, in the butcher's paddocks of our own working and everyday lives, we are often oblivious.

Being told that we have a life-threatening condition is one of the most urgent wake-up calls we can experience. Suddenly, we can avoid the inevitable no longer. After the initial shock, we may pass through phases of denial, anger, bargaining, or depression. Ultimately though, we come to appreciate the value of each day we're alive as never before.

We also review our priorities. Work conducted by the Division of Cancer Prevention and Control Research at UCLA's Jonsson Comprehensive Cancer Center shows that cancer survivors often unexpectedly discover new meaning and positive outcomes from their experience. Patients suddenly sort out who their friends are and what is important to them. Many people have complete transformations in their occupations and interests as a result of cancer diagnosis, and there is often a sense of freedom to change their mind about what they are doing on an everyday basis because life is precious and they want to live it to the fullest.

Similarly, the pioneering work of Ian Gawler in helping people prevent and manage cancer shows that for some people, illness turned out to be a gift: the shock they needed to jolt them from the tracks of an unexamined life; the incentive they needed to find the courage to move on from what wasn't working.

The extent of our preoccupation with outer, material phenomena is also starkly revealed in the face of death. We have already looked at how unreliable these external forces are at giving us pleasure in daily life—how the enjoyment of a favorite meal, for example, is dependent on who we're having the meal with, our state of mind at the time and other circumstances. When facing death, our wealth, our possessions, and our toys become suddenly meaningless. As Shantideva puts it:

> Although I may live happily for a long time
> Through obtaining a great deal of material wealth,
> I shall go forth empty-handed and destitute
> Just like having been robbed by a thief.

Everything we call "mine"—my house, my treasured possessions, and my money—will soon be called "mine" by someone else; even "my" usual cushion in Dharma class will one day be considered "mine" by someone different.

THE CERTAINTIES AND UNCERTAINTIES OF DEATH

One of the most important meditations in Buddhism is contemplating the certainty of death. When we do this regularly, it helps inform our priorities on how to live. For while material considerations are important in our daily life, we need to avoid assuming that they have any greater value than this.

A helpful view of our life of leisure and fortune is to think of it as being like a brief stay in a luxury hotel. It's good to enjoy the view, to make the most of the facilities, to strike up cordial relations with our fellow guests. We may have a favorite seat in the dining room, or talk about "my" room, but we are constantly aware that the facilities are only very temporarily ours to use. Most of us don't suffer from a midholiday crisis on day three, thinking how it's all going to come to an end on day five—we're more likely to book in that jet-ski activity or beach massage, or make other such plans to extract the full value from our stay. And having been mindful all along that we're only making a short visit, we're unlikely to burst into tears in the lobby, overcome with remorse and regret while checking out.

As well as meditating on impermanence and the certainty of death, the Dharma also teaches us to reflect on the uncertainty of the time of our death. Our teaching is to live with the assumption that death is not far off, and therefore not too remote a prospect to dwell on. While the average lifespan for men and women in the developed world is currently in the high seventies, as traditional Buddhist texts point out we are surrounded by more causes for death than for life, and this particular stay on earth could end at any time.

I lost a good friend in my twenties, when the parachute he was using blew onto power pylons, electrocuting him. Since then, suicide, war, illness, and accidents have cut short the lives of quite a few people I knew. You too will almost certainly have encountered many people who have not made it to their three score years and ten. So why should you?

Buddhism encourages us to take seriously the idea that any day may be our last. To relish every meal as though it were our last meal. In particular, not to assume we will have another opportunity to say to someone, "Thank you," "I love you," or "I'm sorry."

Meditating on the uncertainty of the time of death can help us move this idea from an intellectual understanding to a realization. It helps make our own death real. Why wait until the shock of a diagnosis or a close encounter with death in an accident to fully engage with this reality? Whether we believe in an afterlife or not, a committed effort to face our own death, far from being a deeply depressing experience, can be profoundly liberating. When we develop a strong sense that our existence is brief, precious, and could soon be over, it helps us cherish the here and now, and recognize the people and activities that give our life its highest purpose.

BEYOND DEATH

Pema Chödrön tells the story of how she took her children to meet the Sixteenth Karmapa—one of the most important leaders in Tibetan Buddhism. Because they weren't Buddhists, she asked him to tell them something that didn't require any understanding of the Dharma. She writes: "Without hesitation, he told them: 'You are going to die; and when you do, you will take nothing with you but your state of mind.'"

How exactly mind exists after death is the critical question, but we first need to go back a step and ask a prior question: how exactly does it exist *before* we die? While the answer to this may on the face of it seem obvious, it is in fact one of the greatest mysteries of our lives, the realization of which holds the key to our personal liberation—as discussed further in Chapters 14 and 15.

For the moment, we might summarize the Buddhist view as being "the middle way" between nihilism on the one hand and eternalism on the other. The nihilist view is that mind is a function of biology, so that when the body dies, the mind dies with it. The eternalist view is that in addition to body and mind there is a spirit or soul that is our true essence and that separates at the time of death to continue elsewhere. Buddhism suggests that while mind cannot be described in terms of biology alone, when we experience consciousness at its most subtle level we do not find evidence of a soul, spirit, or even a "me." There is continuity, but it is only an aspect of consciousness that is propelled by conditioning, or karma, into its next experience.

Even within Tibetan Buddhism there is debate about the precise nature of this consciousness. However, if we accept as a functioning hypothesis that there is some form of continuity after this life, the implications are vast. Whatever work we do on our mind not only makes our experience of this life happier, but the benefits of rooting out our negativities and replacing them with more positive mental patterns will also have a positive impact on the future as well.

What's more, according to this model, long after we have left behind our friends, loved ones, and even our sense of who we once were, the imprints, or latencies, created by previous actions continue to propel our consciousness into experiences ranging from the extremely pleasant to the deeply unpleasant, and lasting from brief moments to entire lifetimes. Given that so much of our mental behavior has a tendency toward the negative, this notion of continuity is, in fact, far from a reassuring prospect! If we continue to go through life in a cocoon of self-absorption, lacking both mindfulness of the present moment and awareness of the conditioning created by our actions, we put ourselves at risk:

⌒

> Leaving all, I must depart alone.
> Yet through not having understood this,
> I committed various kinds of wrongdoing
> For the sake of my friends and foes.
>
> My foes will become nothing.
> My friends will become nothing.
> I, too, will become nothing.
> Likewise, all will become nothing.

Here Shantideva warns about the consequences of reinforcing our negative conditioning whether for the sake of friends, foes, or inanimate objects; both they and we will cease to exist, but our consciousness will continue to wear the consequences. It is important to remember the context of the latter verse, which might otherwise seem to support a nihilistic view. Rather, Shantideva is indelibly tattooing on our minds the reality that all those people and things for whom we are tempted to act with anger and attachment are just as impermanent and ultimately illusory as ourselves.

OUR GREATEST TEACHER

The Buddha described death as "our greatest teacher." I once heard it said that a good teacher is one who explains, a superior teacher is one who demonstrates, and the greatest teacher is one who inspires. There is no question that meditating on our own death, realizing fully what it means to us, and living with it as a natural, ever-present fact of life is highly motivating.

It makes us realize the value of this precious life. We turn our attention away from distractions toward what truly matters. And if we can conceive of continuity after this lifetime, even as only a hypothetical possibility, recollecting death introduces an urgency to our practice. As Geshe Loden sometimes half jokes, we might think we're too busy watching television or reading the newspaper to practice meditation, but no one is ever too busy to die!

Tibetan Buddhism provides one of the most detailed descriptions of the process of dying. Practices taught by highly realized yogis, whose own subsequent deaths have been far from ordinary, help us navigate our way, stage by stage, through the dissolution of various bodily functions, to a state in which we experience the radiant expansiveness of our true nature. Our ability to master these steps depends to a large extent on the state of our mind when we die.

Analytical Meditation

Before beginning the analytical meditation, stabilize your mind as usual with a breath meditation exercise.

- Contemplate how your death will definitely come and you can do nothing to prevent it. Consider that your lifespan is constantly declining, and how quickly the past year, decade, or several decades have passed by.

- Think how the time of death is uncertain. Your lifespan is unknowable and there are more factors conducive to death than to life. You could die any day from any number of causes. Around us, on planet Earth, death is occurring constantly.

- Imagine that you were told you had only a few days to live. Who or what would be important to you? Is there anything you'd seek to change or "put right"?

- In view of this analysis, how well does your life reflect your real priorities and values?

- Consider the possibility that your consciousness continues after death. Given that you would be leaving your body, family, friends, and belongings, the only thing with continuity would be your state of mind. To what extent are you creating the conditioning, or karma, for this continuation to be a positive experience?

- Reflect how Dharma practice could be the only thing of value to you when you die. Hold on to this thought single-pointedly.

13

Feeding the Good Wolf

THERE'S A POPULAR Cherokee metaphor that's quite Shantideva-like both in style and substance. Instead of crows with the audacity of eagles, or hot and bothered elephants plunging headlong into the cooling waters, this time, appropriately for a North American setting, the analogy is of two wolves.

"There's a battle between two wolves that goes on in each one of us," the wise Cherokee elder tells his grandson. "One wolf is anger, desire, pride, jealousy, and ego. The other wolf is love, compassion, kindness, goodness, and patience."

Staring at the glowing embers of the campfire, the grandson imagines the two wolves circling each other—wary, vigilant, teeth bared.

"Which wolf wins?" he wants to know.

The old man doesn't hesitate. "Whichever one you feed," he says.

It's one of those metaphors to which many of us intuitively respond, "Yes—that's so true!" But after thinking about the imagery and message for a while, questions may arise. Such as, where do we go with this teaching? Isn't it a bit simplistic to describe our inner life in such black and white terms? And how exactly do we feed the good wolf?

Perhaps we shouldn't try to load too much meaning onto a single analogy. But the question of how we go about feeding the good wolf does deserve further exploration.

Mindfulness has to be part of the answer. Unless we're mindful of our thoughts and actions, the bad wolf can have the good wolf on the ground and by the throat before we even know it. Making a conscious effort to practice the six perfections (generosity, ethics, patience, and so on) is, presumably, also part of the answer—reinforcing the positive conditioning that feeds the good wolf.

Environment must also make an important contribution, given that it's so much easier to thrive in some environments than others. The education we receive, the media we consume, and the cultural conditioning to which we're exposed all dramatically affect our capacity to develop our own positive inner conditioning.

More than anything, though, we're influenced by other people.

The truism that "by their friends shall ye know them" is relevant here, but we need to look further than just those we'd regard as friends, to include colleagues, peers, and other social influencers. It's pretty obvious that we'll struggle to cultivate a benevolent and expansive perspective if we're surrounded by people who are absorbed in feuds, dishonest financial dealings, duplicitous relationships, or other such goings-on. But our Dharma journey can be challenging for reasons far less obvious than this. The radical analysis offered by Buddhism about what makes us happy, outlined in Part I of this book, suggests that even those with mainstream conventional values reinforce a worldview from which we would do well to break free.

If we are surrounded by people who are more focused on the dramas of their personal lives than the reality that the life they enjoy is one of amazing leisure and fortune; who believe that happiness, rather than temporary pleasure, is to be found in overseas holidays, a great bottle of wine, or a house in the right suburb; who direct all their energy on self and self's interests, seldom accommodating those of others, then we have an uphill battle in nurturing our own, very different, convictions.

This is a challenging observation. Because most people, ourselves included, are as just described. Nor did Shantideva regard himself as "holier than thou," though he did have a name for this behavior: childish.

Through associating with the childish,
There will certainly ensue unwholesomeness,
Such as praising myself, belittling others,
And discussing the joys of cyclic existence.

When Shantideva gives as an example of unwholesomeness "praising myself and belittling others," he is referring to the very first bodhichitta vow—one of the vows taken when we become Buddhists—which is to abandon doing exactly this. By taking the vow we don't promise never to do it again, which would be an impossibility for most of us, but only to work toward never doing it. As Shantideva points out, though, it's a tough vow to keep if you're in the wrong company.

I once heard an amusing story about a highly regarded lama who traveled to the United States to teach a series of lessons. I can't vouch for the authenticity of this anecdote, but apparently at the end of the lama's well-received first teaching, a member of the very large audience had the temerity to ask him if he had achieved enlightenment.

In accordance with Dharma teachings, which strongly discourage all talk of such matters (i.e. praising oneself), the lama did a great job of explaining that he had achieved no realizations worth speaking of, that his abilities were poor and his knowledge of the Dharma was only slight. Had he been speaking to a Buddhist audience in the Himalayas, his answer would have been seen as confirmation that he was the real deal. But his American audience reacted differently. When the doors opened the following week, hardly anyone had turned up. Who wanted to waste time with such a poorly quali-fied teacher?!

I'm sometimes amazed to catch snippets on TV of various con-testants cheerfully announcing that they are the best dancer/chef/designer/hair stylist, on the basis of nothing in particular, and that they're going to whip the ass of everyone else in the competition. Is this bravado, immaturity, or just the relentless self-promotion expected by our society?

It's truly astonishing how much praising of self and belittling of others goes on in our daily interactions. When we tune in to conver-sations and filter specifically for "praising and belittling," we discover that this is the motivation behind so much of what is said—perhaps not overtly, but as an underlying theme.

So, how do we feed the good wolf in a society that seems so pre-disposed to the bad?

Devoting myself to others in this way
Will bring about nothing but misfortune,
Because they will not benefit me,
And I shall not benefit them.

I should flee far away from childish people.
When they are encountered, though, I should please
*   them by being happy.*
I should behave well merely out of courtesy,
But not become greatly familiar.

In our interactions Shantideva is advocating a "middle way," which is neither to give other people the cold shoulder nor to "devote" ourselves to those whose values are so different from the ones we're trying to cultivate. Or as Pema Chödrön puts it: "Shantideva isn't saying not to have friends or keep company with others. He is giving us advice for becoming less reactive and more wise."

Who we spend our time with isn't necessarily personal choice. It's often the case that there are those we can't avoid, including work colleagues and family members. As much as we might like to flee, that simply isn't an option, or at least not physically. To some extent we can achieve distance by making meditation practice a regular part of life. Once we shut the door, sit on our cushions, and withdraw our minds from conventional reality, it is of no consequence whether we're in our bedroom or a cave in the Himalayas.

CHOOSING ENLIGHTENED INFLUENCERS

We can also give some thought to those who influence us and, where useful, seek opportunities for more enlightened perspectives. Broadening our social circle to include more positive influencers may be helpful. As mentioned in Chapter 5, when we officially become Buddhists we take refuge in the Buddha, Dharma, and Sangha. The example of the Buddha and inspiration of his teachings, the Dharma, are two of the three "gems"—the third, Sangha, is those who accompany us along the path: the ones who help nurture the good wolf.

Strictly speaking, the Sangha in whom we take refuge are those practitioners who have attained high realizations. While such attainments are hard for us ordinary mortals to divine, we can take our cue from those whose behavior suggests they are further down the path than ourselves. Specifically, do they show signs of making others an important priority in their lives? Are they cheerful, peaceful, and consistent in their practice? Do they walk the talk?

Tibetan Buddhist texts sometimes begin, "In the guru and the Triple Gem I take refuge," emphasizing the importance of having a teacher, or *guru*. Of all the people who influence us, our teacher can be the most powerful of all. Because the Dharma is practice-based rather than belief-based, what we do and how we do it is of primary concern. No one would imagine that they could become an elite concert pianist, golfing professional, or NASA astronaut without the benefit of extensive formal training. If we are to achieve enlightenment, we similarly require expert guidance from qualified instructors. Finding such people, and learning as much as we can from them, should be an urgent priority if we don't already have the good fortune to have a teacher.

Traditional texts compare a teacher to a magnifying glass that focuses the rays of the sun. Like rays of the sun, the teachings are powerful and enlightening in their own right, but "concentrating" them in a way that applies directly to us is the job of the guru—a term that translates as "spiritual friend."

A more contemporary analogy is that of a personal trainer. Just as his or her job is to analyze your current physical shape, develop a training program specifically for you, and then provide the right balance of carrot and stick to help you realize your full potential, so too your spiritual coach, or teacher, will tailor the teachings to your spiritual starting point.

Given the objective of making this an important long-term relationship, it's critical to find a teacher you can relate to, perhaps someone who has had similar experiences, and definitely someone you look up to. Dharma texts outline the criteria for assessing whether or not someone is a suitable teacher. First and foremost among these is "a mind controlled by pure morality." In seeking a spiritual friend you should have no doubts about whether or not the person you accept as your teacher represents an ethical role model. Someone who tries to avoid discussing moral issues, or whose private behavior falls well short of Dharma teachings on nonharmfulness, lacks the first quality required of a teacher.

He or she must also have greater knowledge than you, and ideally a wealth of scriptural knowledge. Your prospective coach should have some skill in the area of Dharma teaching, and a track record of enthusiasm and persistence in applying the Dharma to his or her own life, as well as in helping others.

Other traits of the ideal teacher are harder to assess. These include "a mind that is pacified and undistracted through the practice of concentration," and "realization of suchness, the wisdom perceiving emptiness." Additional inner qualities are easier to identify: "having love and compassion." Do the teacher's actions seem motivated by the wish to give others happiness and to help them avoid suffering? In everyday life, does the teacher's behavior show an authentic and ongoing concern for others' well-being?

This isn't to say that all teachers are extraordinary individuals of peerless ethics, superior wisdom, and possessing a pure great love motivated at all times by bodhichitta. But the best teachers are. And it is certainly the direction in which all of us, teachers and practitioners, should be heading. If the Dharma provides us with the tools for spiritual transformation, it makes sense that we should seek as our coaches and mentors those who have already enjoyed some success in effecting personal change in their own lives, rather than those who simply know the theory.

THE BENEFITS OF RETREAT

Another complementary way to feed the good wolf is by going on meditation retreat. Withdrawing from one's normal life and, for a short while at least, following a daily routine that has at its heart meditation—"acquainting the mind with virtue," as defined by Buddhism—is a useful way of gaining perspective on everyday life.

An illustration of one benefit of meditation can be made by considering a glass full of swirling, murky stormwater through which nothing can be seen. Allowed to stand, the sediment settles, the water becomes transparent, and clarity is achieved. So, too, with our minds, usually caught up in the moment-by-moment flurry of daily life: if a period of stability is created, some of that agitation subdues and we're able to gain insights into reality that would otherwise elude us.

The challenge for most of us is that our minds are very, very agitated. Whereas a couple of hours of standing will see all the turmoil subside in a glass of stormwater, the same thing, unfortunately, can't be said for our minds. This is why the repeated practice of meditation is helpful, and why experiencing a number of sessions in a day—as occurs on retreat—can be more beneficial still. After just a few days, as our minds become more settled and we relax into the new rhythm, our customary day-to-day preoccupations begin to slip away and our perspective, quite naturally, broadens.

If something is concerning us, perhaps a major decision we need to make, the benefit of a quieted mind and reminder of our central purpose—bodhichitta motivation based on great love and great compassion—can often help us decide which path to take. Or we might even reach a happier acceptance of decisions or events that have been imposed on us.

When we hear the teachings in a more subtle and receptive mental state, our resolve to engage in more enlightened activities after we return to daily life is strengthened. Positive initiatives, large or small, that we may have pushed aside because of general busyness or other excuses assume a fresh urgency. Ideas for new actions that may never occur to us when our minds are engaged in the frenetic minutiae of daily life arise without effort.

If we're on a formal retreat with others, it's not only the clearer perspective as our mind gradually settles from which we benefit. In the times when we are not meditating, coffee breaks and the meals we share often provide a friendly, nonjudgmental environment in which to discuss what arises. Every retreat is a bit like a mountain trek, and the other meditators are our fellow hikers. The obstacles we face are not soaring mountains or rugged terrain, but the inner landscape of our mind that we carry with us our whole lives but, paradoxically, seldom visit. Just as hikers will pause from time to time to catch their breath and review the paths they have shared, when we go on retreat we usually find others who have encountered the same joys and adversities, who have had to face down the same inner demons, and whose insights can help us break through to new levels of experience and understanding.

In summary, if an informal audit of influencers reveals a high level of those motivated by "childish" pursuits, and a relative scarcity of people concerned with more enlightened living, we do have choices. We don't have to cut other people out of our lives, unless their influence really is toxic. But we can seek to redress the balance, first and foremost by finding the right Dharma teacher as our mentor and coach. Becoming part of a Dharma group also nurtures our practice, and taking part in meditation retreats can be of very real value. These are practical steps we can take to reduce the impact on our lives of those focused only on worldly concerns, to consciously alter the balance of influencers on our goals and values, to feed the good wolf.

Exercise

▶ If you already enjoy the good fortune of having a teacher and belonging to a Dharma group, spend a few minutes reflecting on the following questions: what kind of balance do you have in your life between positive influencers and "childish" ones? Would it be beneficial to be doing more with your teacher or group? And how can you be a more benevolent influence yourself?

▶ If you don't have a teacher or belong to a group, make a resolution to get in touch with at least three Dharma groups in your area, attend teachings in each place, and set about finding a teacher—or allowing him or her to find you!—to support your practice.

14

Emptiness and Santa Claus

So far we have looked at developing a more enlightened experience of reality in two interrelated ways. First, renunciation marks a turning away from our habitual tendency of experiencing our inner lives as a direct, inevitable reaction to what goes on in the world around us. Second, bodhichitta provides a method for replacing unhappiness-creating interpretations of reality with those that not only offer far greater possibilities for happiness but that, over time, effect a profound shift in our whole sense of purpose. Renunciation and bodhichitta are two fundamental elements of the Tibetan Buddhist path.

There is also a third element, known variously as "*shunyata* wisdom," "dependent origination," or "emptiness of self-existence." All of these are clunky-sounding terms for what is, in fact, the most subtle of all truths. It is the truth about the nature of reality, or the way that we and the world around us exist.

On the surface of things, this may seem an obscure subject to explore after the rigorous focus so far on mindfulness and reengineering our thought processes. But this particular wisdom not only complements what we have covered, it takes it to a whole new level. Through it we come to discover that our experience of "me" and "the world around me" is based on a vast scaffolding of assumptions we have never seriously challenged. Shaking at this scaffolding, discovering that what we once believed was concrete reality turns out to be as insubstantial as a film set, can be both disorientating and initially quite scary. But ultimately it is the most liberating discovery we can make. It frees us from the burden of a tightly held sense of self, or an overwhelming experience of the world around us. For people in particular who get unhappy with themselves, suffer from depression and despair, or take themselves too seriously, it offers an enduring wellspring of deep peace. So profoundly transformative is this wisdom that when we realize it—as opposed to merely understanding it intellectually—we relieve ourselves of all our conditioning and delusional habits. We are permanently freed from all suffering.

OUR MISTAKEN ASSUMPTIONS

As a young child I remember the great excitement I felt about Santa Claus. Every year, as Christmas approached, his name would be invoked as a way of making me behave myself. While my parents, being good Presbyterians, didn't allow the frippery of Santa to hijack the sacred annual landmark of Christmas, Santa was allowed a walk-on role. In our home, as in countless millions of others around the world, in the build-up to Christmas, heartfelt letters were written to Santa. What he may or may not bring us was an ongoing topic of conversation—or, in retrospect, expectations management. On Christmas Eve, stockings were draped from the mantelpiece, and a glass of milk and biscuits were left out for our nocturnal visitor, who was in the habit of leaving a lot of crumbs on his plate as though to evidence the gusto with which he'd wolfed down his midnight snack.

One of the highlights of the weeks leading up to Christmas was the visit to see Santa himself. Our particular Santa was to be found in his grotto on the fourth floor of Barbour's, a department store uncannily similar in character to Grace Brothers in the vintage TV series *Are You Being Served?* Quite why Santa chose to visit Barbour's year after year, why he wore a thick red suit in the middle of an African summer, and how he got away from his North Pole workshops at a time of year when they were, presumably, at their most frenetic, were never questions that occurred to me. Instead, I'd line up with all the other kids behind a cordon, as white-gloved security men nodded knowingly at our mothers and allowed us, one by one, through to where Santa sat in a cottonwool igloo decorated with fairy lights. There we'd perch on his knee, blurt out what we wanted for Christmas, hope desperately he believed us when we told him that yes, we had been very good boys and girls, before walking away with a small gift from the large sack of presents he kept by his chair.

For those brief few years, there was no doubt in my mind that Santa existed. Not only had I met him, I had sat on his knee. I knew what he looked like and something about his kindly personality. Why shouldn't I believe in him?

As it happens, most of us have a tendency to believe in a Santafied version of ourselves. While this point may not be immediately obvious, hopefully it will be clearer by the end of this and the following chapter, both of which focus on this important truth.

Generally speaking, each one of us assumes that we are separate and independent from the world around us. We each have a body, a personality, a home, and a variety of things we call "mine." And though we don't usually give much thought to exactly who or what this "I" comprises, we usually think of "me" as an owner and/or controller. We talk about "my body" as being like an important but subsidiary entity belonging to "me." Similarly "my personality" or "my mind" belongs to this "me." "I" am the one running the show. Even those who don't have any religious leanings tend to think of people as having a core, an inner nature, or an essence: some distinctive component that makes them uniquely who they are.

The Buddha's most important teaching, however, is that a person—or any other phenomenon—that exists independently and separately from everything else is an impossibility. As Geshe Loden explains: "Holding an object as self-existent is viewing it as having a self or entity that exists independently of parts, causes, and conditions.... [This] view of self-existence, or inherent existence, is totally mistaken because all phenomena are empty of such a mode of existence."

Geshe Loden explains that it's easier to understand the concept of "emptiness of self-existence" when we apply it to ourselves, rather than to other phenomena. So that's where we'll begin.

DEPENDENCE ON PARTS

Who is this entity we call "I" or "myself," the owner or possessor of my body and mind? This is the subject of our analysis. At functions, we're often given a name tag to pin onto our lapel so everyone can learn one another's names. If you had a name tag labelled "Self," where would you pin it? Presumably, somewhere within your psycho-physical continuum. The idea that "I" could exist separately from my body is illogical because if that were true, "I" would be completely unaffected by whatever happened to the body, which is clearly not the case. So our search for a place to pin our "Self" label is narrowed to somewhere in our body or mind. And as Shantideva explains:

—

Teeth, hair, and nails are not the self,
The self is not bones nor blood,
Neither mucus nor phlegm,
Also not lymph or pus.

Shantideva continues for several verses on the same theme, reviewing every part of the body before dismissing it as not the thing we call "me" or "myself." On one level this may seem an incredibly obvious point, but on another, we're building up a case that has profound implications for the nature of our existence, which is why Tibetan Buddhists frequently repeat an analytical meditation along these lines (provided at the end of this chapter).

To investigate this for yourself, slowly scan upward through your body—feet, legs, torso, arms, shoulders, neck, and head—asking, "Is this the 'I,' or 'myself'? Are my feet 'me'? Are my ankles 'me'? Are my shins 'me'?" What we find, as our body scan progresses, are body parts of "me" but not the actual "me." Like a frustrated receptionist at a conference gathering, we're left holding our "Self" label, unable to find the elusive delegate on whom to pin it.

But then we may decide that we were looking in the wrong place. We were never going to find "Self" closeted away with the kidneys and liver. He or she is far too cerebral for that. "Self" is an aspect of consciousness, a part of our mind, we may decide. Okay, so let's go looking through the various aspects of mental functioning.

Tibetan Buddhism defines six kinds of ordinary consciousness: of sight, sound, smell, taste, touch, and mind. We can make our way through the first five without too much trouble—there's obviously more to "me" than a consciousness of taste, for example, as much as "I" may like Belgian chocolate. Similarly, "I" am a lot more than only an appreciation of sound, scent, or touch. So we might conclude that "I" have to be a part of consciousness of mind, mental consciousness.

Are we getting closer? When we meditate on mental consciousness, however, what we discover, after the agitation settles down, is merely spacious clarity and an ability to cognize things. That is the nature of mental consciousness. There is no other mental factor to be found beyond clarity and cognition, or clarity and awareness. And there's more to "me" than that too. As Shantideva confirms:

Flesh and skin are not the self,
Heat and winds are not the self,
Neither are bodily cavities the self,
Also the six consciousnesses are not the self.

When he talks of "heat" and "winds" he is referring to the four elements—earth, water, heat, and wind—on which Tibetan medicine was traditionally formulated. We may feel uncomfortable with this as a basis for analysis. We may also feel that in defining the mind in terms of six consciousnesses, the deck in this analysis is stacked in such a way that it can result in only one possible outcome.

But we don't have to use the four elements if we don't want to—I personally prefer to think more along Western lines, thinking about the body in terms of skeleton, muscles, blood vessels, organs, and so on. Nor do we have to define the mind in terms of six consciousnesses—we can use whatever method of classification we like. We can go for the Freudian definitions of id, ego, and super-ego—to which of these can I pin the label "Self"? Or if Transactional Analysis is more to our liking, we can look at mind in terms of parent, adult, and child—where does the "Self" nametag go on them?

It really doesn't matter what method of categorization we use for body or mind, the result is always the same—having looked at every component part in turn, we're still left without a specific place to call "me." If we were able to dissect both body and mind, and arrange the various body and mental constituents in front of us, we would be unable to identify an "I" or "self" among any of them.

By the same reasoning, if we were to dismantle my Honda car and arrange all its various component parts on a workshop floor, we would find no specific part on which to pin the name "Honda." That's because "Honda" is simply the label we apply to a collection of parts, arranged to function in a particular way.

And the same is true of me. "Me," "myself," and "I" are only labels for a collection of physical and mental components, arranged to function in a particular way. There is no "me" that exists separately or independently of this collection, in just the same way that there is no car that exists separately from the collection of parts on the workshop floor.

"I" am a label applied to a collection of parts. There is no "I" that owns, controls, or manages the parts. "I" *am* the collection of parts. My whole concept of "I," just like others' perception of "me," is wholly dependent on those parts. What happens if I get a bad knock on the head, and my personality changes from that of a relaxed individual to one with a very short fuse? Or if I lose my legs in a car accident and have to use a wheelchair? Even though I may have the conviction that I, myself, am essentially unchanged, other people wouldn't think of me as just the same person but with a bad temper, or just the same person but without legs. The overall idea of who "I" am would change.

I recently came across the tragic story of a young man who was blinded by a rare illness. Difficult though it was to adjust to life as a sightless person afterward, what made matters even worse was that he was shunned by a number of his former friends. For whatever reason, they couldn't cope with the fact that he'd lost his sight. He would hear their voices in the street, or when he stepped inside his local pub, but they never approached him as they would routinely have done in the past. Even though he felt he was essentially the same person he had been before his blindness—and although he would have cherished their friendship more than ever—to them it was as if he were unrecognizable as their former friend.

The mistaken view we have of a self who is a controller or possessor can be demonstrated in a different way. Tibetan Buddhists, fond of debate, sometimes use the device of supposing, hypothetically, that some misconception is true. What would its implications be? In our example, let's suppose the conference receptionist with

"Self's" label, frustrated at having searched through every "body" and "mind" delegate without success, heads down a corridor to the management suite to report the important missing delegate—and who should she run into, lurking alone by the fire hydrants, but Self!

What would be the implications of that?

Most obviously, if Self really were that independent, it wouldn't matter what was going on with body or mind, he or she wouldn't even know it was happening. Self would have no relationship with them, and would remain unaffected by whatever they went through. Similarly, if Self took off on a Self-development course, whatever he or she learned wouldn't have any impact at all on cognitive behavior, personality, or other mental or physical activity, all of which would continue to operate independently of Self.

Which obviously isn't our experience.

The reality is that, for the most part, we think about ourselves as existing in a way that we just don't. We hold this unexplored assumption of a "me" that is somehow independent or separate from a collection of parts, that is over and above the parts, owns them, and to a large extent controls them.

DEPENDENCE ON CAUSES

That's not the only assumption we make. We also tend to assume that "me," "myself," and "I" operates as a fixed entity, quite separately from the outside world too. There is "self" and there is "other," and for the most part we see a clear distinction between the two. But how much scrutiny can this assumption withstand?

On a physiological basis, it's hard to sustain an argument that we are stable, self-contained systems who exist independently of the outside world. After all, we're so dependent on food that all it takes is a couple of days without nourishment (and just a few hours without water) and we're unable to function. Just a couple of minutes without oxygen and it's Game Over. While the fragility of our life is something we rarely think about, unless brought face to face with it by some shock occurrence, the reality is that our hold on life is tenuous and we are highly dependent on favorable external circumstances. Living in a developed country, most of us are insulated from that harsh reality, but most beings with whom we share the planet aren't nearly so lucky.

Even before we go near matters of life and death, however, our physical and mental state is profoundly influenced by external circumstance. The person who is the life and soul of the party, joking, dancing, and entertaining friends, may seem a very different creature from the withdrawn individual sitting in the corner—but what if the only difference is a few hours and a very different blood-alcohol reading? And which is the real self—the party animal or the more reserved version?

Like chemical cocktails, our physical and emotional state is constantly changing depending on what we put into our system. Food stressors, like sugar, caffeine, alcohol, and chocolate, have a very different impact on the way we feel and behave than food supporters, like water, vegetables, and oil-rich fish. Over a sustained period of time we become what we eat, or don't eat—factors that would be irrelevant if "I" really was a self-sustaining being.

In reality, not only are we wholly dependent on the outside world for our physical continuity, but there isn't a single cell in our body that remains constant. My entire self is comprised of cells that are constantly dying off and being regenerated, not to mention all the bacteria we carry along for the ride, all separate life forms with their own agenda. These components, including all our organs, blood, and bone, are constantly being replaced by materials from the outside, "non-me" world, so that our bodies are not only fundamentally "non-me," they are also in a state of constant flux.

Not even the way in which these outsourced components is arranged is determined by "me." One of the most fascinating scientific inquiries of recent decades is the Minnesota Twin Family

Study, which studied hundreds of pairs of identical twins who had been raised in separate homes. The study showed such striking psychological and behavioral similarities between the twins that researchers concluded that genes affect "almost every behavioral trait so far investigated, from reaction time to religiosity."

Apart from the obvious similarities of physiology, other unexpected "coincidences" were curiously quirky, including such things as the habit of flushing a toilet before using it, the collecting of rubber bands on wrists, reading magazines from back to front and, in the case of one pair of twins, each wearing seven rings on exactly the same fingers, and three bracelets.

It is interesting to note that "religiosity" might be genetically determined—it would certainly help explain why unrelated people who share very similar backgrounds have such different levels of interest in spiritual matters.

Although the term DNA was unknown to Shantideva, he nevertheless recognized the essential truth of our genetic dependence.

—

Although the basis is quite impersonal,
Through constant familiarity
I have come to regard
The drops of sperm and blood of others as "I."

It is hard to think of a greater challenge to our sense of identity than this! Never one to shy away from the uncomfortable truth, Shantideva points out that we're so used to thinking of ourselves as an independent "I" that we have long lost sight of the fact that our whole existence is based on the genetic material of two other people. We tend to forget that our appearance, intelligence, personality, and physical profile is largely determined by genes. But, apart from reminding us of this fact, how much of what we believe to be uniquely "me" really is the result of asserting our conscious will, and how much was decided years ago by the joining of that particular sperm and egg? We may think that "I" am responsible for certain decisions and behavior, but what if much of this is genetically determined?

To advance the analogy of my dismantled Honda, this time taking into account dependence on causes, our challenge is still to find a place to stick the label "Honda," but now we discover that the dismantled car scattered across the workshop floor was codesigned by one engineer from Volkswagen and another from Hyundai; that none of the parts come from a Honda factory, but rather from a wide variety of other sources; and that every component has been exchanged for a different one. How authentic does that Honda label feel now?!

So far we have investigated our dependence on causes from a purely physical perspective. When we look at the workings of our mind, here too we find that everything we take to be "me" actually originates from somewhere else. Counterbalancing nature in the developmental debate is nurture, and this is what we're talking about. The language that we speak, every idea we have about what constitutes "normal," our education, socialization, and attitudes all come from somewhere else. The details of our worldview may be as individual as our experiences, but they originate from outside of us, and so many of our dominant convictions are shaped by the community in which we live.

I'm often struck by the thought that a child born in one part of Jerusalem may be brought up to resent Muslims, while a child born five minutes' drive away may be brought up to resent Jews. What do we consider to be the main issues of the day: the economy, climate change, the impact of globalization? Or where to score our next hit, how to collect more social security money, and what to do if debt collectors show up at the door? Our views about what matters are largely driven by the environment in which we find ourselves.

And our mental components are even more liable to change than our physiological ones: with a different environment, and exposure to powerfully presented new ideas, it's quite possible for us to experience a 180-degree shift in our opinions.

The "I" that exists purely as a label refers not only to a constantly changing group of body parts, but to attitudes and ideas that are also subject to ongoing revision. At university I remember a psychology lecturer playfully suggesting that, to draw a distinction between the different versions of ourselves that evolve over time, people should have date stamps attached to their name. "David Michie: July 2010" may be of the same continuum as "David Michie: July 1980," but the two have very different perspectives and should not be confused. Who do we think of when we hear names like Mohammed Ali or Iris Murdoch? The stars of their prime, or the people of their twilight years? Which versions are the "real" them?

This is the challenge we face when we try to apply a label to a constantly changing collection of parts, each of which in turn is dependent on a wide variety of causes. As Shantideva puts it (here using this reasoning as a caution against anger):

> Hence everything is governed by other factors, which in
>   turn are governed by others,
> And in this way nothing governs itself.
> Having understood this, I should not become angry
> With phenomena, which are like apparitions.

DEPENDENCE ON PROJECTION OF THE MIND

The writing of Professor Richard Gregory, one of Britain's most eminent neuropsychologists, provides some of the most accessible insights into current scientific thinking about how we experience reality.

Most of us become aware, at some point, that our perception of a particular sensation is different from that of other people's. It can seem unfathomable why someone wouldn't love the same piece of music that we do; why, looking at the same vista, they aren't also struck by the same sense of wonder; why, taking a mouthful of the same food, they don't share our delight or revulsion. This is because most of us assume the truth of what's known in neuropsychology circles as a direct-perception theory, which is that the brain acts as a mere receptor for sensations channelled to it through the eyes, ears, and other sensory doorways. This view has long been abandoned as simplistic by neuropsychologists. Advances in technology have revealed a far more complex process.

To use the cognitive visual system as an example, it is now known that some 80 percent of fibers in the part of the brain that processes visual imagery comes from the cortex—which governs functions including memory—and only 20 percent from the retinas. Our eyes may receive images of furry moving fragments behind our neighbor's fence, but we "see" their poodle chasing the postman. Our eyes may receive the profile of a two-dimensional piece of china with a handle, but we "see" a cup. As Professor Gregory explains: "We carry in our heads predictive hypotheses of the external world of objects and of ourselves. These brain-based hypotheses of perception are our most immediate reality. But they entail many stages of physiological signalling and complicated cognitive computing, so *experience is but indirectly related to external reality*." (My italics.)

Far from being simple receptors of images, our brains draw on memory and other brain functions to project a predictive hypothesis onto what we're seeing. In fact, our perceptions may be up to 90 percent memory. "This startling notion," says Professor Gregory, "that perception is projecting brain-hypotheses outward into the physical world—endowing the world with color and sound and meaning—has surprising implications."

The Buddha couldn't have put it better himself. Professor Gregory's explanation concurs exactly with Dharma teachings on dependent arising, specifically on the idea that the existence of an object is dependent on a projection of our mind—or "mind's imputation," as it is sometimes described. Both the Dharma and contemporary neuroscience use the same word to describe the way we perceive reality: as a "projection."

Although our usual experience of reality is that things outside of us exist in a particular way purely from their own side, a more accurate understanding is that we are the cocreators of the way that things exist. According to science, the way that things exist is 90 percent us and only 10 percent them. No wonder everyone doesn't experience the same sights, sounds, tastes, and so on as we do: we may be looking at the same thing, but we are creating very different realities.

Quantum physicists concur on this subject. Just as the direct-perception theory has long been abandoned by neuroscientists as an adequate description of how we experience the outside world, so too the theories of nineteenth-century classical science—which held that an object's properties, such as its mass and length, had definite values—were thrown out by Einstein's Theory of Relativity. To quote physicist David Bohm, "Relativity and quantum theory have shown that it has no meaning to divide the observing apparatus from what is observed." Or as Austrian physicist Erwin Schrödinger summed it up: "[E]very man's world picture is and always remains a construct of his mind and cannot be proved to have any other existence."

Where does this take us in our pursuit of "me," "myself," or "I"?

As science and the Dharma agree, "I" is a projection of my own mind. My perception of "I" is necessarily different from other people's perception of me and, as we well know, can change dramatically depending on what kind of mood I'm in. If I'm feeling depressed I'll be convinced that I'm unattractive, incompetent, and socially inept and will project all kinds of other negativities onto "me." If I'm feeling upbeat and optimistic, I may think of "me" as good-looking, charming, a high achiever, and so on.

Which is the "real" I?

THE SANTA CLAUS–LIKE "ME"

Recognizing that "I" is simply a label for a collection of parts, rather than an owner or controller of those parts; that each part—as well as the collection—is dependent on causes that are constantly changing; and that the entire collection is a construct of the mind, with no independent reality, does this all mean that "I" somehow don't exist?

In a word, no. What it means is that "I" exist in a way that's very different from what I usually suppose.

Here it might be useful to return to the metaphor of Santa Claus. While my annual visits to see Santa and the opening of his Christmas presents were a source of great excitement, at some point in my childhood the sobering truth was revealed. I can't remember whether this was a one-off bombshell or the result of questioning over a period of time, but—one way or another—I came to realize that my idea of Santa was just an illusion. It was impossible for Santa to exist in the way that I thought he did, visiting the home of every child in the world in a single night to give them presents. Nor had he ever existed like that.

Did that mean Santa didn't exist at all? No, it didn't. A man in a red suit and white beard still "Ho-ho-hoed" on Barbour's fourth floor every year. Kids still lined up to see him and mumble their requests. While I would never be fooled about Santa again, I could see why other kids, who hadn't yet discovered the truth, were so excited to see him. I knew the illusion they were under, because I had once believed the same thing.

So it is with "me," "myself," and "I." In the same way that as children we projected a fantasized way of being onto a man wearing a red suit and white beard, so too most of us project a fantasized way of being onto a collection of physical and psychological components. Just as there is no Santa who flies through the night on his sleigh, there is no "I" who owns, controls, or possesses our physical or mental functioning. This "self" who is the powerful center of our particular universe—whose rights we're so quick to defend, and interests we're so keen to advance—is, in fact, nothing but an elaborate fabrication we impute onto a constantly changing collection of parts. Everyone else is involved in their own particular make-believe too, trying to persuade others to believe in the particular projection of themselves that they've created, to concretize this great ghost called "self."

The ease with which we can change the view we have of ourselves, from one mood to the next, should perhaps tip us off to the fact that this imputed self has so little substance. For most of us, all it takes is an encounter with an articulate, confident communicator, and we can come away feeling either wonderful or dejected about ourselves. Would we experience such feelings if we fully understood such a person was talking about something that was just his or her own projection?

LIBERATION FROM "I"

Dharma teachers sometimes talk of "the two I's." The true "I" is just a label for a collection of parts. This is an accurate use of "I." The false "I" is the entity we project onto that collection, the one we attribute with a way of being and all kinds of characteristics that are as real as Santa Claus.

Making the discovery that this "I" is an illusion comes as a shock. Cherishing the "false I" or "self" is among our most powerful instincts, our most deeply ingrained habits. It is the motive behind much of our behavior. To have this "self" unmasked as a fantasy is a truly life-changing discovery. But it is also a wonderfully liberating one.

Because cherishing this false self is also the cause of *all* our dissatisfaction and unhappiness. And while the Buddha's teachings on renunciation and bodhichitta help us to replace our negative mental projections with more positive ones, it is his teachings on dependent arising, or emptiness of self-existence, which provide the direct gateway to permanent freedom. In his book *Confession of a Buddhist Atheist*, Stephen Batchelor sums up the extraordinary contribution made by the Buddha, referred to here by his family name, Gotama:

> Gotama did for the self what Copernicus did for the earth: he put it in its rightful place, despite its continuing to appear just as it did before. Gotama no more rejected the existence of the self than Copernicus rejected the existence of the earth. Instead, rather than regarding it as a fixed, noncontingent point around which everything else turned, he recognized that each self was a fluid, contingent process just like everything else.

In the next chapter I offer some suggestions on how to go forward on the basis of the analysis provided in this one. But I'll close with a few words that might have been used by any Buddhist teacher: "The true value of a human being is determined primarily by the measure and the sense in which he has attained to liberation from the self." This is the enlightened observation not of the Dalai Lama or Shantideva, but of Albert Einstein, who, approaching the nature of our existence from a scientific perspective, reached an identical conclusion.

Analytical Meditation: Where Is the "I"?

It's very important to establish clearly at the outset of this meditation what we are trying to find, which is the "me," "myself," or "I" that we usually assume ourselves to be. We are trying to find the "I" who possesses or controls "my" body and mind. The independent "I" who exists separately from body parts and mental functioning. The "I" who is angry when other people are provocative. The "I" who suffers from depression, stress, or anxiety. Where is this "I" to be found?

▶ As usual, first stabilize the mind through a breath meditation exercise. Given the subtlety of this meditation, you may want to extend this stabilization period so that the mind is as calm and relaxed as possible.

▶ When you are ready, ask yourself: Who am I? Are my feet the "I"? When I talk about "me," are my feet who I feel myself to be? Are my feet who I think of as "I"?" Take your time in this investigation.

▶ Having discarded feet as a possibility, move up to the legs: Are my legs the "I"?

▶ Continue this same analysis, working your way up your body through the torso, hands, arms, shoulders, neck, and head. Can you find the independent, self-existent "I"?

▶ If "I" am not a body part, perhaps I am a functioning of mind or consciousness? Go through each aspect of consciousness: Am I my eye consciousness? My nose consciousness? My ear consciousness? My taste consciousness? My touch consciousness? Look at each of these one by one.

▶ We are left only with mental consciousness—is the "I" to be found here? When the mind is settled, I discover mental consciousness to be nothing more than spacious clarity and awareness. Is that who I think of my "self" as being?

▶ Recognize that, having looked through every element of body and mind, you are unable to find an independent, self-existent "I." Focus single-pointedly on the unfindability of this "I."

15

Adventures in Inner Space

THE REVELATION THAT "I" am not at all as I've always assumed is profoundly challenging, even at an intellectual or conceptual level. Because self-grasping is our most innate instinct, underlying so much of our thinking, it is disconcerting to discover that the self at which we so constantly grasp is an illusion. We may even find this analysis a little frightening—a very typical response is to take the analysis one step too far and arrive at a nihilistic view: if there is no self to become enlightened, there is no point bothering with meditation, Buddhism, or very much else for that matter. We might as well devote ourselves to lives of unfettered hedonism!

We may also feel a sense of sudden loss, and I've come across the phrase "death of the self" in commentaries on this subject. But in reality Self hasn't died, because Self never lived to begin with, in the same way that there was never a "real" Santa who handed out presents to all the world's children. One might even see the hand of Self, or our ego, in coming up with such a deceptive dramatization. For just as a child doesn't die in order to become an adult, no death is required for us to mature in our understanding of how we exist. On the contrary, the benefits of maturity surpass childlike make-believe to an extent that is well beyond our intellectual comprehension. Just because we don't exist in the way we have always assumed, or the way that society seems to tell us, doesn't mean we don't exist at all. In fact, our true existence is a state of far greater subtlety, boundlessness, and radiance than most of us have ever begun to imagine.

Once we begin to understand how we ourselves lack any inherent, independent, objective, or self-sustaining existence, it becomes easier to see how all other beings and things exist in the same way. All of us depend on parts, causes, and our mind's participation and for that reason are dependently existent.

Dharma teachers often challenge students by asking them to think of one thing that does not depend on parts, causes, and mind's participation. While of course there is no such thing, the exercise of trying to think of something that may so exist is a good way to deepen our own understanding of the concept. Nothing, no matter how special or sacred, is self-existent, because it's an impossible mode of existence. All gurus and lamas lack self-existence, as does every buddha and transcendent bodhisattva. Even emptiness of self-existence is itself a mere label. As Shantideva writes:

Upon analysis, this world of living beings is found to
 have no true existence,
Therefore who can die here?
What is there to come and what has been?
Who are friends and who are relatives?

EMPTINESS IS NOT NOTHINGNESS

The Heart Sutra has long been considered one of the most precious of the Buddha's teachings. A text of just a few pages, it focuses on the subject of dependent arising, and both the text and the mantra it contains are regularly chanted in monasteries throughout Asia, sometimes on a daily basis. Of all the phrases in the Heart Sutra, one of the best known is the sentence: "Form is emptiness, emptiness is form; emptiness is not other than form, form too is not other than emptiness."

Taken out of context, this sentence can seem like gobbledygook. Expressing the very essence of his teachings on dependent arising, the Buddha's Heart Sutra is a highly distilled presentation, so it's very useful to receive teachings that help unpack the concepts it contains.

The reason I am including this famous sentence is because I find it very helpful in countering the most common misconception many of us have when first encountering the idea that we have no self-existence, which is to assume that we are therefore left with nothing. This nihilistic view is as incorrect as the opposing, eternalist view that we have a permanent self, or soul, which exists independently of our body and mind.

The first part of the sentence—"form is emptiness"—is shorthand for "everything that exists depends on parts, causes, and mind's participation, therefore is empty of any self-existence." In his commentary *Essence of the Heart Sutra*, His Holiness the Dalai Lama explains this as follows:

> All things originate dependently. Because all things originate dependently, one can observe cause and effect. Cause and effect are only possible in a world that is dependently originated, and dependent origination is only possible in a world that is devoid of intrinsic existence, which is to say in a world that is empty. Therefore, we can say that emptiness is form, which is another way of saying that form arises from emptiness, and emptiness is the basis that allows the dependent origination of form. Thus the world of form is a *manifestation* of emptiness.

The second part of the sentence from the Heart Sutra—"emptiness is not other than form"—is equally significant, because here the

Buddha is countering the idea that emptiness of self-existence equates to a vacuum, a nothingness. Instead he is saying that emptiness of self-existence can only exist as a quality of a thing, a form, which is dependent on parts, causes, and mind's participation. The Dalai Lama again explains this point very clearly: "Emptiness is not a core reality, lying somehow at the heart of the universe, from which the diversity of phenomena rise. Emptiness can only be conceived of in relation to individual things and events…Emptiness exists only as a quality of a particular phenomenon; emptiness does not exist separately and independently of particular phenomena."

UNDERSTANDING EMPTINESS ON DIFFERENT LEVELS

The idea that everything arises in dependence on other things, and is therefore empty of self-existence, is one we can understand at different levels. Knowing it intellectually is both useful and important, but having a direct, nonconceptual experience of it is what transforms us. This is what is meant by the term "awakening": we wake up from believing things exist inherently, independently, or separately and see all things, ourselves included, for the illusion-like appearances they really are. Realizing the true nature of reality in this way is the essence of all Buddhist paths, and in Tibetan Buddhism is known as the sixth perfection—the "perfection of wisdom."

Far from being a depressing experience, this is the realization for which all Buddhists strive! Once we are fully awakened beings, we are no longer subject to delusions. Because we know that those things we once desired are illusion-like, that we are illusion-like, and that the process of us enjoying them is illusion-like, we are no longer enslaved by attachment. Just as we no longer harbor a burning wish to tell Santa what we'd like him to bring us for Christmas, so too we see our attachment-driven goals and wishes, once the cause of such emotional intensity, for the projections they are.

The same holds true of anger. In seeing the objects of our anger as illusion-like, ourselves as illusion-like, and the process of hating others as illusion-like, we shatter the vice-like grip that the superstition of materialism has over us.

You may recall that the "three poisons" are attachment, anger, and ignorance. It is ignorance about the way things exist that is our most enduring and subtle delusion. And as described in the paragraphs above, this ignorance is implicit in both attachment and anger. If we really knew that all the attractiveness of that cute person on the other side of the room was a projection of our mind, and that his or her cuteness was as real as Santa Claus, would we still find them so irresistible? Instead of taking actions based on a deluded view of reality, only deepening our conditioning and further entrenching our samsara, how much better would it feel to be free of it all?

Many people know that nirvana is associated with a blissful, positive state and is the opposite of samsara. As it happens, the word "nirvana" is a Pali reference to extinguishing a flame. On the surface of things this may seem to have little to do with a feeling of bliss, but when we understand that this is a metaphor for extinguishing our false sense of self, understanding becomes easier. And the metaphor points to the fact that nirvana is the ultimate paradox. Instead of continuing with our innate assumption that self-cherishing is the key to happiness, it's only when we realize that there is no inherent "self," "I," or "me" to cherish that we find true happiness. Once we have understood this truth in a state of deep, meditative equipoise, the way in which we interact with "reality" begins to undergo profound change.

We also understand compassion, the "rocket fuel" of our practice, in a more comprehensive way. As the Dalai Lama explains in *Transforming the Mind*:

> Because of the way insight and wisdom affect the development of compassion, the Buddhist literature identifies

three different types of compassion. First, at the initial stage, compassion is simply the wish to see other sentient beings freed from suffering; it is not reinforced by any particular insight into the nature of suffering or the nature of a sentient being. Then, at the second stage, compassion is not simply the wish to see another being free from suffering, it is strengthened by insight into the transient nature of existence, such as the realization that the being who is the object of your compassion does not exist permanently. When insight complements your compassion it gives it greater power. Finally, at the third stage, compassion is described as "nonobjectifying compassion." It can be directed toward that same suffering being, but now it is reinforced by a full awareness of the ultimate nature of that being. This is a very powerful type of compassion, because it enables you to engage with the other person without objectifying him or her, and without clinging on to the idea that he or she has any absolute reality.

When we are able to combine our understanding of emptiness with compassion, our bodhichitta is expressed in its most transcendent form.

THE IMPORTANCE OF DIRECT EXPERIENCE

Before arriving at such an understanding, it's more than likely we'll have a lot of questions. Like—why did I ever think I had an independent self? And where do all these ideas about a separate "me" and "other" come from? You may well have wondered, in the example given in the last chapter, that if "I" am seeking a place to label "I," am I not behaving like a dog chasing its own tail? Or you may be thinking, "This is all messing with my head—exactly what is going on?!"

Developmental psychology offers many fascinating insights into the evolution of our sense of self, and the impact of nature and nurture on personality. Alongside such objective analysis, our subjective experience is that the ideas we have about "me" arise quite naturally in our mind. Whether in our interactions with others, or reflection on our own, thoughts about ourselves arise continuously, effortlessly, and sometimes, if we are honest, quite neurotically. What I look like. How likeable or socially inept I am. How competent or useless I am at certain activities. Thoughts of this nature arise, abide, and pass in our minds, and over time we develop all kinds of stories, ideas, and self-fulfilling prophecies about a self whom we project and concretize onto our constantly changing collection of body parts.

What are we left with when we remove this false, imputed self?

We are left with a collection of body parts and a mind, or mental consciousness, in which thoughts continue to arise, abide, and pass. If we truly want to understand what we are, it is here that we need to focus, becoming aware of the nature of our own consciousness through direct, personal experience.

Tibetan Buddhism teaches that the mind exists on different levels of subtlety. Whether we wish to observe our mind operating at its coarser or more subtle levels, the best way to achieve this is through meditation. This is why Buddhism is a meditative path, because when all is said and done, the only way to penetrate the nature of mind is to do so directly and nonconceptually.

In the introduction to this book I gave an analogy of African cacao workers who had never eaten chocolate. They had all kinds of thoughts and ideas about chocolate but had yet to taste it, until a TV crew arrived and filmed their experience. Suffice it to say, all their thoughts and ideas about chocolate became superfluous on the tasting of it. No further description was necessary. Now they understood why the world wanted their cacao beans!

In much the same way, we could describe various aspects of mental consciousness and what it's like to experience "inner space," but the main thing is to take a bite of it and experience it for ourselves.

MIND MEDITATING ON MIND

The instructions at the end of this chapter provide a guide to this important meditation. But because the mind is such a subtle object of meditation—unlike, say, the breath, which provides a much more obvious focus for attention—it may be useful to expand here on this important meditation.

To begin with, it's perhaps worth saying that this can initially feel like one of the more challenging meditations because our minds, in their untrained states, are usually busy generating new thoughts and ideas. It may seem that, like someone wanting to observe the sky, all we are faced with is constantly changing cloud cover. But there's no need to feel frustrated. Unlike other meditations, where the arising of thoughts is considered to be agitation, here whatever is going on mentally *is* the object of our meditation. The beauty of this meditation is that our agitation is the focus of our concentration, not a distraction.

Beginning your meditation with bodhichitta motivation, it may be useful to extend your stabilizing meditation for a longer period than usual, really concentrating on the breath to settle the mind as much as possible. As your breathing quite naturally slows down, you find you have longer pauses at the end of each out-breath and each in-breath. During those pauses simply be aware. Enjoy the peacefulness of this moment in which there is no breath and no counting.

Little by little, as you repeat the cycles of breathing, try to withdraw concentration from breath-counting, and shift your focus to simply being present. Without losing track of the breath or the count, allow it to fade more and more into the background, so that most of your concentration is on the here and now. Then, when you stop your counting at the end of a cycle of breaths to focus on mind itself, it is as though the breath-counting has faded completely into the distance and you are left with only the present moment.

For a while you may enjoy the experience of relaxed, spacious alertness, free of any mental agitation, but chances are that a thought will appear, and then another one, and then another. How do you deal with these? In short, by observing them dispassionately and not getting caught up in them. This goes completely against our ingrained habit of participating in any idea that pops up in our mind, without even realizing that's what we're doing. Here and now, however, the moment a thought emerges in your mind, your aim is simply to observe it without getting involved in the content of it.

Some people find it helpful to label thoughts as just thought. So, when one appears in your mind you can observe to yourself, "That's just a thought." The content of the thought doesn't matter. Whether it's an idea of immense altruism or utter deviousness makes no difference. From your perspective as an observer/meditator, it's just a thought, and now you can return to abiding in peacefulness.

The First Panchen Lama refers to the curious way in which thoughts vanish when we treat them this way—simply recognizing them as phenomena that arise, abide, and pass through our minds: "When you look at the nature of any thought that arises, it automatically disappears by itself and a bare absence dawns." It's interesting to discover first-hand how focusing on thoughts as just thoughts makes them disappear. This isn't just some theory or the subject of a teaching. It is an important experiment we can conduct for ourselves.

You may prefer simply to cut off your thoughts as soon as they occur. Having settled your mind, the moment a thought emerges, you may prefer to simply switch your attention away from it before you've even fully recognized it as a thought. As gross agitation— the kind that completely interrupts your concentration—subsides, and your main challenge becomes subtle agitation—the kind that doesn't break your concentration, but does create an underlying distraction—this technique of cutting off thoughts becomes particularly appropriate, because even to label a thought as a thought is, at this level, an interruption.

What we discover as we progress in this meditation is that our mind has no form, shape, or color. It cannot be obstructed, and no matter what thoughts pass through it, no matter how virtuous or nonvirtuous those thoughts may be, they leave no residual impact on it, just as clouds leave no trace after they have blown across the sky. This, too, is a highly significant and liberating discovery to make for ourselves, one that points to our fundamental potential for enlightenment. Mind is like an open space, allowing anything to dawn within it as an object of experience. As the Dalai Lama says of mind: "Its nature, in fact, is mere clarity and awareness. If we recognize it properly, we can figuratively 'see' this bare absence that is a mere clarity and awareness vividly in our meditation."

We all have good days and bad days for meditative concentration. If, for example, you are going through a tough time emotionally and are feeling anxious, angry, or bereft, you will probably find it difficult to simply observe another storm of negative thoughts as just thoughts. But even then this meditation practice is very helpful in helping us recognize the true nature of our anxiety, anger, or grief. When we recognize that these are just thoughts, we help liberate ourselves from the hold they have over us. As we observe the unhappiness these thoughts make us feel, we become more determined not to participate in or strengthen them.

Some people may have reservations about this type of meditation, believing that there is no way they can ever stop the ceaseless tide of agitation rushing through their minds, so they might as well not even bother trying. Then there are those who fear the absence of inner chatter, as though if it stops they too will somehow disappear.

But this form of meditation, though more subtle than others, is just the same as other forms in the sense that embarking on it is like the process of learning to walk. Toddlers don't simply wake up one morning thinking, "The day has come," and from that point on walk perfectly. Instead they begin to crawl, and only after doing that for a while are they able to take their first tentative steps—with support. They will fall down many, many times before finally being able to walk unaided for the shortest distance.

When we practice this meditation we need to prepare ourselves in the same way. We cannot experience radiant luminosity of mind simply because we decide it would be a nice thing to feel. First we have to stabilize our mind, develop our concentration, and practice dealing with the arising of thoughts. We will find ourselves getting caught up in thoughts time and again before we're able to observe them simply as thoughts. It will take a lot of practice before we're able to experience our mind free of all agitation or dullness for even the shortest time.

But what a rewarding experience when we are able to sustain our concentration in a relaxed but settled way, if only temporarily! At last we are able to experience our mind free of obstruction—and experience its true nature as mere clarity and awareness. The more we're able to penetrate this bare absence—the more direct, first-hand experience we have of our own primordial mind—the more we want to live in harmony with it, instead of the agitated, fantasized projection of "reality" in which we're usually so caught up. And as we repeat this meditation, perhaps to our own surprise, we find ourselves beginning to experience the most profound happiness. As the Dalai Lama says: "When we achieve a mind focused on mind with the perfect placement of absorbed concentration, free from all faults of dullness or flightiness, we increasingly experience an element of bliss accompanying our meditation."

This meditative state serves as the basis for the most profound realization of emptiness, the dawning of awakening, the experience of nirvana. It is the goal to which Buddhist meditators work, but may also be described as being goal-less, because in our state of absorbed concentration we don't try to achieve anything. We simply abide in the recognition that there is no meditator, no objective of meditation, and no meditative realization. All is nondual, and with the nature of space-like clarity and bliss. This very subtle consciousness is who "we" really are. Boundless and beyond death, we transcend our usual incredibly narrow self-definition to experience a state of being that reveals our true nature to be more expansive, luminous, and blissful than we may ever have conceived.

A MEDITATIVE APPROACH TO DEPRESSION

Mind meditating on mind is not only the most profound meditation in itself, it is also very useful when practiced in conjunction with the analytical meditation outlined in Chapter 14. And as someone who has experienced deep depression, I have found it a very powerful opponent to this miserable condition.

This is how the process works:

▶ First, conduct the mind-watching-mind meditation as already described (and outlined at the end of this chapter). Even if your mind is fairly distracted, you will hopefully still arrive at the recognition that mind, or mental consciousness, is mere clarity and awareness.

▶ Now repeat the meditation process outlined in the meditation at the end of the last chapter, beginning with the question "Who am I?" With familiarity, you can run through the sequence at a speed comfortable to you, asking, "Are my legs the 'I'? Is this torso the 'I'?" and so on. Having gone through all the body parts, then work through the six consciousnesses listed on page 198, ending with mental consciousness. "Is this mental consciousness the 'I'?"

▶ Having just experienced mental consciousness as mere clarity and awareness, you will have a strong conviction that "I," as I am experiencing myself—that is, a depressed I—am definitely not just that. So where is this "I"?

▸ Spend some contemplating the unfindability of "I." And once you have established this firmly, ask, "Where is the 'I' that is depressed?" This is the knockout blow for depression, because such an "I" does not exist. It never existed. It's impossible for it to exist. It is as real as Santa Claus. The longer we can concentrate single-pointedly on the unfindability of an "I" that is depressed, the more powerfully we oppose the delusions on which it is based.

In explaining this process I don't mean to trivialize the experience of depression. I know exactly how it feels to wish you didn't have to wake up in the morning, so bleak is the reality to which you open your eyes. This meditation technique does take practice. But as we become more familiar with it, we find we're able to pull the rug from underneath our depressed feelings. By powerfully reminding ourselves that this self-existent "me," the focus of so much unhappiness, is just our own thought, why continue to perpetuate a creation that makes us feel so unhappy? Reality—that is, blissful, space-like consciousness—is a much nicer place to be, so why dwell in miserable unreality? Even when our meditation hasn't evolved enough to enjoy a blissful, space-like state, it's a very powerful antidote simply to remind ourselves of the conceptual understanding that the depressed I is a myth. Or in Shantideva's words:

If all the injury,
Fear, and pain in this world
Arise from grasping at a self,
Then what use is that great ghost to me?

For some people, meditation practice alone won't necessarily be sufficient treatment for clinical depression. As mentioned earlier, when depression is caused by a chemical imbalance in the body, drugs or other conventional treatment may be necessary and medical advice is recommended.

BEING MINDFUL OF EMPTINESS

In Chapter 9 we looked at the importance of mindfulness in practicing bodhichitta. Our goal is to become increasingly mindful of opportunities for generosity, ethics, and patience, remembering to perfect our practice of these happiness-creating activities by recollecting our bodhichitta motivation. We looked at how, over time, what begins as a contrived performance grows increasingly familiar, until these virtues become spontaneous and quite natural.

To take our ongoing bodhichitta activities to the next level, we add to them the reminder of emptiness. This is particularly powerful because, as already noted, emptiness provides the most direct opponent to all our dissatisfaction by revealing the true nature of reality. It's also the most subtle of concepts, and one with which we need to become very familiar.

For these reasons, next time we drop a coin in the charity collector's box, as well as thinking, "By this act of generosity may I become enlightened for the sake of all beings," the impact of our action is multiplied immeasurably by also remembering, "I am empty of self-existence, this money is empty of self-existence, the charity is empty of self-existence, my act of giving is empty of self-existence."

Ditto when we next find ourselves practicing patience: "I am empty of self-existence, the traffic jam in front of me is empty of self-existence, my practice of patience is empty of self-existence."

If there isn't time to recollect all three, even remembering the emptiness of giving money or practicing patience is most useful. In this way, we can develop our awareness of bodhichitta and emptiness as ongoing themes in our life. We deliberately manipulate our own conditioning, or karma, to predispose us toward positive and enjoyable mental states, away from negative ones—and away from taking our projection of ourselves, and the world around us, so seriously. We also find that when we remind ourselves of emptiness throughout each day, the subject becomes more normalized, more real. If we're sometimes able to reflect on how everything depends on parts, causes, and mind's participation, and is therefore empty of inherent existence, this is also very beneficial.

The familiarity we develop with emptiness in our daily activities supports our meditation on this subject when we sit on the cushion—and vice versa. The better we understand dependent arising, the more we catch glimpses of it in our daily life, and the more we're able to draw on our understanding to help deal with challenges like depression, frustration, anxiety, and loss.

The foundation of our understanding is one we must create for ourselves through meditation. The analytical meditation presented in Chapter 14 and the exercise in single-pointed concentration outlined below provide two important tools for unlocking the secret of reality.

> The remedy for the darkness of the obscurations of
>   disturbing conceptions,
> As well as the obscuration to the knowable,
> is meditation on emptiness.
> Therefore, why do those who wish to quickly obtain
>   omniscience not meditate on emptiness?

Single-Pointed Meditation: Mind Watching Mind

For this meditation, refer also to the extended instructions on pages 206–10.

► As usual, stabilize the mind through a breath meditation exercise. You may want to extend this stabilization period so that the mind is as calm and relaxed as possible.

► Once your mind is to some extent settled, let go of the breath as the object of meditation, and focus on mind itself.

► As thoughts arise in your mind, simply observe them as thoughts. Practice not getting caught up in them. Discover how, by observing each thought that arises simply as thought, it disappears of its own accord. Observe how passing thoughts leave no trace on your mental consciousness.

► As you experience gaps between thoughts, really focus on the space-like emptiness that remains after the last thought has gone and before the next thought has arisen. Observe this in a nondiscursive way. Experience the primordial nature of your own mind—how it is mere clarity and awareness.

► As far as possible, abide in this space-like emptiness without interruption. The more you practice abiding in the unobscured radiance of your primordial mind, the more pleasant and then blissful the experience becomes.

16

The Eight Worldly Dharmas

So FAR in this book we have looked in some detail at our attitudes to material gain and pleasurable experiences. We have seen that, contrary to the assumptions that usually drive us, there are no external objects or experiences that are reliable causes for happiness. We have contrasted this with internally created causes of happiness, specifically our cultivation of great love and great compassion, and its ultimate expression—the wish to become enlightened for the sake of all living beings.

In the past two chapters, we have gained a more detailed insight into *why* no external objects are reliable causes for happiness or misery: because they have no inherent reality and their characteristics are, more than anything, a projection of our mind.

But we haven't looked very much at praise and fame and their opposites, which we'll explore now, completing our discussion of the eight worldly dharmas. The subject is captured by Shantideva with a characteristically vivid metaphor:

> When their sandcastles collapse,
> Children howl in despair;
> Likewise, when my praise and reputation decline,
> My mind becomes like a little child.

We live in a culture where people seem prepared to go to ever more desperate lengths to achieve their fifteen minutes of fame. A flick through the staple fodder of TV gameshows and competitions, where contestants are rewarded for being bitchy or boorish or otherwise humiliating themselves, suggests there are no depths to which some people will not sink just to get on TV. Much of the online world also seems devoted to our hunger for recognition. Why do so many of us feel the need to sign up hundreds of "friends" on social-networking sites when we really have no idea who they are? Why do we feel such a strong need to be known and recognized?

It's not as if being famous is a true cause of happiness. There are many examples of global celebrities who were obviously far from happy and healthy, people for whom fame not only failed to provide a sense of fulfillment and inner peace but almost certainly contributed to their unhappiness. After Michael Jackson's death, one of the themes that emerged from friends and minders was how isolating fame had been for him. How understandably suspicious he had become of other people's motives. How life's simple pleasures, like going out for a meal with friends, had long been an impossibility.

ATTITUDE NOT DEGREE

It's the way we experience something that matters more than the thing itself. Just as the proverb tells us that love of money, rather than money itself, is the root of all evil, so too it's the attitude we have toward recognition and fame that determines how it affects us.

The challenge for Dharma practitioners in all of this is not to lose sight of the fact that the wonderful "me" we are concerned about here is the false one—just an invention. The person in whose appearance, job title, high-status possessions, and reputation we invest so much time and energy cannot be found when we sit down and look for him or her. That one is nothing more than a projection of our own mind—a projection in which most other people have surprisingly little interest, and almost certainly don't share.

This is not to dismiss the value of having a good reputation or of being well thought of. In fact, the Dharma tells us to cultivate a high regard for our superiors, among other reasons because this is a cause for us to enjoy being held in high regard ourselves. Enjoying a good reputation, like possessing wealth and power, enables us to achieve positive things we couldn't do if people thought badly of us or if we had no resources. Just as earlier in the book we looked at how having material goals is very helpful so long as we don't allow ourselves to become too attached to them, being well thought of is also beneficial, as long as we see it for the illusion-like game that it is.

THE BENEFITS OF CRITICISM

Our main challenge is that we're so used to thinking of our false selves as real that other people's approval of this notional identity reinforces it. Far from challenging our erroneous view, their admiration has the opposite effect.

Shantideva makes exactly this point, underlining how praise and approval fuel our experience of samsara—then going on, in typically counterintuitive style, to explain why we should be thankful to those who criticize us.

Praise and so forth distract me,
And also undermine my disillusion with cyclic existence;
I start to envy those who have good qualities,
And all the very best is destroyed.

Therefore, are not those who are closely involved
In destroying my praise and the like,
Also involved in protecting me
From falling into the unfortunate realms?

This is a classic piece of mind-training advice from Shantideva, ever ready to reframe a negative experience as a positive! By reminding us how our concerns about reputation act to bind us all the more tightly to the very view of a self-existent reality from which we're trying to break free, he highlights the "protective" benefits of being criticized. One thing to understand, perhaps, but quite another to remember next time a family member or work colleague takes us to task!

In these lines Shantideva also identifies one effect on our fragile ego of hearing others praised—envy. The reaction seems childish, as indeed it is. We all know how much care we have to take when praising one individual in a group of kids so as not to make all the others feel bad about themselves. It's as though approval is a form of limited currency, and if some people have it, others, by default, do not.

That grand old man of American letters, Gore Vidal, once dryly observed that "It's not enough to succeed—others must fail," a brutal sentiment that applies to public acclaim as much as anything. We might like to think we're immune from such pettiness, and that we're only too happy to see others praised for their sterling qualities or a job well done. But which of us hasn't been irked to see someone we believe to be thoroughly undeserving lavished with praise? Especially when those expressing the approval are people we admire.

We may also like to think Buddhist monks are immune to such jealousies, but from what Shantideva tells us, clearly not. Describing exactly such a scenario, he goes on to ridicule any envy felt by Dharma practitioners toward others when our supposed motivation is no less than to help others become fully enlightened buddhas.

When people describe my own good qualities
I want others to be happy too,
But when they describe the good qualities of others
I do not wish to be happy myself.

If I wish for all sentient beings to become
Buddhas worshipped throughout the three realms,
Then why am I tormented
When I see them receiving merely mundane respect?

Traditional teachings suggest that instead of allowing ourselves to feel "tormented" when others receive approval, by cultivating a sense of happiness for them we create the causes to enjoy the future experience of being approved. When we envy others their fame or good reputation we experience unhappiness at the time, and by empowering such delusions we also reinforce negative longer term consequences.

APPLYING THE "WONDERFUL ME" FILTER

The way we handle praise, criticism, and reputation is an important subject because it underlies so many of our interactions with others. If we're not aware of it, it's interesting to tune in to this aspect of our encounters. When we talk to others in the workplace or socially, how much of the conversation is subtly, or not so subtly, all about me? How much do we, or those around us, seek to assert ourselves, looking for recognition or endorsement? To what extent do we turn conversations in a particular direction because we want to tell people things that will make us seem more successful, daring, popular, knowledgeable, holy, up-to-the-minute, or whatever image it is we're trying to project?

When we start listening to our own conversations with a "wonderful me" filter, the result can be revealing, even embarrassing. And when we listen to others seeking our endorsement or approval, after a while the content of what they're saying just becomes noise as we realize we're dealing with people who, like us—sometimes even more than us—just want to feel loved.

Given that just about everyone we come into contact with has such needs, how should Dharma practitioners respond to them? With love and compassion, is the short answer. Instead of trying to impress them with our own wonderfulness, our challenge is to show appreciation of theirs. Far from trying to assert ourselves as something special, we should follow the example set by the Dalai Lama—*we* should do the bowing.

Significantly, this is exactly the same advice given by Western interpersonal gurus since Dale Carnegie, whose guidance resonates with Dharma teachings: humility, personal warmth, and showing an appreciation for others provide a far more solid foundation for positive relationships than their opposites.

And when we do make mistakes, which is inevitable because we're human, people are far more likely to forgive us for coming clean immediately than if we try to cover up. This particular advice was given to me by a boss early in my career and I've found it very useful. When I've mistakenly sent emails to the wrong people— a potentially hazardous business given that a lot of my email listings are for journalists; when I've erred in my financial calculations; when I forget people's names—a particular blind spot with me—I have found that most people will accept an immediate and genuine apology, and the relationship can move on. After all, if you describe your own behavior as idiotic, deeply regrettable, and something you'll do your best not to repeat, what is left for your critic to say? Or as Shantideva puts it:

Although others may do something wrong,
I should transform it into a fault of my own;
But should I do something even slightly wrong,
I shall openly admit it to many people.

By further describing the renown of others,
I should make it outshine my own.
Just like the lowest kind of servant,
I should employ myself for the benefit of all.

Exercise

For a period of one or two days, apply a "wonderful me" filter to all your conversations. Try to become aware of any tendency you may have to hint or tell people things to make yourself seem more successful, interesting, knowledgeable, well-traveled, and so on.

▶ Notice the way that others use conversation for the same purpose.

▶ Also be aware of how you respond to criticism, direct and implied. If your usual reaction is to become defensive, experiment with the opposite by agreeing with your critic. If appropriate, express regret and the determination never to let the offending action happen again. Observe any changes in the dynamics of the conversation.

▶ Try letting "the renown of others" outshine yours. If you're not in the habit of praising other people's personal or professional qualities, experiment with doing this appropriately, both directly and through a third party. Observe how it feels to do this.

17

A Code of Conduct for Awakening Beings

As we approach the end of this tour through the highlights of Shantideva's *Guide*, I'd like to share with you a few of his verses that are personal favorites but which we haven't covered so far. Some of these verses touch on themes we have already explored, while others cover new ground. Their choice is necessarily subjective. But between them they encapsulate what in modern parlance we might call a "code of conduct" for aspirant bodhisattvas—or awakening beings. They provide a summary of key Dharma teachings to guide us in imbuing our daily lives with greater value and transcendent purpose.

STEERING AWAY FROM ARMCHAIR BUDDHISM

The first of these focuses on the importance of action over thought. Westerners coming to Buddhism almost always find that it provides a feast for the intellect, a smorgasbord of fascinating ideas and concepts that are refreshingly new but also resonate with us at a deeper level. Trying to assimilate all this new material and develop a coherent understanding of the overall Dharma path is an ongoing process because as our experience develops, so does our understanding. The two mutually support our spiritual evolution and ultimate transformation. But we need to be aware of the risk of becoming an "armchair Buddhist"—that is, someone who understands, knows, or delights in Buddhist ideas, but who does little or nothing to put them into practice.

Armchair Buddhists aren't difficult to find. Most of us need only get up and go to the nearest mirror to find someone whose intellectual understanding by far outstrips their willingness to actually do more to help others, develop greater empathy for those experiencing hardship, or apply their backside to a meditation cushion. In the presence of great lamas such as Geshe Loden, I sometimes have the feeling that at a fundamental level I already know all that I need to know to become a more compassionate and loving person. So what's holding me back?

While this challenge is by no means exclusive to Westerners, some of us have the cultural handicap of coming from religious traditions where your stated convictions are all-important. In some religious communities, if you can eloquently articulate what you believe, and support your argument with scriptural references, you are held in high regard as a committed believer.

In the Dharma, by contrast, stated beliefs and intellectual knowledge are only support acts for the main event, which is what you actually *do*. An image traditionally used to illustrate this point is of a man caught in the middle of a thunderstorm who finds himself standing outside the mouth of a large dry cave. "I take refuge in the cave! I take refuge in the cave!" he shouts above the raging elements, while remaining outside all the time, getting soaked through.

Caught in our own storms of samsara, afflicted by the delusions and conditioning that are the root cause of our dissatisfaction, it's equally pointless for us to declare ourselves to be Buddhists with a heartfelt wish to become enlightened for the sake of all sentient beings, while doing little to make that happen. Much better to say nothing and actually start putting the six perfections, for example, into practice. One of Shantideva's verses I particularly like sums this up in the following way:

> Therefore, I shall put this way of life into actual practice,
> For what can be achieved by merely talking about it?
> Will the sick receive benefit
> Merely by reading the medical texts?

Which of us would opt to only read up about an illness from which we were suffering, or to only study medical prescriptions, when we had the opportunity to take the correct medicine? Having outlined a bodhisattva way of life Shantideva asks us bluntly, "What can be achieved by merely talking about it?"

THE THIEF-LIKE PRACTITIONER

Accepting the emphasis on action rather than thoughts and words, we're also encouraged to follow a particular approach, which Shantideva illustrates beautifully in this next verse. Never one to shy away from a challenging image, he suggests we behave, in one respect at least, like thieves:

> The stork, the cat, and the thief,
> By moving silently and carefully,
> Accomplish what they desire to do;
> A Bodhisattva, too, should always behave this way.

I always smile inwardly when I read that verse. Apart from finding the "thief" reference amusing, as a cat-lover I know just what he means. Often when working at my desk I'll turn to discover that our tabby, Mambo—who, weighing in at eight kilograms, is a feline of substance—has materialized on the console right next to me without my even being aware of it. In putting the Dharma into practice, Shantideva advises, we should also take the same care to achieve our purposes without drawing attention to ourselves.

Just as talk without action is baggage we need to dump, so too is the wish to bring our good deeds to the attention of others.

If we are vegetarians, teetotallers, or hold other principles arising from our Dharma practice, we shouldn't make a big deal of them. And we especially shouldn't use the Dharma itself to draw attention to ourselves.

A PEACEFUL HEART

Many of us are pretty high achievers in the field of worry. Some of us, with years of practice under our belt, are so good at it that we do it all the time with little conscious effort. We keep relationship worries, work problems, financial concerns, and health crises—not only those affecting us, but our nearest and dearest as well—bubbling away on the backburner as a constant presence, ready to boil over at any moment.

While the Dharma provides a range of antidotes to deal with worry, those of us inclined to take our (false) selves rather too seriously may allow our Dharma practice itself to become a source of stress. Through force of habit we may co-opt certain teachings or set ourselves expectations that create only more worry rather than less. We may, for example, worry about the extent to which we are slaves to our desires, or how we act out of irritation and anger before we even realize that's what we've done. We can get stressed out that we don't understand the concept of emptiness or that our meditative concentration is really bad.

Enough already!

At the most basic level, the whole point of the Dharma is to help us feel happier and experience greater inner peace—not to give us another stick with which to beat ourselves. If actions rather than words is one of Shantideva's core instructions, and discretion rather than attention-seeking is another, then we also need to embrace equanimity. If we are worriers, this involves being gentle with ourselves and learning to let go.

Which brings us to one of the most quoted verses in Shantideva's *Guide*:

> Why be unhappy about something
> If it can be remedied?
> And what is the use of being unhappy about something
> If it cannot be remedied?

I'm seldom able to read that verse without rereading it. And rerereading it. I find something extraordinarily compelling about it. Its unassailable logic is part of its power, as is the clarity of its meaning. I like the perfect balance it presents as well as the economy of expression.

In our striving to lead more mindful and purposeful lives, we need to do so with a light heart and easy step. There will always be things we should have said or done that we failed to do, and things we did that we later wish we hadn't. But we need to let go. There is no place for guilt in Buddhism. Concretizing thoughts and actions from the past and carrying them around like a self-inflicted burden achieves nothing. The positive response is to feel regret about past actions and to resolve never to repeat them.

This verse has application well beyond our Dharma practice. It is an aphorism for living and deserves to be on fridge magnets, screen savers, and bumper stickers everywhere. How much unhappiness do we inflict on ourselves because we forget the simple truth of this core instruction? Forgetfulness is not always the reason—we may wish, very deeply, to stop the inner torment caused by our minds constantly returning to a subject of fear, or heartache, or bitterness, but find it difficult to turn our thoughts to more positive things. It would be unusual for us to experience rejection, adversity, or other trauma and not feel deeply. But in the aftermath of the event, once the immediate intensity of the experience has passed, Shantideva's verse offers a calming and powerful antidote to help restore our balance.

A SMILING FACE

The development of our inner equanimity should be reflected in the way we behave outwardly, according to this bodhisattva code of conduct:

Now, while there is freedom to act,
I should always present a smiling face
And cease to frown and look angry;
I should be a friend and counsel of the world.

I find the first line of this verse especially meaningful—the reminder not to take our current freedom for granted. Though we may feel constrained by circumstances, in reality we enjoy freedoms beyond the wildest dreams of most beings. Our renovation plans may be sabotaged by petty officials, our love lives dashed by fickle partners, our careers jeopardized by heartless employers, but that doesn't mean we have to turn ourselves into victims or grumble-bums.

For those of us who have a tendency to live in the world of our thoughts, this verse is also a salutary reminder to get out of our heads and be nice to the people around us. To smile. Studies have shown how much more highly we rate the attractiveness of others when they smile, and that we can also tell the difference between an expression where only the mouth is smiling, and one where the eyes are too.

THE PRACTICE IS THE REWARD

There is one reality TV show I love watching—*The Secret Millionaire*. In each episode a multimillionaire goes undercover in a poor community, pretending to take part in a documentary about finding work, but all the while trying to identify individuals and groups in the area who would especially benefit from a cash donation. The individuals and groups are usually people who are doing it tough themselves, but who nevertheless make huge personal sacrifices to help those around them, for example by running community centers to give teenagers in urban wastelands somewhere stimulating to go, delivering groceries to the destitute, providing outings to elderly people who wouldn't otherwise get out of the house, and so on.

Even though the formula of the show is the same, and the audience watching knows more or less what's going to happen at the end, there is something mesmerizing and usually deeply moving about seeing people in the most difficult circumstances having their hard work bountifully rewarded. Their reactions to being handed large checks range from disbelief to tears of gratitude—sometimes they don't feel worthy of the gift and have to be persuaded to accept it.

But the emotions of the millionaires are just as interesting. At the beginning of the show their philanthropy is an ideal, a concept, but by the time they actually make their donation, the people they help have become a living reality and a personal bond has been formed.

In every case I've seen, the millionaires have described the experience as deeply moving. Frequently they say it's the best thing they've ever done. By the end of each show they—the donors—are quite often also in tears. And from the follow-up segments taken weeks or months later, it's evident that the bonds formed by the program have endured well beyond it. In one particular case, a self-made millionaire said she'd enjoyed a closer sense of social connection during her week "undercover" than she had in many years living in splendid isolation. Several other entrepreneurial millionaires said the program had motivated them to go home and make even more money so that they had more to give away.

Whatever the disadvantaged people get out of the experience, it would seem that the no-longer-secret millionaires get as much if not more. It is exactly the same with our Dharma practice. Whether it's material generosity that we're practicing, just like on TV, or one of the other perfections, virtue is its own reward. Or as Shantideva puts it:

⁓

Therefore, although working for the benefit of others,
I should not be conceited or consider myself wonderful.
And because of the joy there is in solely doing this,
I should have no hope for any ripening effect.

By "ripening effect" Shantideva means the positive conditioning, or karma, we have created. To me it is a very significant statement that, in seeking to become happier and more awakened beings, we should do so without future karmic rewards as a motivator. If we do so, we risk our practice becoming calculated and self-focused, rather than spontaneous and grounded in the understanding that there is, in fact, no independent self. Like the secret millionaires, our aspiration is to be secret bodhisattvas, going about what we do without attracting attention to ourselves, or with the expectation of future reward.

LIVING EXAMPLES

In Buddhism we are fortunate to have many great examples, men and women who show that the bodhisattva way of life isn't some hypothetical ideal to which we may one day aspire, but is rather a blueprint for living. Among these are my teacher, Les Sheehy, and my teacher's teacher, Geshe Loden, from whom I have received a number of initiations and who is therefore my "root guru."

Born in 1924, Geshe Loden became a monk in the Gelugpa tradition at the age of seven, and received his full training at Sera-Je Monastery in Tibet, one of the three great monasteries in Tibet prior to the Chinese invasion. The discipline of training in the days before television, email, and mobile phones was austere, and from these rigorous beginnings Geshe-la went on to achieve the highest possible degree of Geshe Lharampa. After the Chinese invasion of Tibet in 1959, he made the dangerous crossing of the Himalayas on foot in order to continue his Dharma studies, subsequently achieving a master's degree in Vajrayana Buddhism and an Acharya degree from Varanasi Sanskrit University in India.

As one of the most highly qualified lamas in the Tibetan Buddhist tradition, one of whose teachers was also a tutor to His Holiness the Dalai Lama, it would have been understandable if Geshe-la had decided to remain in India, where his future as a leading figure within one of the major monasteries, being re-formed in exile, would have been assured. He was already caring for about 150 Tibetan students from all four orders of Tibetan Buddhism. But at fifty-two years of age, a time of life when many people's minds turn to thoughts of retirement, Geshe-la decided to do something completely different. Traveling to Australia at the request of the ebullient Lama Yeshe for a three-year teaching program, he arrived with just ten dollars in his shoe, and a short Tibetan–English translation list of essential phrases like "Where is the bathroom please?"

By all accounts, his early days in Australia weren't easy. Quite apart from having to learn a whole new language, he also found himself in a very different community. His new students were not like the respectful monks back in India but included hippies, surfers, and rebels without a cause who had somehow rolled into the center in Queensland. Geshe-la, who as a senior lama back in India would have had a retinue of staff, not only gave them teachings but would even hand-deliver hot meals to their rooms when some of them couldn't be bothered showing up at the dining room.

But such was the powerful connection he established with his Australian students that when his three-year teaching term was up and he returned to India, there was a clamorous demand for his return. When he did so, after consultation with the Dalai Lama and his two tutors, it was with the decision to make Australia his home and dedicate himself to the development of the Dharma in the West.

Stories are legion of the strange but wonderful events that go on around Geshe-la. These range from the audaciously commercial—like the time he insisted the Tibetan Buddhist Society put in the winning bid at an auction for a sprawling property on the outskirts of Melbourne, now its Australian HQ, even though no one (except Geshe-la) had any idea how the organization could possibly afford the monthly repayments—to the unnervingly personal, such as the time he happened to be standing at the gate of the property when one of the residents returned home still stewing after an angry encounter at work. Geshe-la gestured that he should wind down the window of his car, and before the resident could say a word Geshe-la was treating him to a lecture on the perfection of patience and treating one's professional peers with respect.

Oops!

Having arrived in the West with no knowledge of English, one of Geshe-la's great achievements has been the writing of nine books in the language, setting out the entire Tibetan Buddhist path from sutra school teachings through to the most esoteric, highest yoga tantra instructions. He has distilled the essence of voluminous Tibetan texts into pithy instructions previously unavailable in the West. These writings are of incalculable benefit to English-speaking students, who can now enjoy access to clear and precise directions from a lama whose unrivaled scholarly understanding is matched by his actions in daily life.

Geshe-la also built the first traditional Tibetan Buddhist temple in Australia at the Tibetan Buddhist Society property in Melbourne. He oversaw every aspect of its creation from fundraising to architecture, to the great many internal details required for authenticity, and the result is a uniquely inspiring building of great beauty and purpose, which was officially opened and blessed by the Dalai Lama, and is now used daily.

How many of us would be similarly motivated in our fifties to move right out of our comfort zone to a very different culture on the other side of the world, to teach, write, and build centers for the benefit of the locals? To do so with a peaceful heart and a jovial expression and without any thought of personal reward? When Geshe-la is asked about his activities, he simply says they are repayment to the Australian people for all the food and water, accommodation, and kindness he has received.

Inspired by Geshe-la's example, two of his early students, Les and Margaret Sheehy, returned to Les's home town of Perth, and in 1981 Les began offering Dharma teachings in the lounge room of their home. Just as was the case with Geshe-la's modest beginnings in Australia, more exciting possibilities gradually emerged—first a self-sustaining center, separate from the Sheehy family home, and then a much larger property with the potential to be developed into a retreat center.

Through the past three decades, the commitment of Les and Marg to the Tibetan Buddhist Society has been consistent and untiring. Whatever the demands of running small businesses and bringing up a family, rain or shine Les is always at class on time to deliver that night's teachings—frequently three sessions a week. Retreats— whether for just a weekend or the three-week variety—always run on schedule, thanks to Marg's administrative zeal. And the most recent development has been the construction of a traditional Tibetan

Buddhist temple just outside Perth in Herne Hill, using the same floor plan as the one in Melbourne—the first of its kind in Western Australia, and only the second in the country.

Like Geshe-la, Les's Dharma practice is as much about action as words. He inspires students like me not only because of his understanding of the Dharma and down-to-earth teachings, which would be reason enough, but also because he walks the talk, and is always willing to help or give advice with humility and humor.

At the official opening of the Perth temple, Les made it clear that the building was the result of many people's generosity and hard work. For his own part, he said, he regarded his contribution as repayment for the kindness and inspiration he continues to receive from Geshe-la.

And so the lineage is carried forward, from master to student, each seeking to repay the kindness of those who have taught them and those they live among. When we accept a lama as our teacher—an undertaking we are encouraged to make only with great care—we become part of a spiritual family, a dynasty of successive masters tracing back to the time of Shakyamuni Buddha. Within the four branches of the Tibetan Buddhist family there are numerous role models we can choose from, awakening beings who embody Shantideva's code of conduct, both in words and deeds.

For those of us who develop an interest in following the path, our good fortune in finding ourselves living near teachers like Geshe Loden and Les Sheehy cannot be overstated. And for those of us who accept the explanation of consciousness as an unceasing continuum that flows from one lifetime to the next, the possibilities become even more extraordinary. As trainee bodhisattvas, we cultivate the wish to achieve enlightenment for the sake of all beings. Realized masters, who have achieved this state and who consciously choose to be reborn in a particular time and place, choose their rebirth for only one reason—to help us to enlightenment! We may take up Dharma classes thinking that we have found a teacher we like and trust, but what if it's rather the case that he or she has found us? What if we established a connection with this being in a previous lifetime and, through compassion, he or she has made it possible for us not so much to "discover" Buddhism as to return to a once familiar path? This, perhaps, is the reason that the Dharma teachings resonate with so many of us. We may have been born in the West this time round, but maybe it has not always been so.

Like ripples expanding from a stone cast into a tranquil lake, the teachings pass from teacher to student, each carried further by the energy of actions. Touched by the current of successive waves, perhaps in successive lives, each of us has the opportunity to transmit the energy further, to expand its impact until such time that all beings in universal space realize their own true nature.

Analytical Meditation

Before beginning the analytical meditation, stabilize your mind as usual with a breath meditation exercise.

▶ Consider your attitude to the core Buddhist teaching on the perfection of generosity (see Chapter 6). Explore how this could be the cause of a happier and more meaningful life. How actively do you practice this perfection? What is holding you back from pursuing it more actively?

▶ Consider your attitude to the core Buddhist teaching on the perfection of ethics (see Chapter 7). Explore how this could be the cause of a happier and more meaningful life. How actively do you practice this perfection? What is holding you back from pursuing it more actively?

▶ Consider your attitude to the core Buddhist teaching on the perfection of patience (see Chapter 8). Explore how this could be the cause of a happier and more meaningful life. How actively do you practice this perfection? What is holding you back from pursuing it more actively?

▸ Cultivate the wish to apply the Dharma practices more actively to actions of body, speech, and mind. Hold this wish single-pointedly.

Suggestion: Write out Shantideva's famous verse on equanimity on a card or sticky label and put it somewhere you will frequently see it. Try to apply it to situations you face in your own daily life.

⁓

Why be unhappy about something
If it can be remedied?
And what is the use of being unhappy about something
If it cannot be remedied?

18

Dedication

THE FINAL CHAPTER of Shantideva's *Guide* is a Dedication. It comprises fifty-eight verses in which Shantideva articulates the mind of enlightenment in some of his most beautiful and transcendent stanzas. It seems fitting to end this commentary on the same theme.

I hope you have enjoyed the tour through my subjective "best of" Shantideva. Perhaps we have touched on some interesting concepts or practices to which you can return in your own time to consider in greater depth. Maybe among the reframing techniques and psychological devices Shantideva offers you have found one or two that particularly resonate. In particular, his famous teachings on emptiness, unpacked in Chapters 14 and 15, may have stimulated your own meditation about the way that you and everything around you truly exist.

Most of all, it is my heartfelt wish that *Enlightenment to Go* may encourage you to look beyond the verses quoted here, which comprise less than a tenth of the total number, and explore a lot more of *A Guide to the Bodhisattva's Way of Life*.

In relating some of my encounters with inspiring teachers such as Geshe Loden, Les Sheehy, and Tenzin Palmo, I hope I may have encouraged you to regard Tibetan Buddhism as more than a repository of helpful teachings and practices, but also as a wonderful living tradition, a spiritual lineage of which we can all become a part—and to which we may perhaps have already belonged in the past. And in sharing stories from my own life, I also hope I have shown the very real application and benefits of Dharma teachings to all of us who lead typically busy lives.

So auspicious are Shantideva's verses that when Patrul Rinpoche taught them in the vicinity of Dzogchen Shri Singha for several years in succession in the nineteenth century, it is said that large numbers of yellow flowers, each with between thirty and fifty petals, spontaneously blossomed. They became known as "bodhicharyavatara flowers."

Letting go of our attachment is probably the greatest challenge that each one of us faces. And the object to which we all have such deep, powerful, and enduring attachment is, of course, our own "self." Once we have penetrated the understanding that this self has no real existence, and that it is the great ghost from which arises all our unhappiness, it becomes easier to loosen the bindings of our attachment. To gradually free ourselves from our obsession with "me," "myself," and "I" and focus more on others. To cultivate, step by step, the great love and great compassion that support the heartfelt practice of bodhichitta—a true source of abiding happiness.

I can think of no more inspiring illumination of bodhichitta than Shantideva's Dedication. In it he offers whatever merit has been achieved by his writing of the *Guide* for the benefit of all living beings. He does this not as some hypothetical exercise or ritualistic way of ending a text, but with a heartfelt conviction that's evident in the poignancy of his language:

May the blind see forms,
May the deaf hear sounds,
And just as it was with Mayadevi,
May pregnant women give birth without pain.

May the naked find clothing,
The hungry find food,
May the thirsty find water
And delicious drinks.

May the poor find wealth,
Those weak with sorrow find joy;
May the forlorn find new hope,
Constant happiness, and prosperity.

May all who are sick and ill
Quickly be freed from their illness,
And may every disease in the world
Never occur again.

While some of these verses evoke the Christian Prayer of Saint Francis, or Jesus's Beatitudes from the Sermon on the Mount, Shantideva's scope is even broader, envisioning the end of suffering and the attainment of enlightenment for beings from every realm of consciousness. Among his dazzling range of examples are the transformation of hellish states, projected as forests of razor-sharp leaves turning into pleasure groves, burning coals becoming heaps of jewels, and rains of molten lava transforming into rains of flowers. He describes animals living free from the fear of being eaten by one another, lost travelers finding their way, lower life forms being reborn in higher realms, and all embodied creatures uninterruptedly hearing the sound of Dharma issuing from birds, trees, beams of light, and space itself.

Evoking a world that contemporary book reviewers might describe as magical realism, Shantideva's vision is not, however, an exercise in ninth-century literary fiction so much as a personal manifesto. In the deeply moving ending to the book he wrote to motivate his own Dharma practice, Shantideva makes it clear that the immeasurable and transcendent purpose of freeing every living being from suffering is a challenge for which he takes direct responsibility—"I alone shall do this."

I can think of no more motivating way to end this book than with one of Shantideva's own final verses. A stanza that expresses the ultimate purpose of compassion, the extraordinary vision of bodhichitta, in some of the most selfless, challenging, and inspiring lines of the whole book. It is a verse we might work toward making our own heartfelt purpose too, a statement of intent unrivaled for the sheer scope of its limitless altruism.

For as long as space endures
And for as long as living beings remain,
Until then may I, too, abide
To dispel the misery of the world.

Appendix

How to Meditate*

MEDITATION IS THE PATHWAY to wisdom. As explained in the introduction, the accumulation of knowledge at an intellectual level can
be helpful, but unless this information changes the way we think or
act, its impact on our life is questionable. A frequently used illustration of this point, as mentioned earlier, is that of the sick man who
spends hours studying the label of his medical prescription and who
complains that he never gets any better. Knowing about the medicine is one thing: taking it is quite another.

Meditation helps us understand ideas at a deeper level. When we
subdue our minds through meditation, we create the possibility of
seeing things as they really are, free of the agitation or dullness that
afflicts us for much of the day. As illustrated in Chapter 13, a glass of
swirling stormwater may be cloudy and agitated but left to stand for
a while will settle, providing a clear medium through which things
can be seen clearly.

Many of the meditations provided throughout this book have
been designed as the focus of analytical meditation, the purpose of
which is to develop our understanding of a subject to the point at
which we fully understand it—we realize it at the most profound

---

*This appendix is adapted from Chapter 4 of *Hurry Up and Meditate*, Allen &
Unwin, 2007.

level. Even if we understood a concept before on an intellectual basis, this is qualitatively different from knowing it directly, in much the same way that no amount of watching movies or reading books can compare to an intensely life-changing experience such as falling in love.

And just as our whole world is unlikely to change on the very first date we ever go on, the process of meditation is one that requires time, patience, and repeated effort. It is a process that will almost certainly cause us moments of intense frustration, as we come to terms with the reality of our out-of-control minds. But it is probably also the most life-affirming thing we can do. Practiced regularly, even the most mediocre meditation sessions deliver powerfully positive physical and psychological benefits, as described in my book *Hurry Up and Meditate*. And from a Dharma perspective, meditation offers the only way to realize our own true nature; to experience the reality that our consciousness is free of obscurations and concepts and is in the nature of boundless clarity and abiding peace. So profound is this sense of reconnection that many different meditators find themselves choosing the same phrase to describe it: meditation is like coming home.

WHERE AND WHEN?

A quiet room with the door shut, first thing in the morning, is recommended for meditation. Until we get to be very advanced meditators, able to withdraw from external stimuli, it helps to be able to shut them out physically if at all possible. And first thing in the morning suits most people because after a good night's sleep we tend to be more refreshed, and our minds less cluttered, than in the evening.

If there is no possibility that you'll be able to meditate until you get the kids off to school, or even before the end of the day, don't use this as a reason not to start meditating. And if the laundry room or garden shed is the only place to avoid noise and interruptions, then welcome to your new meditation sanctuary!

FOR HOW LONG?

I would suggest you start with ten or fifteen minutes. All the meditations in this book can certainly be completed within this time. It's important that meditation is not a chore for you but something you want to do, at the very least a matter of curiosity, and hopefully developing into the source of greatly enhanced inner peace. Ideally you will end a session feeling positively about what you've just done, instead of relieved it's all over. By starting with bite-sized chunks, you will want to increase the length of your sessions quite naturally as your concentration improves. While some meditators put a watch in front of them to keep track of time, if you find this creates a distraction you may like to use an alarm clock. I have a friend who does this—leaving the clock in the next room so she doesn't get too startled when it goes off!

POSTURE

The seven-point meditation posture has been used for at least two and a half millennia and across most meditative traditions. Before assuming the following posture, for the sake of comfort you should remove your shoes and loosen any tight clothing such as belts and ties. Ideal meditation clothing is simply a T-shirt or sweatshirt, shorts or tracksuit pants, or a comfortable dressing gown.

If you can't adopt the posture outlined, for example because of an injury, troublesome joints, or some other physical disability, this doesn't mean you can't meditate. As outlined below, a normal seating posture will also provide a perfectly useful basis to begin. Even if you are confined to bed, as long as you are able to maintain a straight spine, you have the most essential element to begin meditation.

1. **Sit cross-legged on a cushion on the floor.** The purpose of the cushion, which should be firm, is to tilt the pelvis so it's easier and more comfortable to sit for a longer period of time. Having three points of contact—the butt and both thighs—provides good stability. While meditation cushions are generally available online, in specialist shops, or from meditation centers, to get started you may want to try out a few different cushion alternatives from your home until you find one that provides comfortable but firm support.

   Some meditators prefer to use a low wooden stool on which they sit, essentially in a kneeling position, with their legs tucked behind them. Alternatively, they kneel astride a cushion. If sitting cross-legged is very difficult or painful for you, these postures provide another option.

   If neither the cross-legged nor meditation stool posture is possible for you, you can simply sit on a chair or bench. In this case it's recommended that you plant your feet flat on the floor for good stability.

   From time to time, whether sitting cross-legged or in a chair, you may want to alternate which foot/leg is in front. This helps even out any imbalance in your posture.

   Some meditators use a mat, rug, or carpet under their cushion, so that their knees don't press into the hard floor. However, this pressure is only likely to become painful if you have long meditation sessions, which will not apply to begin with.

2. **Rest your hands in your lap.** The three most common hand positions are:
   ▸ resting palm down, one on each knee

- resting one on each knee, palm up. The tips of the thumb and the index or middle finger of each hand may touch
- resting with the right hand in the left, palms upward, like a pair of shells, and thumb tips meeting approximately at the level of the navel

Most teachers and groups have their own preferences, but I am not aware that any one of the above alternatives has advantages over the others. Try each out for yourself and see which feels most comfortable.

3. **Keep your back straight.** Of all the posture instructions, this is the most important because your spine is the main conduit of your central nervous system. Your back should be straight, but following its natural tendency to be slightly curved in the lower back. When you meditate, it's important to keep the spine relaxed, neither slumped nor artificially straight. This instruction holds true whether one is sitting on a meditation cushion or a regular chair, or even lying in bed.

4. **Relax your shoulders.** Ideally they should be slightly rolled back, down, and resting level. Your arms will therefore rest loosely by your sides, not held tightly in.

5. **Tilt the head slightly forward.** Keeping the head evenly balanced, tuck your chin slightly inward. Tilt angle can be a useful control. If your mind is going particularly crazy, try deepening the tilt, moving your face down toward the floor. If, on the other hand, you start to feel very sleepy, try lifting your head, like a sunflower, to get rid of drowsiness.

6. **Relax your face.** Your mouth, jaw, and tongue should be neither slack nor tight and your brow should be smooth. By placing the

tip of the tongue behind your front teeth, you can help control the build-up of saliva.

7. **Close your eyes.** Not too tightly, just gently resting your eyelids. While keeping your eyes half-opened, unfocused, and gazing downward is recommended for some kinds of meditation, at the beginning most people find that keeping the eyes fully closed is better for eliminating distraction.

YOUR MEDITATION OBJECTIVE

To give structure to your practice it's a good discipline to start with a clear affirmation, which you use both to begin and end the session. This should encapsulate what you're wishing to achieve from meditation in a way that's powerful to you. The most commonly used Tibetan Buddhist affirmation, which succinctly combines the three practices of taking refuge, a commitment to practice, and bodhichitta motivation, is as follows:

To the Buddha, Dharma, and Sangha
I go for refuge until becoming enlightened.
By the practice of giving and so on,
May I achieve buddhahood to benefit all beings.

It's useful to learn this affirmation off by heart so you can repeat it three times, eyes closed, at the start of a session. In this way you associate a relaxed physical and psychological state with this verse. Every time you repeat it, the associated state is deepened, enabling you to further develop your calm abiding and concentration. In so doing you are also transforming your practice of meditation into a "perfection" by endowing it with bodhichitta motivation. The perfection of meditation is the fourth perfection.

STABILIZING THE MIND THROUGH
BREATH MEDITATION

The meditations provided in this book include analytical meditation, visualization (such as tonglen), and mindfulness. Before engaging in the meditations outlined, however, it would be useful to first calm the mind through single-pointed concentration. Probably the best meditation practice to achieve this is breath-counting. This is a practice used widely across most meditative traditions, and through all levels, from novice meditators to the most advanced practitioners. There are a number of reasons for this. The breath is a convenient object of meditation because we have no difficulty finding it. Making it the focus of our attention is an entirely natural process. When we do, our breathing tends to slow down quite naturally, thereby slowing our entire metabolism and making us feel more relaxed. And achieving a calm but focused state serves as a very useful stabilization practice.

With the following breath-counting exercise, the objective is to actively shift our focus to the breath. We do this, quite simply, by mentally counting each breath on exhalation, for a set number of breaths—typically between four and twenty-one—before repeating the exercise.

The process is as follows: place the focus of your attention at the tip of your nostrils, like a sentry, and observe the flow of air as you breathe in and then out. Ideally all the air you inhale and exhale should be through your nose, with your mouth kept firmly shut. However, if you have a condition that makes this difficult, by all means part your lips slightly to inhale and exhale.

As you breathe out, count the number "one" in your mind, then on the next out-breath "two," then "three," "four," and so on. Don't focus on anything else—for example, don't follow the air traveling into your lungs, or your rib cage rising and falling. Don't allow your mind to wander from the tip of your nostrils. And try not to fall asleep!

What we're setting out to achieve is really very simple—but not necessarily easy. The best way to discover this for yourself is to try it. Pretty soon, you'll find all kinds of thoughts demanding your attention. Even though you've set this time aside for meditating, habitual agitation or drowsiness may very soon kick in, to the point that you may discover you can't even count to ten!

This is called gross agitation and it happens to us all. When it does, once you realize you've lost the object of meditation—the breath—simply refocus on it and start back at one again. Try not to beat yourself up about your lapse of attention or fall into the trap of believing that you're one of the few people who can't meditate. Your experience is, in fact, totally normal. Our minds are amazingly inventive at coming up with reasons to avoid self-discipline: you shouldn't buy into any of them!

If you experience a lot of gross agitation in the beginning, don't even attempt a count of ten, but see if you can reach four, and only when you feel comfortable with that build up to a regular count of seven. When I first started meditating, for many months my main practice was simply to spend ten minutes each day counting to four. It was a simple practice, but one which provided a very strong foundation and was to have far-reaching effects.

Another tip: when doing this particular meditation you may like to include the word "and" on the in-breaths between numbers. This provides the mind with some extra support between the numbers. However, like the stabilization wheels on a child's first bicycle, you should aim to get rid of the "ands" as your concentration improves.

As this happens, your focus on the breath will become sharper. Try paying more concentrated attention to the detail of your practice. The subtle, physical sensation at the tip of your nostrils as you breathe. The coolness of the air coming in. The warmer sensation as you exhale. You can note the start of each in-breath, how it builds up, then how it tapers off. The gap between in- and out-breaths.

Then the start, middle, and fading away of each exhalation. The much longer gap at the end of each exhalation.

As you progress into a meditation session, your breathing will probably slow, and you'll become more and more conscious of the gaps between out-breath and in-breath. What do you focus on then? Only the absence of breath and the complete relaxation you experience with nothing to distract you, and no demands being put on you. This may not seem an ambitious goal but, rest assured, it is not only profoundly calming, it is also a stepping stone to other, more advanced meditation practices.

ANALYTICAL MEDITATION

Having settled your mind to some extent, then open your eyes to the page of this book on which your chosen analytical meditation is described. It would help if you have the page already open in front of you, so that you don't have to move from your meditation posture to read it. If you need to place the book on a low table or shelf, that may also be useful preparation.

The purpose of analytical meditation is to penetrate the meaning of a specific truth. We sometimes call this "realizing" a particular subject. Each analytical meditation in this book is structured to help lead you, step by step, toward the experience of an idea at a direct or nonconceptual level. This will help complement the intellectual understanding you have acquired by reading about it in the main part of the chapter.

Read each bullet point in turn and think deeply about the meaning of the words. To make the meaning real, it is useful to bring specific ideas and images to mind. In each meditation I have suggested a few of these. But by all means use specific examples that are more personally significant to you.

When you discover that your mind has wandered from the object of the meditation, simply bring it back.

When you reach the final point of each analysis, the specific concept you wish to penetrate, try to let the meaning of the words touch you so deeply that you can allow the words and concepts themselves to fall away. Abide with this meaning as a direct experience, free of words. Sustain this single-pointed, nonconceptual focus for as long as possible.

AGITATION AND DULLNESS

Early on in your meditation practice you will discover the two main obstacles to meditation: agitation and dullness. Each of these exists on a spectrum from major to minor, or from gross to subtle.

Gross agitation is, for example, the recollection, midway between contemplating the rarity of your life of leisure and fortune, that you have failed to transfer sufficient money to cover a check you wrote two days ago. This leads to you imagining the call you're going to have to make to your bank, the endless automatic prompts you're going to have to follow before you finally end up speaking to a human being, the lack of help or support you're likely to receive, the overdraft fee you'll be forced to pay, and the embarrassment of having to call the recipient and reissue a check.

Heart pounding and palms starting to perspire, you suddenly remember—I'm supposed to be meditating! What was I thinking about? My material well-being or the good fortune of having time to meditate? Unable to remember, you have to bring the mind back, gently but firmly, open your eyes, and read the point again. With gross agitation, you've quite simply lost the plot, or to put it more formally, you've lost the object of concentration.

With more subtle agitation you are still able to maintain your analysis, but experience the distraction as background chatter. The more advanced meditator who has failed to transfer money may also have the thought pop into his or her mind, but instead of giving it any attention, such a meditator will continue to focus on counting, not allowing concentration to be disturbed. The thought simply dissolves away.

I once heard the story of a writer who decided that a meditation retreat would be just the thing to stimulate some creative thinking. Arriving at his first session with a pen and brand-new notepad on which he intended jotting down his freshly inspired ideas, he was dismayed when the meditation teacher swooped down, confiscating the tools of his trade. "Our job is to starve our thoughts of attention," the teacher admonished him, "not to develop them!"

This is no easy thing, of course, because it goes against our habitual tendency to focus on a thought before taking that thought in any number of directions. Trying *not* to develop thoughts goes against what we've done all our lives and is actually very hard work.

The other meditation obstacle, dullness, is when our concentration is threatened by sleepiness or heaviness. Gross dullness means discovering that we have nodded off completely. On retreat, the first, post-lunch session of the afternoon is often a time when minds grow dull, postures slide, and it's even been known for snoring to be heard, before familiar neck-snaps back to concentration. Gross dullness, like gross agitation, means the complete interruption of our meditative concentration.

Subtle dullness ranges from a state of deep—and quite possibly enjoyable—relaxation in which we are nevertheless no longer alert and focused, to an even greater state of relaxation that threatens to turn into sleep. Maintaining the clarity of our focus is the main challenge.

When most people start out meditating, they often find they have a tendency to experience one obstacle rather than the other. We should use common sense to try to reduce any external factors—for example, if we are always overwhelmed with tiredness and we're trying to meditate at 9 p.m. every night, could we move our session to an earlier slot? Would a shower beforehand help wake us up?

But apart from trying to get our external environment right, there are two meditation tools that are essential to our practice.

MINDFULNESS AND AWARENESS

Mindfulness means keeping the object of meditation in your mind and not allowing your concentration to stray. In this case, the object is the sensation of the breath entering and leaving your nostrils during preparation, or the subject of your investigation during analytical meditation. Making sure your focus stays where it's supposed to is the application of mindfulness.

Awareness means being watchful of what your mind is actually doing and safeguarding it from wandering. This may seem very similar to mindfulness, but it's subtly and importantly different.

The best illustration I've heard to explain the difference between mindfulness and awareness is what happens when you carry a very full mug of coffee across a room. The surface of the liquid near the rim of the mug could easily spill over, so you are treading with great care. Mindfulness equates to the very close watch you keep on the surface of the coffee to make sure it doesn't spill.

But as you carry the mug, part of your attention is also taking in the bigger picture, making sure you're not about to trip over the dog or bump your elbow against a doorframe. That part of your attention is awareness. While working toward the same objective as mindfulness, it is nevertheless a slightly different aspect of your consciousness.

When I first began to meditate, I really didn't get the difference between mindfulness and awareness. No one had explained the cup of coffee analogy to me—that came much later, at which time it all started making a lot more sense. But at the beginning, I thought that making a distinction between mindfulness and awareness was really a case of splitting hairs—probably because we tend to use the two words interchangeably in everyday life.

It may also be worth mentioning that I had a hard time with subtle agitation too. Did it really exist? Surely you were either focused on something or you weren't? My problem in understanding this concept was quite simply that my own mind was so agitated I had never knowingly experienced subtle agitation. It was all very much at the major, or gross, level. There I'd be, sitting down to concentrate on my breath-counting and, the next thing I knew, I was thinking about next Saturday night. I'd have to start again at one. It was hardly surprising, then, that I thought subtle agitation was up there with Santa and the tooth fairy.

How mindful should we be when we meditate? Probably the best way to answer this is to quote the Buddha himself when he taught meditation to a famous vina player who had become a monk.

"How did you get the best sound out of your vina? Was it when the strings were very tight or when they were very loose?" The Buddha asked him.

"Neither. When they had just the right tension, neither too taut nor too slack."

"Well, it's exactly the same with your mind," said the Buddha.

ENDING THE SESSION

It's useful to end a meditation session with a structured close that also reinforces your ultimate purpose. The affirmation you use at the end of the session can reinforce the one with which you began it. Here is one dedication verse, translated by my own root guru Geshe Loden:

> By this virtue may all beings
> Complete the collections of wisdom and merit
> And attain the two holy bodies
> Arisen from wisdom and merit.

May the precious, superior mind of enlightenment
Be generated in those who have not yet generated it,
And not decrease in those who have developed it,
But increase continuously.

The "two holy bodies" of the first verse refer to a buddha's body and mind. In essence the meaning of the dedication is the wish for our meditation session to be a direct cause for all beings to achieve enlightenment and, until then, for all beings to discover and develop their enlightened nature.

Meditation Checklist

1. **Physical posture:** Legs are crossed, hands resting, back straight, shoulders rolled back, arms loose by your sides, head tilted slightly down, face relaxed, eyes shut.

2. **Psychological posture:** Give yourself permission not to think about your usual concerns. Be a person, in this moment, with no history and no future.

3. **Mentally establish your bodhichitta motivation:** You may like to repeat the following verse three times, focusing on its meaning.

To the Buddha, Dharma, and Sangha
I go for refuge until becoming enlightened.
By the practice of giving and so on,
May I achieve buddhahood to benefit all beings.

4. **Stabilize your mind for a few minutes by breath-counting:** Do this for about a third of the session, or for longer if your mind is very agitated.

5. **Follow the analytical meditation provided, holding the final point single-pointedly:** Try to penetrate the meaning so that you can allow the words and concepts themselves to fall away. Abide with this meaning as a direct experience, free of words. Sustain this single-pointed, non-conceptual focus for as long as possible.

6. **Use mindfulness and awareness:** Remember what the focus of your mind is supposed to be on and watch what your mind is really doing. Bring your attention back every time it wanders.

7. **End the session:** However good or bad your concentration during the session, try especially hard to focus strongly at the end—finish like a winner. You may like to use these dedication verses, discussed on pages 253–54:

> By this virtue may all beings
> Complete the collections of wisdom and merit
> And attain the two holy bodies
> Arisen from wisdom and merit.
>
> May the precious, superior mind of enlightenment
> Be generated in those who have not yet generated it,
> And not decrease in those who have developed it,
> But increase continuously.

Allow yourself a few moments as you open your eyes, and come back to the room.

References

3. Inner Experience or Outer Appearance?
Work by Daniel Gilbert referenced in Carlin Flora, "Happy Hour,"
Psychology Today, January/February 2005.

4. Shifting the Focus from Self to Other
Work by Dr. Richard Davidson referenced in Daniel Goleman,
Destructive Emotions: How Can We Overcome Them?, Bantam
Books, London, 2003, pp. 3–27.
His Holiness the Dalai Lama, "the dynamics of self-absorption . . . ,"
Ethics for the New Millennium, Riverhead Books, New York,
1999, p. 139.

5. Bodhichitta: The Compassionate Mind of Enlightenment
His Holiness the Dalai Lama on compassion, *Transforming the
Mind*, Thorsons, London, 2003, p. 59.
His Holiness the Dalai Lama, "Our bodhichitta may not yet be spon-
taneous . . . ," *A Flash of Lightning in the Dark of Night*, Shamb-
hala, Boston, 1994, p. 18.
His Holiness the Dalai Lama, "Everyone has at least some unselfish
tendencies . . . ," ibid., p. 57.

6. Open Heart, Open Hand: The Perfection of Generosity
Geshe Loden's definition of generosity, *Path to Enlightenment in
Tibetan Buddhism*, Tushita Publications, Melbourne, 1993, p. 649.

Publication in *Science* magazine by Dr. Michael Norton referenced in *Harvard University Gazette* online: http://news.harvard.edu/gazette/story/2008/04/money-spent-on-others-can-buy-happness/ [accessed November 10, 2009].

Jonathan Haidt, *The Happiness Hypothesis*, Basic Books, New York, 2005.

Peter Singer, *The Life You Can Save*, Text Publishing, Melbourne, 2009.

Warren Buffett, quoted in a profile published by *New Internationalist*, January/February 2007.

7. A Practical Approach to Ethics

His Holiness the Dalai Lama, "those individuals whose conduct is ethically positive . . . ," *Ethics for the New Millennium*, Riverhead Books, New York, 1999, p. xii.

Samuel Pepys, *The World of Samuel Pepys*, HarperCollins, London, 2000, p. 263.

Geshe Loden, "As a fragrant perfume delights . . . ," *Path to Enlightenment in Tibetan Buddhism*, Tushita Publications, Melbourne, 1993, p. 681.

His Holiness the Dalai Lama, "It is worth saying again that ethical discipline . . . ," *Ethics for the New Millennium*, Riverhead Books, New York, 1999, p. 146.

8. Thank Buddha for Aggravation!: The Perfection of Patience

Geshe Loden on anger, *Path to Enlightenment in Tibetan Buddhism*, Tushita Publications, Melbourne, 1993, p. 706.

His Holiness the Dalai Lama, "In the Tibetan medical system . . . ," *Ethics for the New Millennium*, Riverhead Books, New York, 1999, p. 92.

Pema Chödrön anecdote on angry man, *No Time to Lose*, Shambhala, Boston, 2005, p. 101.

The Buddha, "Though one man conquers...," verse 103, Dhammapada.

9. Mindfulness and the Yoga of Coffee Drinking

Center for Mindfulness in Medicine, Healthcare, and Society, University of Massachusetts: www.umassmed.edu/content .aspx?id=41252 [accessed November 11, 2009].

The MRC Cognition and Brain Sciences Unit, "A new treatment for depression: mindfulness based cognitive therapy": www.mrc-cbu .cam.ac.uk/research/emotion/researchtopics/mindfulness.html [accessed November 11, 2009].

10. Breaking the Cycle of Dissatisfaction

Definition of delusion, Geshe Loden, *Path to Enlightenment in Tibetan Buddhism*, Tushita Publications, Melbourne, 1993, p. 416.

Geshe Loden, "The source of cyclic existence . . . ," ibid., p. 416.

11. The Four Laws of Spiritual Success

Pema Chödrön on finding joy in what we do, *No Time to Lose*, Shambhala, Boston, 2005, p. 227.

His Holiness the Dalai Lama, "Spiritual practice is difficult in the beginning . . . ," *A Flash of Lightning in the Dark of Night*, Shambhala, Boston, 1994, p. 87.

12. Our Greatest Teacher

UCLA's Jonsson Comprehensive Cancer Center website: www .mesotheliomaweb.org/jccc.htm [accessed November 11, 2009].

Ian Gawler, The Gawler Foundation: www.gawler.org [accessed November 11, 2009].

Pema Chödrön on the Sixteenth Karmapa, *No Time to Lose*, Shambhala, Boston, 2005, p. 42.

13. Feeding the Good Wolf

Pema Chödrön on friends, *No Time to Lose*, Shambhala, Boston, 2005, p. 276.

14. Emptiness and Santa Claus

Geshe Loden on self-existence, *Path to Enlightenment in Tibetan Buddhism*, Tushita Publications, Melbourne, 1993, p. 837.

Minnesota Twin Family Study, discussed in T. J. Bouchard et al., "Sources of human psychological differences: the Minnesota Study of Twins Reared Apart," *Science*, vol. 250, issue 4978, pp. 223–28.

Professor Richard Gregory, "Brainy Mind," www.richardgregory .org/papers/brainy_mind/brainy-mind.htm [accessed March 28, 2010] (originally published in the *British Medical Journal*, vol. 317, issue 1693, 1998).

Bohm and Schrödinger on the perception of reality, *Einstein and the Buddha*, Seastone, Berkeley, 2002, pp. 70 and 64.

Stephen Batchelor, *Confession of a Buddhist Atheist*, Spiegel & Grau, New York, 2010, p. 133.

15. Adventures in Inner Space

His Holiness the Dalai Lama, *Essence of the Heart Sutra*, Wisdom Publications, Boston, 2005, p. 117.

His Holiness the Dalai Lama on insight and compassion, *Transforming the Mind*, Thorsons, London, 2003, p. 60.

The First Panchen Lama quotation from His Holiness the Dalai Lama and Alexander Berzin, *The Gelug/Kagyü Tradition of Mahamudra*, Snow Lion Publications, Ithaca, 1997, p. 99.

Further quotations from His Holiness the Dalai Lama and Alexander Berzin, *The Gelug/Kagyü Tradition of Mahamudra*, Snow Lion Publications, Ithaca, 1997, pp. 139 and 142.

Further Reading

Commentaries on Shantideva's *Guide to the Bodhisattva's Way of Life*

His Holiness the Dalai Lama, *A Flash of Lightning in the Dark of Night*, Shambhala, Boston, 1994.

Pema Chödrön, *No Time to Lose*, Shambhala, Boston, 2005.

Other Related Reading

Stephen Batchelor (translator), *A Guide to the Bodhisattva's Way of Life*, Library of Tibetan Works and Archives, 1979.

Stephen Batchelor, *Buddhism without Beliefs*, Riverhead, New York, 1998.

Stephen Batchelor, *Confession of a Buddhist Atheist*, Spiegel & Grau, New York, 2010.

Geshe Acharya Thubten Loden, *Path to Enlightenment in Tibetan Buddhism*, Tushita Publications, Melbourne, 1993.

His Holiness the Dalai Lama, *Ethics for the New Millennium*, Riverhead Books, New York, 1999.

His Holiness the Dalai Lama, *Essence of the Heart Sutra*, Wisdom Publications, Boston, 2005.

His Holiness the Dalai Lama and Alexander Berzin, *The Gelug/Kagyü Tradition of Mahamudra*, Snow Lion Publications, Ithaca, 1997.

His Holiness the Dalai Lama, *Advice on Dying and Living a Better Life*, Rider, London, 2002.

His Holiness the Dalai Lama, *Transforming the Mind*, Thorsons, London, 2003.

Jon Kabat-Zinn, *Mindfulness Meditation for Everyday Life*, Piatkus, London, 1994.

Lama Surya Das, *The Big Questions*, Rodale, New York, 2007.

Vicki Mackenzie, *Cave in the Snow*, Bloomsbury, London, 1998.

David Michie, *Buddhism for Busy People*, Allen & Unwin, Sydney, 2004.

David Michie, *Hurry Up and Meditate*, Allen & Unwin, Sydney, 2007.

Padmakara Translation Group, *The Way of the Bodhisattva*, Shambhala Dragon Editions, Boston, 1997.

Peter Singer, *The Life You Can Save*, Text Publishing, Melbourne, 2009.

Tenzin Palmo, *Reflections on a Mountain Lake*, Allen & Unwin, Sydney, 2002.

Index

childish behavior, 175, 181, 220
children, education of, 29. *See also* education
chocolate, 55, 187, 191, 207. *See also* cacao plantations
Chödrön, Pema, 110, 158, 168, 176–77
Christianity, 9, 46, 86, 89, 184, 241
Christmas, 184–86, 204. *See also* Santa Claus
Clarke Institute of Psychiatry, 126
cockroaches, 60, 82
code of conduct, 225–27
coffee, 7, 121–22, 128–29, 254
compassion, 9, 53–54, 65–77, 173
  Dalai Lama on, 205–6
  defined, 55–56
  ethics and, 9, 100
  generosity and, 82, 93
  happiness and, 56–58
  Loden on, 226
  meditation retreats and, 180
  non-objectifying, 206
  purification through, 153–54
  as the "rocket fuel" of our practice, 205–6
  self-other relation and, 59–64
concentration, 160, 210–13, 248, 249–51
Confessions of a Buddhist Atheist (Batchelor), 12, 199
consciousness
  broader perspectives and, 32–33
  continuation of, from one lifetime to another, 48
  death and, 168–70
  six kinds of ordinary, 187–88
consumerism, 42, 44–45
Coolidge, Calvin, 29
Copernicus, 199
creativity, 62, 130, 253
criticism, dealing with, 219–23
crow-turned-eagle metaphor, 155, 156, 173
cynicism, 39, 139

D
Dalai Lama, 1–2, 13, 62, 68–70, 72, 82
  on anger, 108
  bowing by, example of, 222
  on compassion, 68, 205–6
  on emptiness, 204
  Essence of the Heart Sutra, 203
  on ethics, 97, 98, 100
  Geshe Loden and, 233, 234
  on leisure, 33
  on the mind, 210, 211
  on religion as kindness, 55
  on self-absorption, 59
  teachings from, receiving, 152
  Transforming the Mind, 205–6
  tutors of, 233
Davidson, Richard, 53, 61
daVinci, Leonardo, 33
death, 43, 163–72
  certainties and uncertainties of, 166–68
  as our greatest teacher, 170–71
  of the self, 201
  values and, 164–66
delusion, 21, 134–45
  long-term impact of, 135–37
  why we tolerate, 137–41
dependent origination, 183, 196, 203. *See also* emptiness
depression, 18, 20, 124–26, 154
  anger and, 109–11
  brain activity and, 53
  consumerism and, 44
  death and, 163, 165, 167
  emptiness and, 184
  gratitude and, 35
  meditative approach to, 212–214
  negativity and, 23
  self-discipline and, 154, 155
  tonglen meditation and, 75
desire, 41–42, 73, 137, 145
  cultivating compassion and, 173
  as one of the three poisons, 126
  Shantideva on, 46

despair, 18, 58–59, 64
  emptiness and, 184
  gratitude as the antidote to, 34–36
Dhammapada, 69
diet, effect of, 191. *See also* digestive
    system; eating
digestive system, 108. *See also* diet;
    eating
direct/nonconceptual understanding,
    5–6, 152, 195, 206–8
divorce, 43
dog, wounded, story of, 153–54
Dongyu Gatsal Ling, 50
Drukpa Kagyu lineage, 50
dualism, 13, 55, 108
dullness, 252–55
Dunn, Elizabeth, 84
dying. *See* death
Dzogchen Shri Singha, 240

E
eating, 7, 11, 191
  austerity and, 19
  mindfulness and, 123, 130
  pleasure and, 43
Eddington, Arthur, 13
education, 28–29, 31, 37, 174
effort and reward, trade-off between,
    41
egalitarianism, 10
ego, 72, 173, 188, 201, 220. *See also*
    self
Einstein, Albert, 196, 199
elephants, at watering holes, 159,
    162, 173
emotion(s)
  awakening and, 17–18, 20–21
  brain activity and, 53
  emotional intelligence (EQ) and, 29
  self-other relations and, 53–64
empathy, 55, 60
emptiness, 183–200, 214–16
  compassion and, combining our
    understanding of, 205–6

Dalai Lama on, 204
form and, 202–3
nothingness and, comparison of,
    202–4
realization of, 211–12
understanding, on different levels,
    204–6
enemies, 73, 125, 145
  patience and, 108, 116–18
  tonglen meditation and, 76
  "true," 136–37
Engaging in the Middle Way
    (Chandrakirti), 87
equanimity, 138, 230–31
  bodhichitta and, 66, 68
  generosity and, 94
  patience and, 115
  Shantideva on, 238
Essence of the Heart Sutra (Dalai
    Lama), 203
eternalism, 168
ethics, 9, 33–34, 97–100
  generosity and, 85–87, 89
  mindfulness and, 128, 130
  perfection of, 81, 95–103, 237
  practical approach to, 95–103
Ethics for the New Millennium (Dalai
    Lama), 100
evangelism, 72
evil, 218
exercise regimes, 160–61. *See also*
    sports training

F
face, smiling, 230–31
fame, 44–45, 219–23
family. *See also* relationships
  bodhichitta and, 65
  love and, 53
  patience and, 117–18
  tonglen meditation and, 75–76
  trade-offs and, 39
fear, 33, 64, 107
  mindfulness and, 124, 125

patience and, 117
  tonglen meditation and, 75
firmness. *See* self-discipline
First Panchen Lama, 209
four elements, 188
France, 63
Freud, Sigmund, 3, 188
friendship, 53, 174, 189. *See also*
  relationships
  bodhichitta and, 65–66, 73
  death and, 165, 169
  rebirth and, 60–61
  spiritual, 178–79

G
gamma-wave activity patterns, 47
Gawler, Ian, 165–66
Gelugpa tradition, 233
generosity, 87–88, 93–94, 214
  ethics and, 85–87, 100
  happiness and, scientific linkage
    between, 84–85
  mindfulness and, 128, 130
  perfection of, 81–94, 237
  privilege of, 83–85
  Shantideva on, 89, 90
  as a state of mind, 88–90
genetics, 192
Gilbert, Daniel, 43
globalization, 193
goal-setting, 150–52, 161, 162
God, 46
grasping, overcoming, 90–91
gratitude, 24–26, 38, 47, 128
Gregory, Richard, 194–96
guilt, 97–98
Gujarat, 10
gurus, 177–78, 201. *See also* teachers

H
Happiness Hypothesis, The (Haidt), 85
Harvard Business School, 84
Harvard University, 43
hatred, 42, 73, 126, 136, 145

heart
  attacks, 6
  goal-setting and, 151
  peaceful, 228–30
Heart Sutra, 202–4
Hebrew language, 85
hedonism, 201
hellish states, 125–27, 241
Himalayas, 49, 63, 175, 233
homosexuality, 6, 61
hospice movement, 163
human nature, 2
humility, 222
hungry ghosts, 89
Hurry Up and Meditate (Michie), 159,
  243, 244
hypnotherapy, 57

I
id, 188
identity, sense of, 40. *See also* self
ideology, 73
ignorance, 72, 107–8, 126, 205
illness, 57–58, 135, 227
  anger and, 110
  awakening and, 17
  death and, 165, 167
  mindfulness and, 124
  realization and, 6
India, 10–11, 49–50, 152
injustice, 106, 133, 135, 138–39
inner experience, focus on, 29–30,
  39–51, 201–16
instinct, force of, 165, 201
intelligence, 28–29, 31, 107
interconnectedness, 47, 58, 75
intoxicants, 18, 35, 68
IQ scores, 29, 107. *See also*
  intelligence
Islam, 85–86

J
Jackson, Michael, 218
jealousy, 102–3, 134, 173

checklist, 256
death and, 166–68
depression and, 110
as fundamental to transformation,
46–47
goal-setting and, 151
gratitude and, 34
the importance of inner development and, 48–51
instructions for, 243–57
length of, 37
meditative equipoise and, 205
mindfulness, 110
"mind-watching-mind," 127, 208–12,
215–16
objective of, 248
patience and, 115–16
perfection of, 81
posture, 245–48
self-discipline and, 152–53, 156
sessions, ending, 255–57
time for, 48, 244–245
tonglen, 74–77, 249
meditation retreats, 151, 152, 154. *See
also* meditation
benefits of, 179–91
starving thoughts of attention during, 253
merit, 255–56
"middle way," 160, 168, 176
mind. *See also* thoughts
Dalai Lama on, 210, 211
existence of, on different levels of
subtlety, 207
luminosity of, 211
non-virtues of, 96–97
as open space, 210
projection of, dependence on,
194–97
"sesame seed," 50
use of the term, 4
-watching-mind meditation, 127,
208–12, 215–16
mindfulness, 24–25, 38, 110–12, 131

awareness and, comparison of,
255–56
-based cognitive therapy, 126–27
"bridging the disconnect" through,
122–23
compassion and, 174
death and, 169
emptiness and, 183, 214–16
meditation, 110
science of, 123–25
transformation and, 149
using, 257
and the yoga of coffee drinking,
121–32
Minnesota Twin Family Study,
191–92
morality. *See* ethics
mortality, 163–72. *See also* death
motherhood, 60–61
music, 3, 91, 150–51, 178, 195
Muslim tradition, 61, 193

N
Nalanda Monastery, 10–11, 159
needs, hierarchy of, 29–30, 32, 37, 87
Nepal, 152
neuropsychology, 13, 194–95. *See also*
psychology
neuroscience, 13, 53, 194–95. *See also*
science
nihilism, 168, 170, 201, 203
nirvana, 205, 211–12
nonconceptual/direct understanding,
5–6, 152, 195, 206–8
normality, sense of, 27–30, 31, 35
Norton, Michael, 84, 85

O
Olympic athletes, 150. *See also* sports
training
Ornament of Clear Realization, 67–68
ownership, taking, 113–15

P

Palmo, Tenzin, 49–50, 239
panoramic view, of life, 7, 34, 35, 48, 65
parable, of two calves and a piglet, 133–35
Path to Enlightenment (Loden), 99–100
patience, 100–101, 173
  anger and, 105–11, 113–15, 118–19
  mindfulness and, 128, 130
  perfection of, 81, 101, 105–19, 237–38
Patrul Rinpoche, 240
peak experiences, 64
Pepys, Samuel, 99
persistence, importance of, 29
personal trainers, 178. *See also* sports training
Perth, 22–23
physics, 13, 196. *See also* science
plantation workers, 5–6, 207
pleasure, 43–44, 55
poverty, 10–11, 83, 86, 90, 100
prefrontal cortex, 53. *See also* brain, anatomy of
prescription drugs, 18, 35, 44, 110, 214
psychology, 19, 42–43, 72, 150
  cycles of dissatisfaction and, 134, 136, 140
  mindfulness and, 124
  neuro-, 13, 194–95
  patience and, 105
  selfhood and, 62–63, 190–91, 207
  twin studies and, 192
public housing, 27

Q

quantum physics, 13, 196. *See also* science

R

radio stations, 49
rebirth, 37, 48, 60–61, 236. *See also* karma

Reflections on a Mountain Lake (Palmo), 50
"reframing," of experience, 1–2, 22, 113–17, 127, 136, 239
refuge, taking, 68, 177–78, 248, 256
relationships. *See also* family; friendships
  awakening and, 17, 18
  cycles of dissatisfaction and, 135
  patience and, 117–18
  self-other relation and, 53–64
  trade-offs and, 39
  well-being and, 53
renunciation, 18–19, 183
Rinpoche, Patrul, 115–16
"ripening effect," 232
royal families, 10–11

S

Saint Francis, 241
salespeople 138
samsara, 205, 219, 226
  delusion and, 135–36
  the lotus flower and, 149
  Shantideva on, 159
  use of the term, 135
sandcastles, metaphor of, 217–18
Sangha, taking refuge in, 68, 177–78, 256
Santa Claus, 184–86, 197–98, 201, 204–5, 213
Schrödinger, Erwin, 196
science, 13, 84–85, 123–27, 168, 196
Science (magazine), 84
Scotland, 9
Secret Millionaire, The (television show), 231–32
Segal, Zindel, 126
self. *See also* ego
  bodhichitta and, 65–66, 240
  death of the, 201
  direct experience and, 206–8
  -discipline, 29, 31, 105, 152–57, 161, 162

emptiness and, 185–90, 198–99
equalizing, with others, 59–60
-esteem, 30, 42, 154–55
exchanging, for others, 61–62
false, 205, 207, 219
liberation from, 198–99
praising of, and belittling of others, 176
-sabotage of, truth of, 21
Shantideva on, 213
shifting the focus from, to others, 53–64
-talk, 7, 25
"wonderful me" filter and, 221–23
sense experience, 187, 195, 200
sentient beings, use of the term, 32
Sermon on the Mount, 241
"sesame seed" mind, 50
sexuality, 42, 68, 96–98
Shakespeare, William, 2
Sheehy, Les, 20, 23, 97, 233, 235–36, 239
Sheehy, Margaret, 235
shoes, wearing, metaphor of, 40, 19–21
shunyata. See emptiness
Singer, Peter, 86–87, 100
six perfections, 174, 226–27, 237–38
  perfection of ethics, 81, 95–103, 237
  perfection of generosity, 81–94, 237
  perfection of meditation, 81
  perfection of patience, 81, 101, 105–19, 237–38
  perfection of wisdom, 81, 204
Sixteenth Karmapa, 168
sleep, 11, 130, 244
  depression and, 35
  lack of, 108, 160
snails, 60, 82
social networking, 218
sociology, 55
South America, 30
speech, non-virtues of, 96–97, 101–2, 105

spiritual friends, 178–79. See also friendship
sports training, 150, 156, 160–61, 178
stealing, 68, 96
stress, 75, 125, 228
  patience and, 117
  reduction clinics, 124
suicide, 44, 167
super-ego,.188

T
taboos, 163
teachers, 177–79, 181, 236
Teasdale, John, 126
television, 30, 44, 96–97, 130, 170. See also Secret Millionaire, The (television show)
  fame and. 176, 218
  news, 5–6
ten commandments, 96
ten non-virtues, 96–97
ten virtuous actions, 96
thief-like practitioner, 227–28
thought(s). See also mind
  the Buddha on, 69, 91, 125
  labeling, 209
three poisons, 126, 205
Tibet, 50, 152
Tibetan Buddhist Society, 91, 233, 235
Tibetan medicine, 188
tonglen meditation, 74–77, 249. See also meditation
trade-offs, 39–42, 47, 164
Transactional Analysis, 188
Transforming the Mind (Dalai Lama), 205–6
true causes, concept of, 51, 56–58
turtles, metaphor using, 32, 37

U
UK Medical Research Council, 126
University of British Columbia, 84
University of California at Los Angeles, 165

University of Massachusetts, 123–24
University of Nalanda, 10–12
University of Toronto, 126
University of Wales, 126
University of Wisconsin, 53

V
Vajrayana Buddhism, 233
values, 164–66
Varanasi Sanskrit University, 233
Vidal, Gore, 220
visualization, 76, 77, 91, 102, 249

W
warfare, 167
watering hole, elephant at the, 159,
  162, 173
wealth, 10, 31, 51, 134
  consumerism and, 44–45
  death and, 166
  eight worldly dharmas and, 218–19
  ethics and, 100

generosity and, 82, 84–88
millionaires and, 231–32
Shantideva's abandonment of, 10–11
widow's mite, example of, 89
Williams, Mark, 126
wisdom
  affirmations and, 255–56
  exchanging self for others and, 61,
    62
  perfection of, 81, 204
  tonglen meditation and, 74
"wise selfishness," notion of, 62
wolf, "feeding the good," 173–81
wrong view, 96, 97

Y
Yahweh, 46
yoga, 115–16, 170, 234

Z
Zimbabwe, 138

About the Author

 DAVID MICHIE is the bestselling author of *Buddhism for Busy People* and *Hurry Up and Meditate*, as well as the Buddhist thriller *The Magician of Lhasa*. His books have been published around the world and translated into many languages.

David works as a corporate communications consultant specializing in the financial services sector. Born in Zimbabwe and educated at Rhodes University, South Africa, David has lived and worked in both Johannesburg and London. He is now based in Perth, Western Australia. www.davidmichie.com

About Wisdom Publications

WISDOM PUBLICATIONS IS dedicated to offering works relating to and inspired by Buddhist traditions.

To learn more about us or to explore our other books, please visit our website at www.wisdompubs.org.

You can subscribe to our e-newsletter or request our print catalog online, or by writing to:

Wisdom Publications
199 Elm Street
Somerville, Massachusetts 02144 USA

You can also contact us at 617-776-7416, or info@wisdompubs.org.

Wisdom is a nonprofit, charitable 501(c)(3) organization and donations in support of our mission are tax deductible.

Wisdom Publications is affiliated with the Foundation for the Preservation of the Mahayana Tradition (FPMT).